Facets of Neurodivergence

Our Brains, Our Health, Our Lives

Ash Banks

Facets of Neurodivergence: Our Brains, Our Health, Our Lives.

© Copyright 2022 by Ash Banks. All rights reserved.

Written by Ash Banks.

Cover Illustration © Copyright 2022 by Ash Banks.

Cover design by Ash Banks.

ISBN: 9798410401470

All rights reserved. Without limiting the rights under the copyright reserved above, no part of this publication may be reproduced, stored in, or introduced into a retrieval system, or transmitted in any form or by any means (electronic, mechanical, photocopying, recording, or otherwise) without prior written permission of Ash Banks.

While every effort has been made to ensure the accuracy and legitimacy of the references, referrals, and links (collectively 'Links') presented in this book, Ash Banks is not responsible or liable for broken Links or missing or fallacious information at the Links. Any links to a specific product, process, web site, or service do not constitute or imply an endorsement by Ash Banks of same, or its producer or provider. The views and opinions contained at any Links do not necessarily express or reflect those of Ash Banks.

Material in this book is for educational purposes only. This book is sold with the understanding that neither the publisher nor the author is engaged in rendering legal, medical, psychological, or any other professional service. Neither the publisher nor the author assume any liability for any errors or omissions or for how this book or its contents are used or interpreted or for any consequences resulting directly or indirectly from the use of this book. For legal, medical, psychological advice or any other, please consult the appropriate professionals.

For updates, new releases, and totally unrelated stuff I just happen to be writing, please check out:

> https://www.amazon.com/Ash-Banks/e/B08TMMNPZH
> https://www.amazon.com/A-R-Banks/e/B09JHP4FT5
> https://www.amazon.com/Robin-Banks/e/B01MU5VWGL
> https://godsbastard.wordpress.com/

Contents

Introduction.	1
Terminology.	8
Methodology.	9
Of causal links, cheese, and asshats.	12
Results.	17
Participation.	18
Personal Information.	19
Cognitive and learning styles.	24
Types of neurodivergence.	29
Traits.	34
Exposure to painful stimuli	46
Restlessness, fidgets, and stims.	50
Focus and stimulation.	58
Memory.	69
Time management and decision-making.	76
Interest and hyperfocus.	84
Communication.	93
Eye contact and facial recognition.	103
Functioning in groups.	109
Emotional regulation.	116
Interoception.	123
Sleep.	126
Food.	140
Environmental sensitivities.	148
Blood pressure and sugar levels.	153
Dissociative states.	162
I am tired and everything hurts.	173
Hormonal imbalances	190
Relationships and trauma.	198
Mental health.	209
Stress.	214
Crisis points.	218
Achievements, or lack thereof.	228
Conclusion.	234
Appendix 1: The original survey.	249
About the author	275

"You're more than your diagnosis"

is the "You're not fat, you're beautiful" of ableism.

A.B, 2022

Introduction.

Hi! My name is Ash. I am the author of "Going Official!: On Getting a Diagnosis of Adult ADHD, and What to Do with It."[1] If you've heard about me at all, it's probably as Modgoblin, occasional wielder of the banhammer on The ADHD Gift.

In January 2022, I ran a public survey about neurodivergent traits and co-occurring conditions. This book is not an in-depth statistical analysis of the results, a scientific/medical/academic report, or anything brainy like that; it's just me, looking at the most obvious patterns that emerged from the survey and ranting about what they suggest. If that's not what you are looking for, this is your chance to save yourself some money or buy something else instead! But if you want to know more about some of the most common issues that affect our corner of the neurodivergent community, this may be a good place to start.

Now that we've got this down, and before you go any further, let me spell out what this book *isn't*:

1. It is not the report of a scientific or medical study. No medical specialists were harmed, or even consulted, in the making of this production. Having said that, one of my backgrounds is applied genetics, which means that I am trained to examine patterns in phenotypes (i.e., the set of observable characteristics of an individual resulting from the interaction of its genotype with the environment) and to use statistical methods to reverse-engineer how they might have come about.

2. It is not a diagnostic guide. While it includes the descriptions of some medical conditions that may be relevant to you, these descriptions are not sufficient for self-diagnosis. Seriously, don't even go there. And if you are curious about something you read here but you can't ask your doctor, please be careful about the sources you consult.

3. It is not an oracle of doom. If you look at the survey questions and you find many of them relevant, that doesn't mean that you're a hopeless mess, for two solid reasons. First of all, the survey focused solely on negative traits and symptoms. That really sucks, because there already

---

[1] https://www.amazon.com/dp/B09LBT4JZZ

is enough negative stuff about neurodivergence out there. However, when compiling an extremely long survey aimed at a community of people who often struggle with reading, completing long or tedious tasks, and maintaining their focus, 200+ questions seemed more than enough. I simply could not add questions about the good stuff without either taking out some that I needed answered, or making the survey so long that it would be inaccessible to too many of us.

Secondly, many of the issues mentioned in the survey are linked and treatable – in fact, because they are linked, they can sometimes be treated by doing the same things. This doesn't mean that there is a magical remedy that will make all of your problems go away forever. However, it might mean that, with the help of your doctor(s), you might be able to considerably decrease the impact of some bothersome traits and symptoms by taking relatively simple steps.

Or not: I am not promising you a miracle solution. I don't think there is one, and I definitely don't think there can be a miracle cure for neurodivergence, because neurodivergence is not a disease. I think, however, that there is one overarching issue that affects us all: a huge disconnect between us and the medical specialists responsible for our care.

It can be very hard for us to get heard by our doctors. This is partly due to the biases that are the natural result of the medicalization of neurodivergence, and partly due to the fact the Western medical care is the opposite of holistic.

Some doctors don't take us seriously when we report symptoms, because they have been trained to believe that we are oversensitive, over-reactive, or simply unable to take adequate care of ourselves. We are not really experiencing a case of X; we just think we are, because we are wired to feel too much of everything and overreact to it. And if we really are experiencing a case of X, it's probably because we are doing something wrong. If we could just behave like normal people...

The above is the worst-case scenario, but it's more common than it should be. This is particularly critical for those of us who are at the receiving end of a number of biases due to our ethnicity, gender, sexuality, weight, socioeconomic status, and so on and so forth. There is plenty of information out there on the impact of implicit and explicit biases on medical care.[2] I discussed the specific impact of biases on ADHD diagnoses in "Going Official!" This subject is vast and I won't cover it here, but suffice to say that research has proved that medical biases exist, and their impact is serious. They can prevent our access to adequate medical care, unnecessarily delay our treatment, or even kill us.

Even if we are lucky enough to avoid these issues and find a doctor who believes in us and our symptoms, that does not mean that our problems will be addressed adequately. In most Western countries, family doctors or GPs treat common medical conditions, but refer patients to hospitals and other medical services for specialist treatment. This is not a bad thing, because we cannot expect any doctor to know everything there is to know about modern medicine. Specialization is essential to ensuring that we get the best possible care for each of our conditions. However, it becomes an issue when the resulting information doesn't filter back in a way that creates a picture of us as a single person with a constellation of symptoms, rather than as a collection of disparate conditions.

Just like the constellations in the sky, any pattern formed by our symptoms only becomes visible if all the individual elements are examined together. Also, the observer has to look out for it. They have to know that a pattern could be there, and what it looks like, before they can recognize it.

That does not always happen in modern medicine. We might be treated, and treated well, for each of our symptoms. But if each of them falls under the scope of different specialists, a complete picture may never emerge. Even when all the information is put together, not all doctors are trained to recognize it as a pattern.

In some situations, this lack of information can translate into a lack of care. Rather than seeing us as a patient with a constellation of real symptoms, our doctor might dismiss all of our issues because there are just too many of them. There can't possibly be that much wrong with us, right? We must be exaggerating our symptoms, making them up, or have genuine psychological issues that fall outside of the scope of a primary care physician. So, rather than get a lot of separate treatments, we might get none at all.

None of this should happen, but it does, and all too often. It will

---

[2] https://www.medicalnewstoday.com/articles/biases-in-healthcare
Not a conclusive article, but a good starting point.

continue happening until our doctors are better informed about what neurodivergence really means – that our neurodivergence is not "just in our heads," literally or metaphorically, because our brains and our bodies do not exist independently of each other. That change in perspective won't happen until a lot more research is put towards treating neurodivergent patients, rather than towards treating neurodivergences as if they were diseases to be cured. Until that happens, many of our doctors will continue to lack the knowledge essential to ensuring that we receive the best possible treatment. And until that happens, they will not be able to tell us what the constellation of our symptoms shows. If we want to figure that out, we might have to do the work by ourselves.

That is one of the many important goals the #ActuallyAutistic movement has achieved: they have generated a wealth of easily-accessible information about what it means to be Autistic. Autism is a package deal including a constellation of mental and physical traits and symptoms that fall outside of the current diagnostic criteria. Managing these co-occurring conditions can have a huge positive impact on the lives of Autistic people.

Unfortunately, other neurodivergences have not benefited from the same kind of activism yet. Even more unfortunately, many of us have failed to benefit from the #ActuallyAutistic activism, for two main reasons.

1. The neurodivergent community is not immune to anti-Autistic stigma. There are plenty of non-Autistic neurodivergent people whose ableism does not allow them to accept that they could learn anything from the Autistic community. This is especially true if what they could learn is personally relevant to them. Some are so invested in maintaining their identity as "neurodivergent, but not like *that*" that they will refuse to admit that they have any traits commonly associated with Autism, even when they are ready to admit that they show the relevant symptoms.

2. Some members of the Autistic community attack non-Autistic people who claim to have traits most commonly associated with Autism, because they see that as appropriating the Autistic identity or diluting Autistic struggles. While that reaction is perfectly appropriate when dealing with those who insist that "We are all a little bit on the spectrum," telling people who exhibit certain symptoms that they aren't allowed to because they are not Autistic is a whole other story. It goes beyond gatekeeping and into gaslighting.

The combination of these factors has resulted in a rift within the neurodivergent community which is preventing the dissemination of information. That is the kind of thing that really gets up my nose, and it's partly why I wanted to run this survey. To the best of my knowledge and according to current diagnostic criteria, I am not Autistic, but my neurodivergence includes a number of traits and symptoms I would have not learned to recognize if I did not have the opportunity to learn from the #ActuallyAutistic movement. I wanted to see how common these traits and symptoms are in the neurodivergent community at large.

The other reason is that I needed some information and I couldn't find it. A few years ago, I wrote "Trauma-Aware Self-Defense Instruction: How instructors can help maximize the benefits and minimize the risks of self-defense training for survivors of violence and trauma."[3] I wrote that because I was spending a lot of time in the self-defense community, and realized that too many instructors do not understand the consequences of trauma and how to best take care of students affected by it. As a result, many students recovering from trauma end up quitting their self-defense training, or risk being re-traumatized during it.

I have been trying to write something similar about neurodivergence, because too many neurotypical instructors fail us badly without meaning to; they just don't understand the impact of what they are doing, because they do not understand how our brains and bodies work. Current representations of neurodivergence in popular media are unlikely to help bridge that information gap, for the simple reason that too many of them suck. I wanted to find some official numbers to back up my assertions and I couldn't, so I decided to generate them, or at the very least to see how hard it would be to generate them.

The third reason is personal. In October 2021, I discovered that taking melatonin supplements to treat my rampant seasonal insomnia had a significant impact on the symptoms of six other chronic conditions I have been suffering from. After I stopped wondering whether I had finally lost the plot, I did a bit of research. I found a number of studies in which melatonin supplements were used to successfully manage the symptoms of those conditions, and of other "unrelated" conditions, too.

I knew from previous research that sleeping disorders linked to melatonin production – or the lack thereof – are rife in the neurodivergent

---

[3] https://www.amazon.com/dp/B09JGDTK28
And yes, I might have a bit of a problem thinking of concise titles.

community. I also knew from the anecdotal evidence compiled by the #ActuallyAutistic movement that many of the conditions whose symptoms can be managed with melatonin supplements are over-represented in the neurodivergent community. While I try very hard to avoid sounding like someone who fashions tin foil into hats, sometimes a pattern becomes too glaring for me to leave it alone. This one really bugged me, so I decided to pick at it.

From personal experience, I suspected that asking people whether they had this or that condition would not necessarily lead accurate results, because people aren't born with a medical dictionary implanted into their brain. Unless we are told about a condition from our doctors or the people around us, we might not only not know what it's called, but not even realize that it's an issue. If something is all we know, why would we suspect that it's not "normal"? And if we repeatedly tell our parents, teachers, or doctors that we are experiencing a symptom and they don't take it seriously, why should we?

Happily, that lack of awareness was something a survey could give me the opportunity to explore relatively easily. If I ask the questions "Do you have this condition?" and "Do you have these symptoms?" any discrepancy in results suggests a lack of information.

Which brings us to what my survey tried to achieve:

1. To explore the most frequent traits of neurodivergence, and how often they occur together;

2. To see how many of us exhibit symptoms of co-occurring conditions that are anecdotally associated with Autism, to see whether they also show a correlation with other neurodivergences;

3. To see how many neurodivergent people exhibit symptoms of melatonin deficiency, and also have co-occurring conditions that can be managed with melatonin supplements;

4. To get a rough idea of how informed we are about traits and co-occurring conditions in order to assess how many of us are receiving adequate information and medical treatment.

I also asked a bunch of other questions; for instance, about people's sexuality and gender identity. I asked them because anecdotal evidence suggests that sexual and gender minorities are more common within our community, and I wanted to know the numbers.

This book aims to summarize what I found out. I hope that it will be of use to you. While you cannot use it to diagnose yourself (seriously, *do not*), it can provide you with information that might help you in getting your doctor to look at your symptoms from a different angle, and as a whole. Hopefully, that will enable you to get better treatment, if you need it.

If that does not work, that doesn't mean that this was a waste of time for you or me. If the only person who takes your survey results seriously is you, that's still a major win. You might learn that things you have put up with all your life are actual symptoms of actual conditions; and while that might not make you delirious with happiness, it can hopefully give you a better handle on how to manage them. If nothing else, I hope it will stop some of us from punishing ourselves for things we have no control over.

That's the last thing a survey of this nature can tell us: that "we" are a "we" – that there is a community of people who share our struggles. We are not alone. In a world with 7.9 billion inhabitants, the answer to "Am I the only one who..." is almost guaranteed not to be "no." That doesn't mean that we can't feel alone with our problems, particularly when those around us don't take them seriously.

This is my biggest hope for this work: that it will be taken seriously by someone in a position to use the information we have generated to guide future studies. Most studies of neurodivergence have a serious flaw: they do not answer the questions we are asking. As a result, many of them do not help us. They generate useful information – or some of them do, anyway – but they often do not address the issues that could have the greatest positive impact on our lives. They aim to unlock the mystery of neurodivergence, rather than to help us live our best possible lives.

This book, and the survey it is based on, cannot replace scientific or medical studies carried out by actual professionals. What they might do, however, is stimulate actual professionals to run similar, better surveys, and to direct specialist studies towards the issues that most affect us.

And heck, if I achieve none of the above, at least I found this interesting – frustrating, often depressing, and extremely infuriating, but definitely interesting. I hope that you'll find it interesting, too.

Terminology.

Throughout this book, I am going to assume that my readers are neurodivergent. When I talk about "us," I mean "neurodivergent individuals" or "the neurodivergent community." This is not an attempt at false teaming [4] on my part; it's just shorter.

If you are not neurodivergent and you are still reading this, please note that I am not an official spokesperson for neurodivergent people. I am particularly not qualified to speak on behalf of people with a different neurotype. Also, I might be wrong. That happens sometimes.

I will use identity-first language, so I will talk about people who are ADHD/ADHDers, Autistic, dyslexic, disabled, and so on and so forth. This is a personal choice, as well as being increasingly the preferred choice of the communities in question. Discussions of the pros and cons of identity- vs. person-first language abound on the internet, and I do not wish to repeat what has already been said more eloquently than I ever could.[5] The bottom line for me is that any insistence that "I am more than my diagnosis" ultimately stems from the belief that my diagnosis makes me less. I don't agree with that, so I won't go along with it. That doesn't mean that I don't respect people's rights to use person-first language for themselves, or that anyone has the right to impose identity-first language on others because that's what I use.

This book will likely include many medical terms you have never heard of. Do not let this make you feel bad, because that's one of the points I was trying to make. None of us is born knowing these terms. If we learn them, it's usually because a doctor teaches them to us, or to the people around us. If you discover a new term that applies to you, it's not your fault if you have never heard it before. And if you re-discover a term that you have heard before but didn't stick, that's also not your fault. Sometimes our brains are pesky like that. (For me, it's prosopagnosia. I don't know why, but I just cannot retain it.)

---

[4] https://en.wikipedia.org/wiki/The_Gift_of_FearPINS_(Pre-Incident_Indicators)
[5] https://neuroclastic.com/2019/04/19/person-first/
https://blog.usejournal.com/how-person-first-language-isolates-disabled-people-61a681a4fac4
https://thebodyisnotanapology.com/magazine/the-problem-with-person-first-language/
https://www.ncbi.nlm.nih.gov/pmc/articles/PMC3519177/

Methodology.

The survey was carried out on Google Forms, purely because it's free. I have come to regret that decision since, as extracting useful data from there is about as straightforward as milking a weasel.

The survey comprised of over 200 questions divided roughly into 20 themed sections of around 10 questions each. This breakdown was partly to make the survey less overwhelming to respondents, and partly to make it easier for me to look at the results section by section.

Most sections could be answered on a five-point scale. I deliberately chose a five-point scale and kept it consistent across most of the sections in order to make the survey easier to navigate for those with working memory issues or dyslexia. It can be very hard for some of us (me included) to find the right box to tick, particularly if the answers and questions do not fit on our screen. We scroll up, find the right column, scroll back down, forget which column we wanted, scroll up again... and rapidly lose the will to live, let alone the will to complete a questionnaire.

The survey was launched on the 26th of January 2022 and closed on the 4th of February 2022. It ran for a total of 203 hours, during which time 1426 respondents filed their answers. It was briefly opened again as some respondents had started it but had not managed to file it yet, which led to a total of 1433 respondents.

The survey was publicized primarily through "The ADHD Gift", a Facebook page posting ADHD-themed humor.[6] At the time of the survey, "The ADHD Gift" had 274,839 followers. The survey was advertised through three public posts, on the 26 January, 28 January, and 2 February. It was also advertised through a post in "Neuro Pride Ireland Community," a private group with 356 members. Any other advertising has been through individuals and groups sharing the survey link.

The survey was not evaluated by a Research Ethics Committee because it did not meet the criteria for 'research' as stated by the UKRI MRC.

Participant's anonymity was ensured by the simple means of not collecting names, email addresses, or current locations. Anyone who wished to be kept abreast of results was invited to request them via email.

---

[6] https://www.facebook.com/TheADHDGift

The survey included questions that covered the following subjects:

1. The main traits of some commonly-known neurodivergences, including ADHD, Autism, Dyscalculia, Dysgraphia, Dyslexia, Dyspraxia, Hyperlexia, Sensory Processing Disorders, and Synesthesia. (Note: for the main traits of Autism, I referred to the article "'Autism is a Spectrum' Doesn't Mean What You Think" by C.L. Lynch[7] rather than to the current diagnostic criteria. I did so because this article is the clearest explanation of Autism I have read to date, while the current diagnostic criteria are an ableist mess. And yes, I might be biased about this, but that does not mean that I am wrong.)

Please note that the survey did not include any of the positive traits of neurodivergence. This was purely because it was already massive, and making it any bigger would have made it inaccessible to a significant proportion of the neurodivergent community. Positive traits exist, and they matter.

2. The co-existing conditions that, according to the anecdotal evidence gathered by the #ActuallyAutistic movement, are most commonly present within the Autistic community.

3. Some of the chronic conditions whose symptoms can be managed with melatonin supplements, particularly those which seem to be more prevalent in the neurodivergent community.

4. Other aspects that seem to be more prevalent in the neurodivergent community than in the general population, such as minority sexualities and gender identities.

5. Aspects that are relevant to my current writing project; i.e., issues that affect the ability of neurodivergent students to participate in and benefit from the training of physical skills and sports in general, and self-defense instruction in particular.

A copy of the original survey can be found in Appendix 1. Please note that while it was a decent first attempt, some problems with its structure became obvious while the survey was still running.

The main issue was revealed in comments to our posts advertising the survey. I structured the survey so that a question about a trait or condition (e.g., Synesthesia) was followed by questions about the main symptoms of

---

[7] https://neuroclastic.com/its-a-spectrum-doesnt-mean-what-you-think/

said trait of condition (e.g., "Cross-overs between sensory or cognitive pathways."). I did so to be able to quickly and easily evaluate how well-known the technical terms for some traits or conditions are within our community. If somebody answer that they do not have a trait or condition but that they do have the symptoms of that trait or condition, this suggests that they lack information about that trait or condition. (In the case of synesthesia, for instance, 17% of respondents answered that they have synesthesia, while 24% answered that they have the symptoms of synesthesia.)

While this approach seemed good in theory, it became apparent that a number of respondents had failed to notice the instructions regarding technical terms – i.e., to select "not sure" if they were not familiar with them. Also, a number had read them, but refused to follow them. It was impossible to address this issue without completely restructuring the survey. As we had already gathered a considerable amount of data, I decided to carry on as we were.

It also became apparent that lack of an option for "suspected but not officially diagnosed" meant that the "not sure" category included respondents who are aware of their symptoms and their likely implications, but have not been able to receive an official diagnosis and are not comfortable self-diagnosing. This issue further weakens this aspect of the survey, as we cannot assume that anyone who is "not sure" simply does not have the necessary information.

The survey also suffered from other limitations and problems. These are discussed section-by-section.

Of causal links, cheese, and asshats.

This was supposed to be a section about correlation versus causation, but it ran away from me. You can skip it if you want. Unless you want to read about smacking me in the face. And cheese. The cheese is important.

When we look at how things are connected, sometimes a causal link seems obvious. If you smack me in the face and I get a nosebleed, we can make an informed guess that the former caused the latter. If we wanted to be thorough and scientific about it, we could stick an endoscope up my nose and have a proper look, but I would not appreciate it, and most of us would not deem it necessary. There might be other issues going on – for instance, I might have a condition that makes nosebleeds more likely – but most people would be happy to assume that smacking my face caused it to bleed. Obvious cause led to obvious effect; the end.

Sometimes, however, causal links are not that obvious. If you smack me today and in three weeks' time I start to show the symptoms of an intracranial hematoma, it might be hard for anyone, me included, to connect the dots. The interval of time between cause and effect is so long that the connection between them is just not that obvious. And even if we suspect that one thing caused the other, it might be impossible to prove it.

Sometimes the problem is that we do not have enough information to connect an effect to its cause. If you give me a cheese crêpe – nicely: don't throw it at me! – and half an hour later I get a nosebleed, we might not put two and two together. It might not occur to us to think along those lines unless we know that allergies, including allergies to dairy, can cause nosebleeds. Even then, we won't know the exact cause for sure unless we get more data. We could run a little experiment, if we wanted. For instance, over a number of days, you could feed me crêpes without cheese and crêpes with cheese to see where the problem lies.[8] Is it the cheese? Is it the crêpes themselves? How does my nose react to pancakes?

Over time, we might come to the conclusion that there is a connection between cheese going into my mouth and blood coming out of my nose. That gives us no information about the underlying mechanism, but we could look that up. If we found research that supports our findings, we could form a theory: cheese gives me nosebleeds, which suggests that I have an allergy to cheese, or to something in cheese. We could run further

---

[8] Please do. I already know that the problem is the cheese, but I am all about free food.

experiments to find out the details. Is it that one cheese, or all cheeses? Do other dairy products produce the same results?[9] However, we might just call it a day, and be happy with the knowledge that a causal link between your cheese and my nosebleeds exists.

I like that kind of thing – working out causal links, I mean. Getting nosebleeds isn't fun. I like it when I can extract a little bit of sense out of the world, particularly when that means that I learn something new in the process. Thing is, a lot of people don't. They like to think that they know how the world works. When life throws up evidence that doesn't fit their worldview, they reject it. It doesn't matter how often A leads to B: if what they know about A and B doesn't support a causal link between them, then there can't be one. Cheese doesn't make their nose bleed, so it can't make my nose bleed, either. If my nose is bleeding, it can't be because of the cheese, because noses and cheeses do not work like that. The end.

Repetition of evidence doesn't always change their mind. If I eat cheese 384 times in front of them, and I get 384 nosebleeds, this may convince some people, but not everyone. In fact, too much repetition will cause some to lose any respect they might have had for my theory. My nose is always bleeding, so how could I possibly know what's causing it? It's definitely not the cheese, though. My nose is just suboptimal.

This isn't a statistical issue; it's a human issue, but it's an issue that affects a lot of people who have atypical responses to certain stimuli. However obvious the connection may seem to us, it can be very hard for us to convince some people that, for us, A causes B. That can make it hard for us to get them to accept that we don't do A because we don't want B. We are clearly just being ridiculous, because there is no link between A and B! If only we gave it a go, we would find out. And if we do give it a go and our theory is proved right, it's only because we made that happen. It's. Not. The. Cheese.

It can be hard enough to deal with this kind of thing when we have a handful of these asshats in our lives. When they are in the majority, they can really mess us up. Being constantly told that our reactions, perceptions, memories, and beliefs are fundamentally wrong can make us question our judgment and sanity. If done deliberately, it's gaslighting, which is a form of abuse. Even when it's done by accident, by people who genuinely believe that we are wrong and they are right, it can leave scars.

---

[9] Send me a couple of tubs on Ben & Jerry's, and I promise to report back.

If none of this applies to you, hey, that's great. But if this sounds familiar, there is a chance that you might benefit from having a bit of a think about it. You might need the time and space to work out how much of your experiences you have been ignoring, blocking off, or denying because you were brought up to believe that it was the right thing to do. That's some heavy stuff right there, and you might have a lot of feelings about it. Or not: I can't tell you how to feel any more than I can tell you how your nose should react to cheese.

Anyway, let's go back to causes and effects. Way I see it, they are a lot safer than feelings.

Sometimes, if we don't have enough information, we might see that two things are linked, but not be able to work out how. For instance, say that you have been smacking me in the face every day for two weeks. I am slow, but I do learn, so when I see you on the fifteenth day, I might duck out of the way because, shockingly, I don't actually like having my face smacked. If that tactic works, I might do it again the following day, and keep doing it forevermore. Hey presto, no more smacks, and no more nosebleeds.

An external observer unaware of the history between my face and your fist may watch this and wonder what is going on. Why did I duck as you approached me? They don't have the necessary data to see my action as a reaction to your past actions, so they might put it down to coincidence. You were there, I ducked, no link. They might formulate theories as to why I ducked, but these might not include you as a factor.

If we keep repeating our little skit, however, they might start to wonder whether there is a connection between your proximity and my ducking. That doesn't mean that they'll work out what it is, though. They simply don't have enough information for that. If they are the kind of person who relies solely on the evidence of their own eyes and ears, they might determine that I duck when you approach for no valid reason. You are not making me duck; I am clearly doing it without any input on your part.

If one day I don't duck in time and you manage to sock me one in the snout, they might decide that you smacked me because you got fed up of me being a silly blighter. I made you smack me by provoking you. And you weren't right to do it, because hands are not for hitting, but you did not start this, either. I did.

If you think this is bullshit, so do I, but that doesn't mean that it doesn't happen in real life, and often. Every time someone reacts to stimuli other people cannot perceive, the first conclusion the majority jumps to is that there is something wrong with them, or at the very least with their behavior. Maybe they are just being silly. Maybe they are misbehaving on purpose. Either way, the only problem with what's going on is them.

If their "overreaction" is followed by a negative outcome, well, it's pretty obvious what happened, right? They did something weird, and in response, something bad happened. Hardly a mystery for the ages.

Sometimes we can fix this by explaining ourselves, and sometimes that works, but not always. And if we are not able to explain what our problem is because we can't find the right words, or we can't speak them, then we don't stand a chance.

Sometimes all we are left with is flight or fight. We may be able to get away from the stimulus by literally moving or by disconnecting ourselves from our perceptions and surroundings – that's learned dissociation, FYI. Sometimes we might just get desperate or triggered enough that we end up fighting it out. And if that happens, whatever comes next is definitely going to be seen as our fault.

I am writing this here because it is relevant to many of us – or, rather, to too many of us. Being neurodivergent in a neurotypical world means being constantly bombarded with stimuli we struggle to tolerate and demands we struggle to meet. When we can't hack it, we are often punished.

Sometimes we know that it's unfair, that what we are being asked to do is wrong or impossible, but often we don't. This is particularly true if we do not realize that there are fundamental differences between our perception of the world and that of those around us. And how are we to know that, when we are constantly being told that what we are feeling isn't real?

Sometimes we know that we are different, because we have been told, but nobody bothered to explain how, or why. That hardly seems to matter, anyway, because our difference provides a handy reason for everything that's wrong with our lives. Nobody needs to bother working out why we are struggling, or how to help us struggle less, because they already have all the answers they need. There is something fundamentally wrong with us, and that's why there are so many things wrong with our lives.

When that happens to us at home, it really sucks. It's not very nice growing up knowing that those who are supposed to love us unconditionally wish that we were fundamentally different; that they love us despite of who we are, rather than because of it. Knowing that doesn't just hurt; it wounds, and it can teach us not to expect any better from anyone else.

We deserve better, though. All of us. At a very minimum, we deserve to be believed. When we say that X hurts, or that we just cannot do Y, *we deserve to be believed*. And when we "react badly" to X, or "fail to achieve" Y, our explanations should be taken into account. Our behavior doesn't happen in isolation from everything that's going on in and around us. We are responding to our experiences, and our experiences are just as real and as valid as everyone else's. They might not be common, they might not meet most people's expectations, but that doesn't make them less real or less valid.

If you have been struggling with this kind of thing all your life, the results of this survey will not prove that you were right all along, and you have been wronged. They will not prove that your "misbehaviors" and "failures" were the natural consequences of you responding to the stimuli you were perceiving, and operating within the abilities and limitations your brain and body granted you. They will not prove that the people around you got the causes and effects all wrong because they couldn't or wouldn't accept that your experiences were different from theirs. And that's not because this survey was bad, or because I am not a doctor: it's because your reality does not need further proof. It is what it is, and nobody has a right to tell you otherwise.

You might, however, find solace in the fact that you are actually not that special. You might be the only person you know who would answer certain questions a certain way, but you're not the only person *I* know. That's why I'm asking these questions: because they are so relevant to so many of us. There is an "us," and you are part of it.

So, yeah, don't look for validation here, because you don't need it. If you ever need ammo, though, maybe we can find you some. Next time someone tries to shove cheese down your throat, it might help to be able to say, "Actually, a recent survey indicated that X% of neurodivergent people have food allergies or intolerances, and these can cause nosebleeds in susceptible people by drying up the nasal membranes." You shouldn't have to do that, but you might need to, and it might work. Or not – some people will not hear you, not matter what you say.

What do I know, anyway? I can't even eat cheese right.

Results.

This survey did not aim to be a scientific study. It was not rigorous enough to allow for complex data analysis, and it definitely cannot "prove" anything conclusively, but that is not what it was designed to do. I was trying to find out how many of us are affected by certain issues and to what extent, and this survey achieved that.

The results cannot be assumed to apply to the entire neurodivergent community and all its members because we did not get enough respondents in certain groups. The fewer respondents we got, the less solid the results are. This doesn't make them invalid, but it does make them less reliable: they are true for the respondents, but they might not be representative of that particular group as a whole.

The picture created by the results is more of a watercolor than a boxplot, but I am OK with that. Most people can't read boxplots, anyway.

Throughout the survey, unless otherwise specified, I considered the people who reported that they often or always have a symptom or issue as "testing positive," so to speak. I did not include those who reported that they have it only sometimes, because I took the view that for most (but not all) issues, most people experience them sometime. This is along the lines of "Everyone needs to pee, but if you need to pee 80 times a day, you should probably see a doctor about it." Based on this highly scientific approach, those who answered "sometimes" and "not sure" were included in the data tables, but not in the percentage of people who have this or that symptom.

This approach doesn't work for all symptoms. To carry on the previous metaphor, if you pee blood, you need to see a doctor asap. In situations where I used different criteria, I explained which and why.

Most results are presented with no decimals for simplicity's sake. If some figures do not add up – for instance, if 15% of respondents answered "often" and 14% answered "always" but I added that up to 30% - it's because of rounding issues.

Participation.

The survey was completed by a total of 1433 respondents. Six respondents didn't report any neurodivergences, so their answers were removed from the dataset. Some respondents left portions of the questionnaire uncompleted, so their results could not be included in the analysis for that section. However, we obtained in excess of 1400 viable responses for most sections.

This is a result in its own right: a meme page, with no back-up from any research or medical institution, investing zero money into advertising, managed to collect over 1400 sets of results in just over 200 hours. And this for a large questionnaire riddled with technical language, aimed at a community whose members often struggle to navigate and complete this type of task.

This suggests that it's actually not that hard to get neurodivergent people to share their experiences. Other surveys ran by neurodivergence advocates have obtained similar or better results – for instance, the "Autistic Not Weird" survey was completed by 11,212 respondents.[10]

This raises a question: if we can do it, why isn't it been done by actual grown-ups? Why is our willingness to invest time and spoons into this kind of project not put to good use by the scientific and medical community?

It is not unusual to see "groundbreaking" studies of neurodivergence with sample sizes so small that all respondents could fit in a minivan. And this isn't solely an issue with studies that require in-person participation or expensive medical testing.

While surveys such as this may not be able to provide definitive answers, they could do something else: they could guide research towards the issues that most affect our lives. This is something that simply cannot be done by studies driven by the interests of researchers, or of pharmaceutical companies, rather than by the needs of our community. Our needs cannot be decided by neurotypical people, regardless of their investment in our lives. They can only be discovered by consulting us, and broad-stroke surveys such as this can help with that.

---

[10] You wanna check it out. It's seriously awesome.
https://Autisticnotweird.com/Autismsurvey/?fbclid=IwAR0tinc159KaZYZMi0cwcKgnjbboInZkfCAVT_QX8ADruod8JKnGYWmwbKY

Personal Information.

This section looked at the age, gender, and sexuality of the respondents. It also included a section on the country where they spent their childhood (under the age of 12), as that might have an impact on their diagnosis. The questions were:

- In which country/countries did you spend your childhood until the age of 12?
- How old are you?
- What gender were you assigned at birth? Tick all that apply. (Male / Female / Intersex)
- Are you heterosexual? (Yes/No/Not sure)
- Do you still identify with the gender you were assigned at birth? (Yes / No / Partly)

Country of residence (under 12)	
Aotearoa - New Zealand	3%
Australia	8%
Canada	9%
UK	12%
USA	52%
Other	12%
Multiple	4%

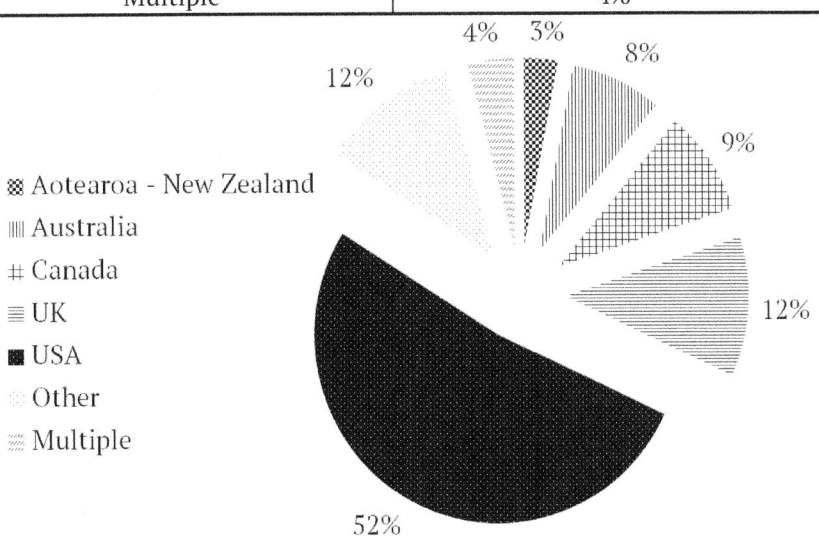

52% of respondents spent their childhood in the USA. Of the remaining 48%, 3% are from Aotearoa – New Zealand, 8% from Australia, 9% from Canada, 12% from the UK, and 12 % from other countries, including Argentina, Austria, Belgium, Brazil, the British Virgin Islands, Denmark, Egypt, Finland, France, Germany, Greece, Honk Kong, Hungary, India, the Republic of Ireland, Israel, Italy, Lebanon, Mexico, Morocco, The Netherlands, Norway, Philippines, Poland, Portugal, Puerto Rico, Romania, Serbia, Slovak Republic, South Africa, Sweden, The Isle of Man, Trinidad, Tunisia, Turkey, Yugoslavia, and Zimbabwe. 4% of respondents spent their childhood in multiple countries. These percentages broadly reflect the geographical spread of the followers of "The ADHD Gift."

The number of respondents from outside of the USA was not large enough to allow an investigation into a correlation between country and diagnosis. A larger survey would be required to facilitate that.

However, collecting country data was not a waste of time. It showed that over half of the respondents spend their early childhood in the USA. This survey is, therefore, very US-centric, and might not reflect the experiences of neurodivergent people from other countries.

	AFAB	AMAB	AIAB	TOTAL
13-17	1%	0.07%		**0.63%**
18-24	10%	2%		**12%**
25-34	34%	5%		**39%**
35-44	28%	4%	0.07%	**33%**
45-54	10%	2%		**12%**
55-64	2%	1%		**3%**
65+	0.28%	0.07%		**0.35%**
TOTAL	85%	15%	0.07%	

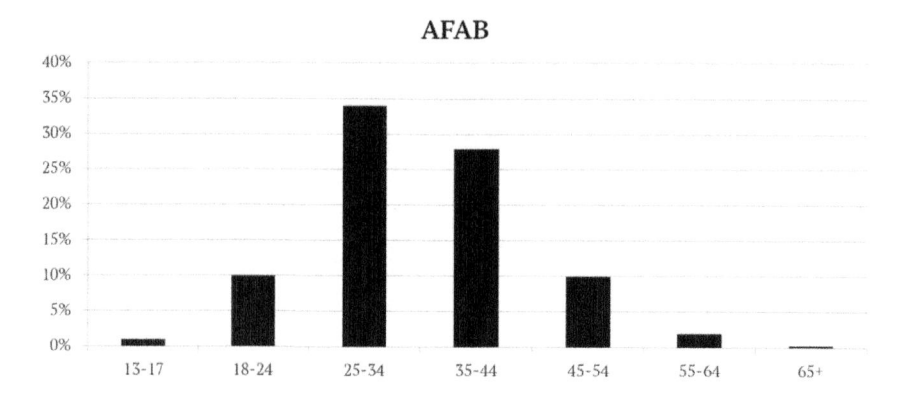

AFAB

AMAB

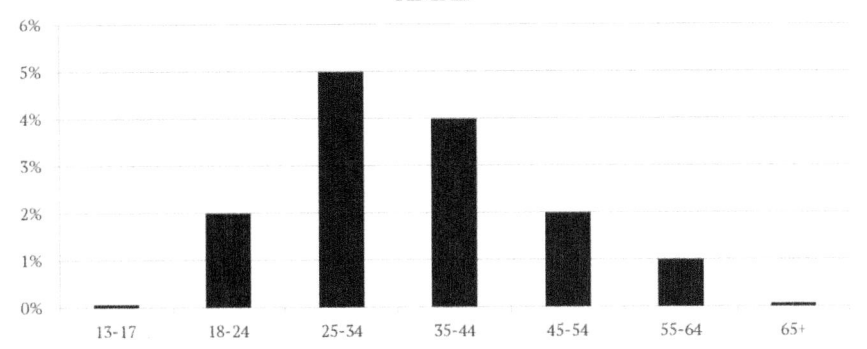

The spread between genders was also very uneven. 85% of respondents were assigned female at birth (AFAB), 15% were assigned male (AMAB), and one participant was assigned intersex. This also broadly reflects the gender of the followers of "The ADHD Gift."

The age distribution was also uneven. 39% of respondents were between 25 and 34, while 33% were between 35 and 44. The average age was 35, and the median 34. Respondents under 17 and over 65 were particularly scarce on the ground.

All these factors combine. Over 33% of respondents were AFAB 25-44 year olds from the USA. While this does not invalidate the results of the survey, it does mean that it is not necessarily representative of our community as a whole. We might all be neurodivergent, but that does not mean that we all live the same lives. The bottom line is that if you wish to find answers about groups that were unrepresented or poorly represented by this survey, this isn't the place to look for them.

Heterosexual	
yes	42%
not sure	9%
no	49%

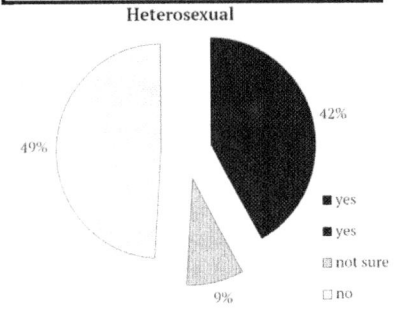

Identify with assigned gender	
yes	75%
partly	15%
no	10%

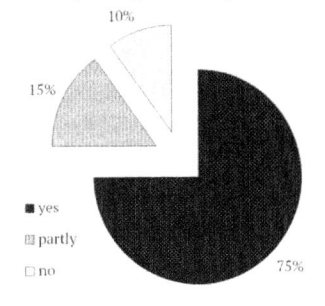

42% of respondents were heterosexual and 75% were cisgender. These figures are much lower than the current worldwide estimates of 80% heterosexual[11] and 98% cisgender.[12] Only 41% of respondents were both heterosexual and cisgender.

This is important, so I am going to state it, even though it's obvious: **according to the results of this survey, cis-het people are not the majority in our community**.

While these results are likely affected by the geographical spread of our respondents, one could argue as to exactly why that is. Is the issue one of opportunity, access to information, or a proof of the success of the (in)famous queer agenda?

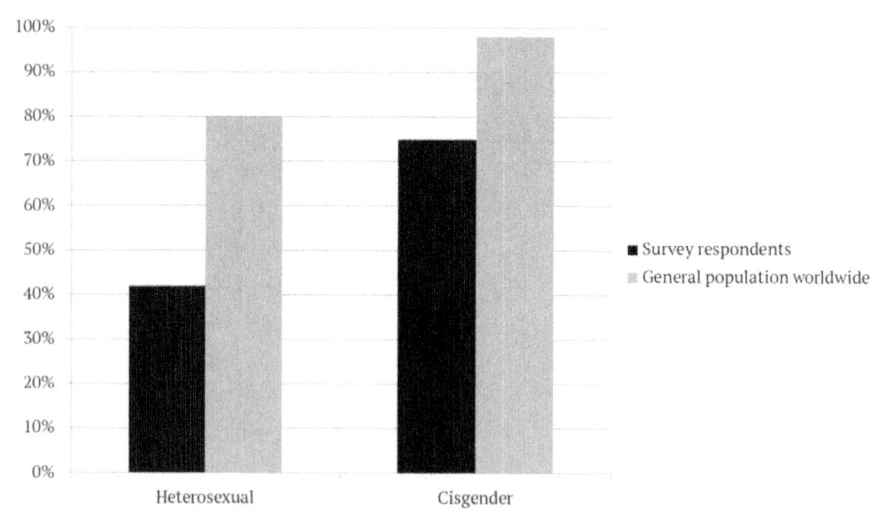

While such concerns are beyond the scope of this kind of survey, one consideration is not: the truth about the proportion of neurodivergent people who are not cis-het is more likely to be revealed by anonymous, volunteer surveys such as this one than by any official statistics. This is particularly true if we are interested in the number of trans neurodivergent people. Homophobia, biphobia, acephobia, and other phobias against non-heterosexuality are still a serious issue in many if not most countries, and may discourage people from revealing their sexual identity unless they have to. Many trans people, however, are not only at risk of experiencing transphobia, but in a unique position with regards to

---

[11] https://www.ipsos.com/en/lgbt-pride-2021-global-survey-points-generation-gap-around-gender-identity-and-sexual-attraction
[12] https://www.statista.com/statistics/1269778/gender-identity-worldwide-country/

their medical needs.

Not all trans people want or need gender-affirming medical care, but plenty do. For us, gaining access to such care often means negotiating an extremely fine line: we have to prove that our gender dysphoria affects us enough to make us worthy of the care we want, but not so much that we might be deemed incompetent to make life-changing decisions. If we are deemed incompetent, we might be denied access to gender-affirming medical care.

Having a diagnosis of neurodivergence is enough for some care providers to deem us incompetent. It absolutely shouldn't be, but it is. For this reason, trans people who do not have an official diagnosis of neurodivergence may find out, unofficially but accurately, that they are better off not seeking one, or they might be excluded from gender-affirming care. On the other hand, people who already have a diagnosis of neurodivergent may be refused a diagnosis of transness, as it were. That may prevent their access not only to gender care, but also to the processes associated with a change of legal gender, and sometimes also with a change of name. As a result, some of us end up being classified as trans but not neurodivergent, some of us end up being classified as neurodivergent but not trans, and most of us end up exhausted and disgusted by the medicalization of our identities.

These issues only apply to those of us who feel the need to formalize our trans status. Many of us do not, for a number of reasons, and their transness may therefore not show up on official statistics.

Also, these issues only apply to those of us who are lucky enough to have access to the relevant diagnostic services. There are no official statistics on the number of people who meet the criteria for diagnosis but cannot get it, because nobody official is collecting those numbers. However, there is some research and plenty of anecdotal evidence suggesting that this issue may be depressingly common.

The fact that a high proportion of our community isn't cis-het isn't just a social issue; it's a medical issue, but not because not being cis-het is a disease. Anything that raises our chances of being subjected to discrimination, bullying, social ostracism, or social isolation increases our stress levels – and this is a physiological issue, not an emotional or psychological one. This issue is so important that I am going to address it in its own section – see "Stress."

Cognitive and learning styles.

This section looked at the different ways in which people think and learn. Respondents were asked to select their main mode(s) of thinking and how they learn best.

In the cognitive styles section, the options were:

- **Verbal/logic thinker:** you think verbally, with your mind narrating your experiences as you go through them. You might have an affinity for words, literature, or languages.

- **Visual thinker:** you think in pictures and need to see things – either in your mind or physically – in order to process information. You use language as a secondary tool to narrate the photo-realistic pictures that pop up in your imagination.

- **Pattern thinker:** this is a more abstract form of visual thinking. Thoughts are in patterns, rather than photo-realistic pictures. You might have an affinity for finding seemingly meaningful patterns in both meaningful and meaningless data.

- **3-D or spatial-mechanical thinker:** you automatically create a 3-D model of the world around you in your head, and can rotate and manipulate the resulting picture so you can view it from all angles. You might have an affinity for spatial problem solving (e.g., solving visual puzzles, rotating or arranging objects so they fit in small spaces.) You might be able to mentally picture something with such detail that you can run mental experiments on your creation, tweaking it until it works.

- **Not sure**

I asked this question because I have read a number of articles that suggest that 3-D thinking is more common with dyslexics, and in fact can be a cause of some forms of dyslexia. As I am dyslexic and a 3-D thinker, I wanted to check this out. I have also read articles suggesting that pattern thinking is more common with Autistics.

Unfortunately, giving people the opportunity to select multiple answers backfired, because a large proportion selected several options, including "not sure." That is not surprising given that pondering one's cognitive style(s) is not something everyone does, but it did make a number of responses unusable.

Of 1281 viable answers, the results were:

verbal/logic	33%
visual	16%
verbal/logic + visual	12%
verbal/logic + pattern	9%
pattern	8%
not sure	6%
3D	5%
visual + pattern	3%
verbal/logic + 3D	3%
visual + 3D	3%
pattern + 3D	2%

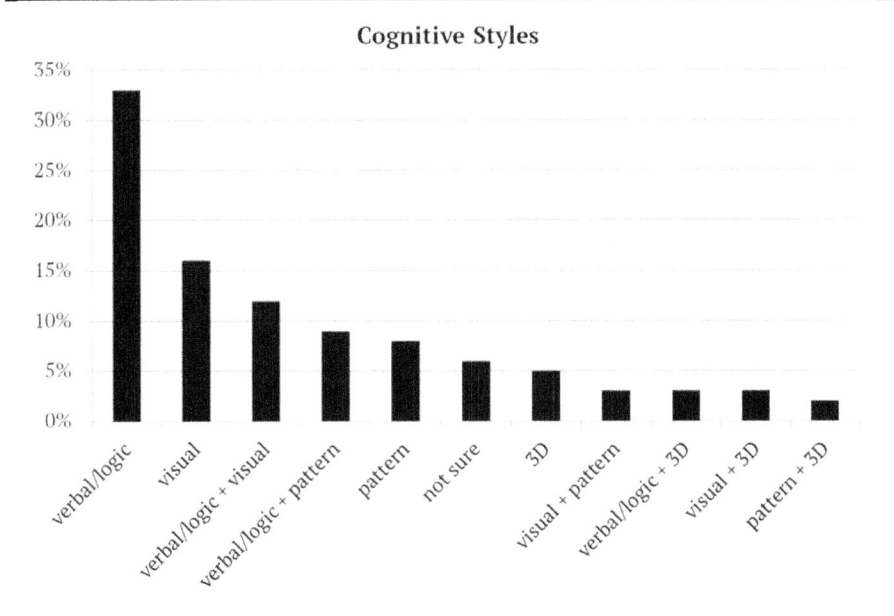

Cognitive Styles

The option of selecting multiple answers made it impossible to look at any correlation between neurodivergences and cognitive styles. Restricting answer options may resolve this issue, but as only 56% of respondents selected a single cognitive style, it might also result in answers that are factually incorrect, or an increased number of "not sure."

The question about learning styles was far more illuminating. The options were:

- Visual learning: understanding and retaining information presented in a visual way – e.g. as pictures, diagrams, written directions, visual demonstrations, and more.
- Reading/writing learning: understanding and retaining information presented in writing – e.g. as text only.
- Auditory learning: understanding and retaining information presented verbally rather than visually – e.g. as a spoken lecture rather than written notes.
- Kinesthetic learning: understanding and retaining information through physical activities - e.g. carrying out manual tasks, physically handling objects, acting out events, or translating concepts, even abstract ones, into physical sensations in your body.
- Combined: when the same information is presented in multiple formats at the same time.

Only 47% of respondents selected a single learning style. Of these, more than half selected "Combined", while only 2% selected "Auditory." "Kinesthetic" came in second, "Visual" came in third, and "Reading/writing" was second-to-last.

Combined	52%
Kinesthetic	23%
Visual	14%
Reading/writing	9%
Auditory	2%

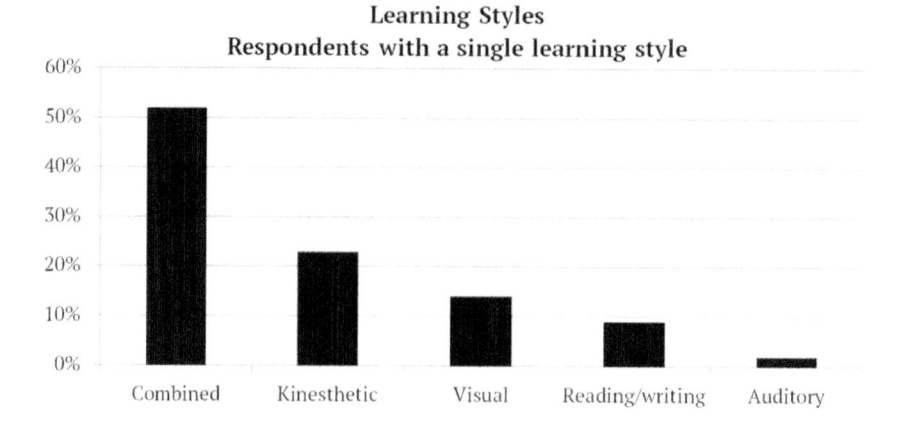

Learning Styles
Respondents with a single learning style

When we include the answers of people who selected multiple learning styles, the order of preference remains the same. 56% of respondents selected "Combined," while only 10% selected "Auditory."

Combined	56%
Kinesthetic	48%
Visual	43%
Reading/writing	26%
Auditory	10%

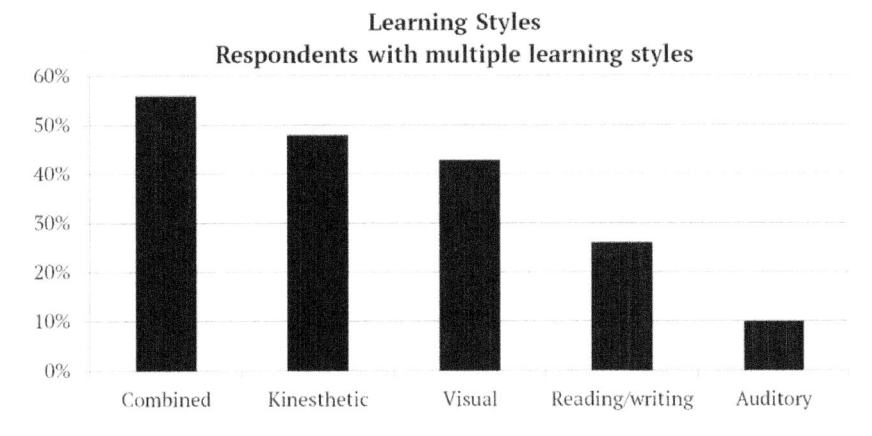

Learning Styles
Respondents with multiple learning styles

I have looked for comparable statistics for the population at large, but I cannot find reputable studies that are not very narrow (e.g., only including students of a particular discipline, which skews the results). At any rate, that's not the key issue here. The most important thing we can learn from these results is that the modern school system is setting us up for failure.

Most classroom learning consists of listening to an instructor riff on a subject. If graphic information is provided, it is usually to support or enhance verbal information rather than to duplicate it. Only 10% of us are wired to learn like that.

The act of note-taking may help some of us, as it effectively turns auditory learning into combined learning. However, it might not help those of us with dyslexia, dysgraphia, poor fine motor skills, auditory processing disorders, short-term memory problems, or any other issue that interferes with that activity.

I don't know about you, but this makes me really angry. We are forced to learn in a way that does not come natural for us, and if our results don't meet expectations, we are the ones deemed to have failed.

This is particularly annoying to me as there is no valid reason for this. Classroom lectures are not the only way of teaching. They were just the cheapest way for one person to impart information to a number of students, but that hasn't been true since the digital age. We now have plenty of alternative learning options that would either cost nothing (e.g., making lecture notes available to students prior to a lecture), or have a set-up cost learning institutions would only have to pay once (e.g., producing documentary-style presentations with a much higher proportion of visual content).

This type of approach might not help primarily kinesthetic learners, but adaptations can be made to help us, too. Not forcing us to stay still during lectures, or punishing us if we find workarounds that help us listen (e.g. crocheting or knitting to keep our bodies occupied so our brains can focus), would be a good starting point. A common objection to such adaptations is that our movements may distract other learners, but this raises a question: why is their ease of learning prioritized over ours? And has anyone bothered to ask them whether they would also prefer to be able to move while listening? Also, if that is really the primary concern here, why is stillness still routinely enforced during long-distance learning?

There is no reason why neurodivergent students – or in fact any student who is not an auditory learner – should have to waste most of their school time failing to learn from lectures. It is high time that we stop framing these issues in terms of learning difficulties, because our learning potential is not at the core of this problem.

Types of neurodivergence.

This section looked at the most commonly-known types of neurodivergence, whether people were officially diagnosed or self-diagnosed, and the age of diagnosis.

Of 1433 respondents, 94.3% were ADHDers – not surprising, given that the survey was advertised primarily on an ADHD page. Other neurodivergences were not as well represented.

	DX<12	DX <18	DX >18	Self DX	TOTAL	not sure
ADHD	13.0%	4.5%	49.4%	27.4%	**94.3%**	1.7%
Aphasia/dysphasia	0.3%	0.0%	0.3%	2.9%	**3.5%**	17.8%
Autism	1.0%	0.8%	7.0%	21.6%	**30.5%**	17.9%
Dyscalculia	1.2%	0.5%	2.1%	11.7%	**15.5%**	15.4%
Dysgraphia	1.3%	0.2%	0.6%	2.5%	**4.6%**	16.3%
Dyslexia	3.1%	0.8%	1.9%	4.9%	**10.7%**	14.8%
Dyspraxia	1.1%	0.4%	0.9%	5.9%	**8.3%**	17.3%
Hyperlexia	2.4%	0.2%	0.1%	7.5%	**10.3%**	17.4%
Sensory Processing Disorders	1.7%	1.0%	5.2%	31.3%	**39.2%**	11.7%
Auditory Processing Disorder	2.1%	0.8%	4.8%	30.1%	**37.8%**	12.5%
Synesthesia	0.3%	0.1%	0.1%	7.0%	**7.7%**	15.9%
Tourette's	0.4%	0.0%	0.3%	1.1%	**1.8%**	15.4%
Other	2.0%	1.5%	4.7%	4.7%	**12.8%**	12.6%

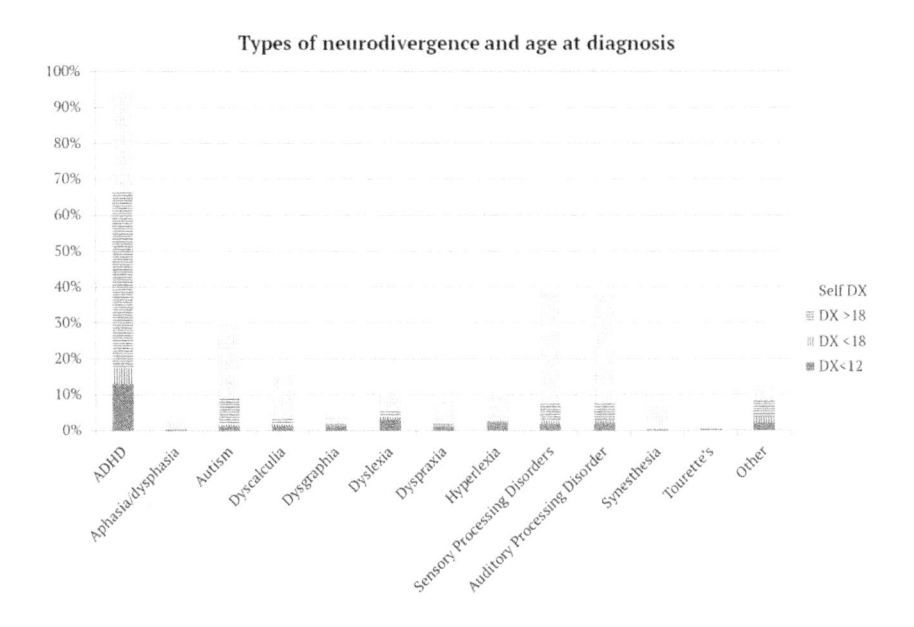

Types of neurodivergence and age at diagnosis

If we do not include those who responded "not sure" in the calculations, 73% of respondents had multiple diagnoses. The mean number of diagnoses was 2.8, and the median was 2. Of the 27% of respondents who only had one diagnosis, 94% were ADHDers. One respondent had the lot.

If we include those who responded "not sure" in the calculations, the mean number of diagnoses increases to 4.7, and the median to 3. 19% of respondents only had one diagnosis. Of these, 96% were ADHDers.

After ADHD, the most prevalent diagnoses were Sensory Processing Disorders (39.2%), Auditory Processing Disorder (37.8%), and Autism (30.5%). 80% of those who reported sensory processing disorders are self-diagnosed. I was surprised by the relatively high incidence of processing disorders reported, as I very rarely hear them mentioned outside of Autistic communities. Lo and behold, 49% of respondents who reported Sensory Processing Disorders and 47% of those who reported Auditory Processing Disorder were also Autistic.

12.8% of respondents stated that they have a neurodivergence not included in the list. As I did not allow respondents the opportunity to add additional neurodivergences, I cannot know what they are. This should be rectified in future surveys.

The survey allowed self-diagnosed NDs to participate, for one simple reason: I am aware of the barriers to diagnosis that affect a large proportion of the neurodivergent community. If you'd like to know the details of this issue as they apply to ADHD, I wrote a whole book about it.[13] The TL/DR version is that, while diagnostic paths and methodologies vary between countries, if you are young, male, thin, otherwise healthy, sociodemographically advantaged, straight, cis, white, and with no history of substance abuse, addictive behaviors, or legal entanglements, you have a better chance of getting an official diagnosis. If you do not meet all of the above criteria, there are visible and invisible barriers in place that may prevent you from getting diagnosed, regardless of how obvious, pervasive, and impactful your neurodivergent traits may be.

Some of these barriers can be overcome if you have enough money to throw at them, but not everyone can do that. This is particularly true for those of us who were not diagnosed in childhood, and whose neurodivergence is a barrier to full, regular employment. Also, some barriers, most notably the absence of experts willing and able to assess

---

[13] https://www.amazon.com/dp/B08TKJ6LV7

adults, simply cannot be overcome by the average individual.

The results of this survey highlighted the significance of this issue. Although our neurodivergences are with us from birth, and diagnoses are only granted to those who could prove that their symptoms started before a certain age, many of us were not diagnosed in childhood. This is incredibly important, as many neurodivergences have an impact on the effectiveness of classroom learning. Early diagnosis and the appropriate academic adaptations can ensure that we achieve our academic potential.

As most respondents were ADHDers, we have the greatest amount of data about ADHD. Unfortunately, we did not get enough respondents under 18 and over 55 to warrant further analysis. For the remaining age groups, only 14% were diagnosed under 12. 5% were diagnosed under 18, 53% over 18, and 28% were self-diagnosed.[14] This indicates that 86% of us were diagnosed too late to get support and accommodations during our early school years, 81% were only diagnosed after high school, and 28% of us are still undiagnosed. And, of course, that 28% only includes people who are aware enough of the experiences of having ADHD (as opposed to unrepresentative stereotypes) to feel it may apply to them and to seek out information and support. The real number of undiagnosed ADHDers could be much higher.

These results look even less positive if we look solely at those of us who have managed to get an official diagnosis of ADHD. Broken down by age group, the results indicate that most people are diagnosed over 18.

	<12	<18	>18
18-24	25%	14%	61%
25-34	24%	7%	69%
35-44	16%	4%	80%
45-54	8%	5%	87%

The low childhood diagnostic rates in older age groups are to be expected, given how ADHD only hit the medical mainstream in the 80s. However, that does not justify the fact that only 25% of 18-24 year olds were diagnosed under 12.

---

[14] 2% responded not sure, so I excluded them from these calculations.

Age at diagnosis by age group (ADHD)

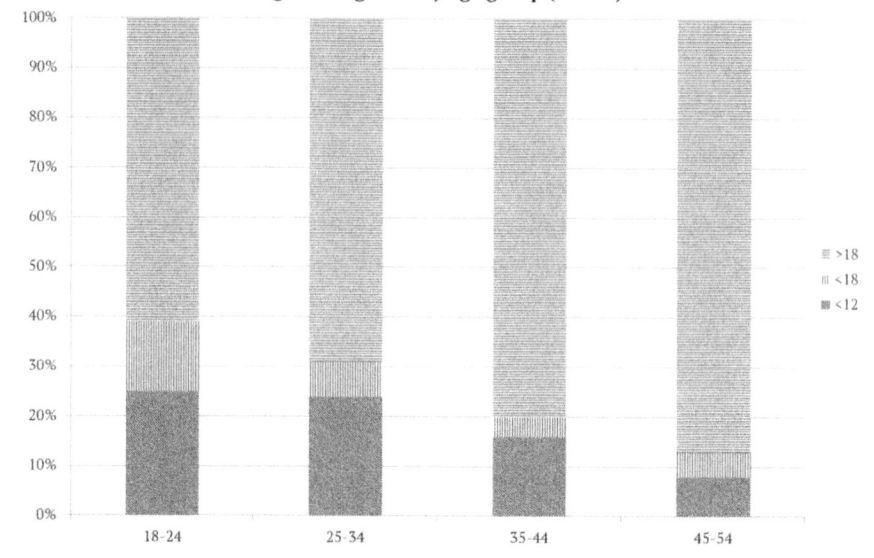

Legend: >18, <18, <12

This is an interesting result, given how often people, including "experts," suggest that ADHD is overdiagnosed in school-age children. While our results cannot inform us as to diagnostic rates in younger generations, they indicate that past generations, including Millennials, have been massively *under*diagnosed. This might have had a detrimental impact on those of us who were forced to complete our education without any support or accommodations.

The results were worse for Autism. 33% of respondents were Autistic. Of them, 71% were self-diagnosed. Of the 29% with an official diagnosis, only 12% were diagnosed under 12, while 80% were diagnosed over 18.

These results suggest that the need for specialist services for the diagnosis and treatment of adult NDs is very real. In many areas, this need is not currently reflected in the availability of services. ADHD and Autism in particular are still largely seen as childhood disorders, and not only by the general public. In many areas, there are no diagnostic services for adults – as in, it is literally impossible for adults to be diagnosed, because no experts are available to carry out that diagnosis. While it is absolutely true that neurodivergences should be diagnosed in childhood, the fact that they so often are not should be taken into account by service providers.

With a sufficiently large number of respondents, the discrepancy between symptoms exhibited and diagnoses received could be used to quantify the impact of biases. If diagnostic rates are different between people who are subjected to a bias and people who are not, that difference suggests that the bias in question has an impact on diagnostic rates.

Gender has been reported as having a significant impact on the diagnosis of ADHD and Autism. As I explained in an earlier section, this survey did not receive enough AMAB respondents to compare results by gender. It also did not collect information to facilitate an analysis of the impact of other biases in early life.[15] However, this could be done in future, larger studies.

---

[15] While trans adults were once trans children, transness is not always apparent in early years, and I did not ask the relevant questions.

Traits.

This section looked at the traits of some of the most common neurodivergences. The questions were:

Traits you have had since childhood. (Mark only one oval per row. Never / Sometimes / Often / Always / Not sure)

- Difficulties writing.
- Difficulties reading.
- Difficulties with math.
- Poor gross motor skills (i.e., are you uncoordinated or "clumsy").
- Poor fine motor skills (i.e., do you struggle to pick up, hold, or manipulate small things.
- Synesthesia.
- Cross-overs between sensory or cognitive pathway? (e.g., you can see music or smell colors).
- Alexithymia.
- Inability to recognize your feelings.
- Inability to recognize other people's feelings.
- "Mental juke-box" that plays a constant soundtrack.

In an ideal world, the Venn diagram of people who display neurodivergent traits and people with a diagnosis of neurodivergence would be a perfect circle. Alas, we do not live in an ideal world. Due to a combination of issues – lack of awareness, lack of resources, academic and medical biases, ableism, and more – a large number of neurodivergent people do not get diagnosed in childhood and are unable to get diagnosed in adulthood, even though they meet current diagnostic criteria.

By comparing individuals' ND traits and diagnostic status, surveys such as this one could help identify just how many of us fell through the diagnostic cracks. If a person has the traits of a neurodivergence and does not have a diagnosis, that's what we call A Clue. It doesn't necessarily mean that they should be diagnosed – they could be subclinical, have underlying conditions whose symptoms mimic neurodivergent traits, and so on. However, this kind of comparison is a good place to start.

	Alexithymia	Inability to recognize your feelings	Inability to recognize other people's feelings
Never	38%	20%	28%
Sometimes	11%	41%	46%
Often	9%	27%	20%
Always	4%	9%	4%
Not sure	39%	2%	2%

Alexithymia is a fascinating neurodivergence because it has a huge impact on our ability to self-regulate, communicate, and socialize, but most people have never heard about it.

Alexithymia is a difficulty experiencing, identifying, and expressing emotions. The word comes from Greek: 'a' meaning lack, 'lexis' meaning word, and 'thymos' meaning emotion. However, alexithymia is not just a "lack of words" to describe emotions. People with alexithymia[16] struggle to express their emotions to others because they struggle to identify them in themselves. This can be linked to problems with introspection (the examination of one's own mental and emotional processes) and/or interoception (the perception of the state of the body). The latter concept is so important that it's going to get its own section.

Alexithymia can make it difficult for people to identify and respond to emotions in others. This can lead to interpersonal and social issues.

Alexithymia is not currently classed as a neurodivergence or condition in its own right. It is usually diagnosed as co-occurring with Autism and some mental health conditions. This is somewhat problematic, to put it mildly, and the issue isn't just one of diagnosis; it's the lack of information that matters.

Alexithymia can have a profound and serious impact on a person's life, but people who have always lived with it may not be aware that they are missing a key tool. It's not that we don't realize that we can't tell how we feel; it's that we don't even suspect that we should be able to do that. We might not feel a lack, because we do not know that there is something we are missing. We may not look for ways to compensate for our issues,

---

[16] I don't believe "alexithymic" is currently in use, but I could be wrong! Apologies if I messed up.

because we are not aware of that possibility. Also, we might be aware that the people around us are operating on a different level, but we won't know why, which gives us no chance to bridge that gap.

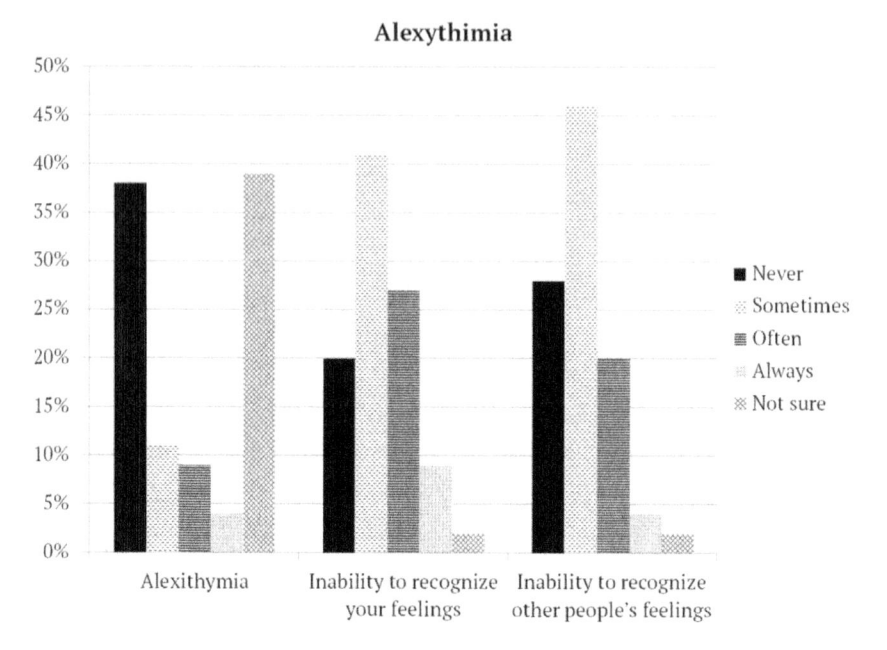

Alexythimia

[Bar chart showing percentages for three categories — Alexithymia, Inability to recognize your feelings, Inability to recognize other people's feelings — across five response types: Never, Sometimes, Often, Always, Not sure.]

The results of this survey reflect this lack of information. 13% of respondents said that they often or always have alexithymia, which is in line with current estimates of the prevalence of alexithymia in the general population (10-13%, dependent on studies). However, 36% of respondents are often or always unable to recognize their feelings, and 24% are often or always unable to recognize other people's feelings. While the latter issue may be caused by communication problems – or, if you live in a culture that promotes emotional suppression, by the absence of a crystal ball – the former suggests that alexithymia is a possibility.

If we correlate the responses about alexithymia with those about Autism, we find that 62% of respondents with alexithymia are Autistic, as are 47% of those who often or always unable to recognize their feelings, and 50% of those who are often or always unable to recognize other people's feelings. While these correlations may seem high, they still leave out half of the respondents who, lacking an Autism diagnosis, are currently unlikely to receive a diagnosis of alexithymia, or even to be told about it. Lacking information about the problem, we are unlikely to stumble upon any solutions.

Ultimately, I don't think it really matters whether people have "real" alexithymia or "just" problems identifying emotions. The issue is that being unable to identify emotions, for whatever reason, can make it difficult for us to function. When information and support is only targeted towards a section of our community, the rest of us can't benefit. The results of this survey suggest that this approach is leaving a lot of us out in the cold.

Similar issues apply to other less-known neurodivergences, like Synesthesia.

Synesthesia		Cross-overs between sensory or cognitive pathways	
% total	8%	Never	68%
<12	5%	Sometimes	17%
<18	2%	Often	5%
>18	2%	Always	4%
SD	92%	Not sure	7%

Synesthesia is a perceptual phenomenon in which stimulation of one sensory or cognitive pathway leads to involuntary experiences in a second sensory or cognitive pathway. The results vary depending on the senses involved, but common symptoms include:

- Involuntary perceptions that cross over between senses.
- Sensory triggers that consistently and predictably cause interplay between senses.
- Ability to describe these perceptions to other people.

The results of this survey indicate a partial overlap between people who know that they have synesthesia and people who experience sensory cross-overs. 8% of respondents have synesthesia, of which 92% are self-diagnosed. However, the percentage of people who experience sensory cross-overs is greater: 4% experience them always, 5% often, and 17% sometimes. Assuming that those cross-overs are not induced by chemicals, the results suggest that up to 18% respondents may be experiencing symptoms of synesthesia without being aware of it.

Happily, this may not be much of an issue. There is no treatment for synesthesia, but as most synesthetes enjoy their experiences, that is not a major concern. However, synesthesia can cause people to feel socially isolated. In that eventuality, finding other synesthetes or talking to a therapist may help. Unfortunately, that hinges on synesthetes being aware that synesthesia is a thing, either by being told or by working out that their sensory experience is different from that of the majority.

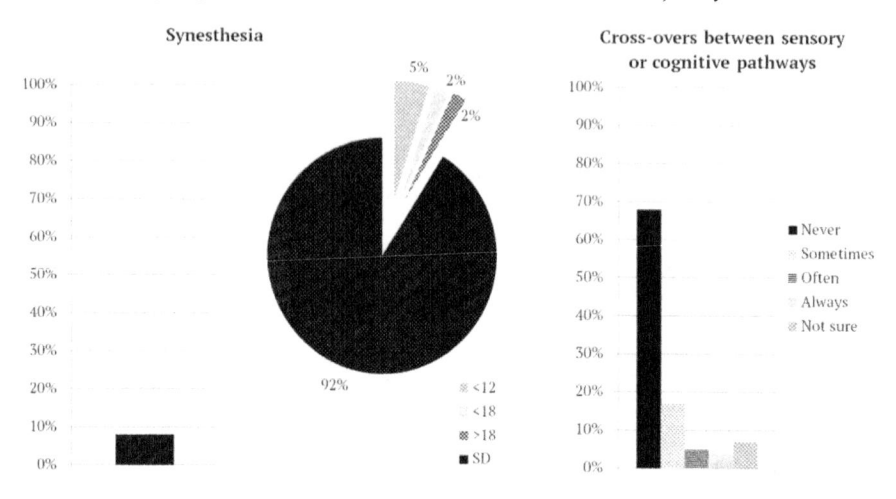

[Chart: Synesthesia — pie chart showing 92%, 5%, 2%, 2% with legend <12, <18, >18, SD]

[Chart: Cross-overs between sensory or cognitive pathways — bar chart with legend Never, Sometimes, Often, Always, Not sure]

That is one of the issues with many neurodivergences: although they might make our experience different from that of the majority, we might not realize that, or not realize why. That isn't because, as some "experts" suggest, NDs lack "theory of mind"; quite simply, it isn't always possible to compare our experience to that of other people, particularly if that experience is purely internal. Neurotypicals routinely fail to understand or to accept that the way in which we experience the world is fundamentally different. Why are we expected to succeed where they fail? And how are we supposed to do that when we are constantly bombarded with messages about how our ND traits and symptoms aren't real?

Realizing how we differ from the majority can be even harder when we are not in the minority – not locally, anyway. Many neurodivergences run in families. Not all of us are blessed with neurodivergent parents, but many of us have one or more relatives who share our traits and symptoms. This can create the impression that what we are going through is "normal," even when it statistically rare in the general population or is the symptom of a serious condition. We might be chronically sleep deprived, unable to breathe properly, allergic to a staggering amount of stuff, unable to move without spraining a joint, eternally late, lost, dissociated, overwhelmed, bored, or so staggeringly confused by other humans that we wonder whether we are the first wave of an alien invasion. But so are Grandma, Uncle Bob, and three of our cousins, and there's nothing wrong with them! Our family is just like that!

Some aspects of our neurodivergence are picked up when we "fail" to perform like our neurotypical peers. Often, this happens at school. School is one of the few settings were every aspect of our productivity is tested. Doing well in school isn't just about delivering a product that meets certain standards; it also means producing it at the right speed, following the right set of steps, while behaving the right way, and all in an environment that is totally outside of our control. We may produce good quality work and still be punished because we worked too fast, too slowly, too intuitively, too precisely, while concentrating too hard or not hard enough, while we did not look like we were paying attention, while were not staying still, while we were not sitting properly... the list of potential transgressions is endless. Most workplaces have some of those restrictions, too, but very few have all of them.

School is, therefore, ~~hell~~[17] a good place for individual differences to become apparent, and this includes differences that stem from neurodivergences. While that often sucks for the kids involved, it does give them the opportunity to get the support they need to try and improve their performance. This support can have a huge positive impact, particularly in primary/elementary school, because learning is cumulative. The earlier we fall behind, the harder it is to catch up.

Identifying neurodivergences in childhood gives us the chance to develop coping mechanisms and workarounds that can help us keep up with our classmates and maximize both our current achievements and our future potential. From a practical point of view, it's helpful. From a psychological point of view, however, it sucks. Educational interventions often focus on what we can't do and ignore all the areas in which we excel. If we are constantly described in terms of our shortcomings, they can end up defining us, and we risk growing up with an identity that centers around negatives. That is suboptimal, to put it mildly, but so is failing at stuff without knowing why or getting any help. At least the deficit-based approach gives us the chance to get help instead of getting punished for "failures" entirely outside of our control.

---

[17] I actually loved elementary school, but as my teacher was Montessori-trained, I feel like I cheated. And moving to a regular secondary school *sucked*.

...or rather, it would if it worked, but that's not always the case.

Let's look at four of the most famous neurodivergences: dyslexia, dysgraphia, dyscalculia, and dyspraxia. The first three are classed as learning difficulties or disabilities, and the fourth is a neurological motor disorder. All four manifest in childhood and will persist throughout life, especially if they go "untreated." All four affect the development of skills essential to academic performance, namely:

- **Dyslexia** affects the skills involved in accurate and fluent word reading and spelling.
- **Dysgraphia** affects the mechanics of writing as well as grammar, syntax, comprehension, and the ability to put thoughts on paper.
- **Dyscalculia** affects the ability to understand numbers, perform accurate calculations, and perform basic math skills.
- **Dyspraxia**, aka Developmental Coordination Disorder (DCD), affects fine and/or gross motor skills.

These descriptions are horrifically reductive – in fact, there is so much wrong with them that it would take a whole other book to dissect all the issues.[18] However, they do serve a key purpose: they are so simplistic that the least neurodivergent-savvy person in the world should be able to draw a connection between struggles in a certain domain and the possibility that the relevant "learning difficulty" may be in play. If a kid struggles with reading, they might be dyslexic; if they struggle with coordination, they might be dyspraxic; etc.

Obviously, this approach doesn't always work, because dozens of issues can cause difficulties in any domain. For instance, difficulties with reading could arise from poor eyesight, motor skills issues affecting eye movement, poor working memory, or lateralization issues. Difficulties with motor skills could arise from neurological factors, musculoskeletal conditions, lack of practice, or adrenalization. Furthermore, a child could be able to perform a task provided that certain conditions are met, but be unable to perform the same task if the conditions change; for instance, they might be able to read to themselves in a quiet room, but be unable to read in a room full of distractions, or if they are being observed. Also, a child may be able to perform a task but be unable to demonstrate that to

---

[18] No, I am NOT writing that. I am finishing this and I'm going back to writing neuroqueer fiction forever, thank you very much.

the adults around them; for instance, they might be able to read, but not be able to talk about what they just read when asked to.

Ultimately, though, the whole point of classifying kids according to their deficits is to enable educational institutions to provide them with the extra support and adaptations they need.

Let's see how this works in practice:

Dyslexia		Difficulties reading	
% total	11%	Never	59.3%
<12	29%	Sometimes	27.3%
<18	8%	Often	10.1%
>18	17%	Always	2.7%
SD	46%	Not sure	0.6%

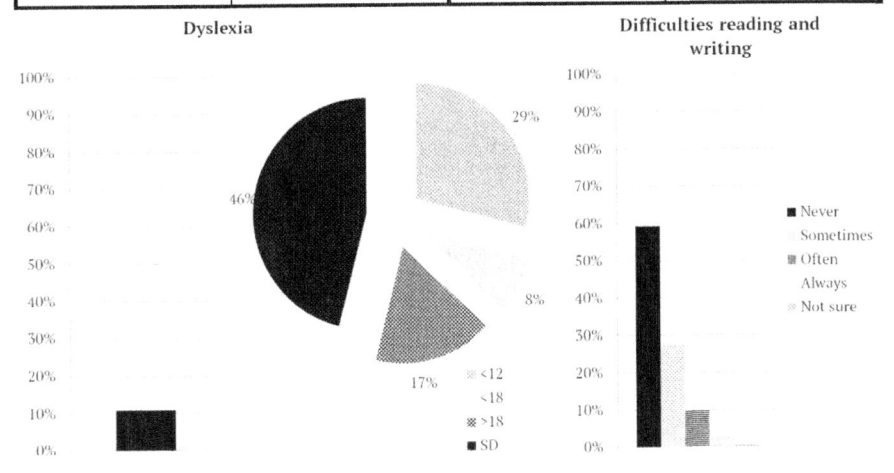

11% of respondents are dyslexic, of which 46% are self-diagnosed. By contrast, 13% of respondents often or always have difficulties reading.

Dysgraphia		Difficulties writing	
% total	5%	Never	48.5%
<12	28%	Sometimes	31.2%
<18	4%	Often	13.0%
>18	12%	Always	6.5%
SD	55%	Not sure	0.8%

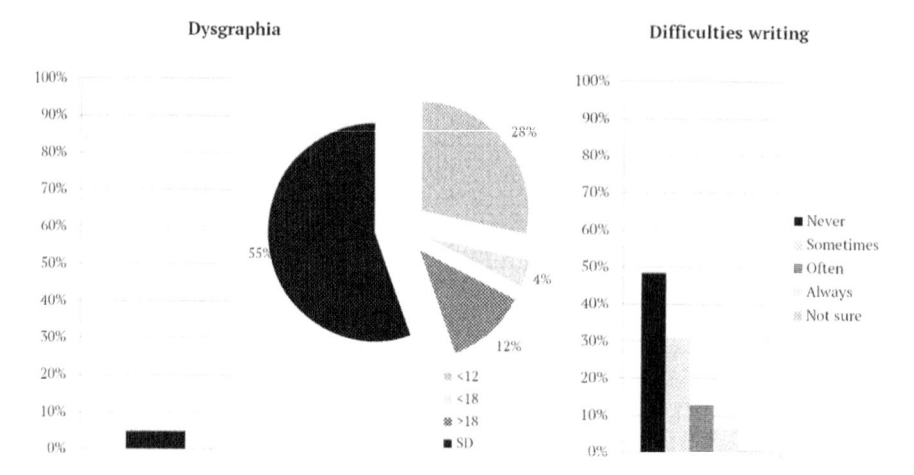

5% of respondents are dysgraphic, of which 55% are self-diagnosed. By contrast, 19% of respondents often or always have difficulties writing.

Dyscalculia		Difficulties with math	
% total	16%	Never	27.5%
<12	8%	Sometimes	29.9%
<18	3%	Often	20.8%
>18	13%	Always	21.3%
SD	75%	Not sure	0.6%

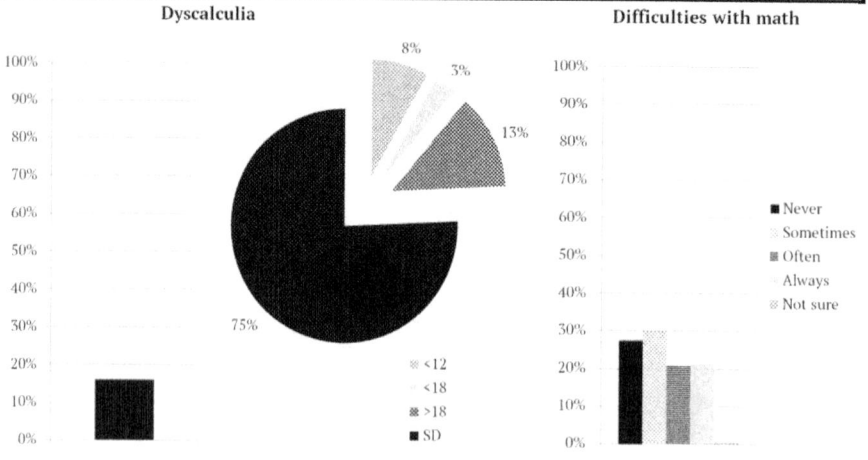

16% of respondents are dyscalculic, of which 75% are self-diagnosed. By contrast, 42% of respondents often or always have difficulties with math.

Dyspraxia			Poor gross motor skills	Poor fine motor skills
% total	8%	Never	13.2%	46.9%
<12	13%	Sometimes	33.9%	34.6%
<18	5%	Often	31.7%	12.2%
>18	11%	Always	20.7%	5.5%
SD	71%	Not sure	0.5%	0.7%

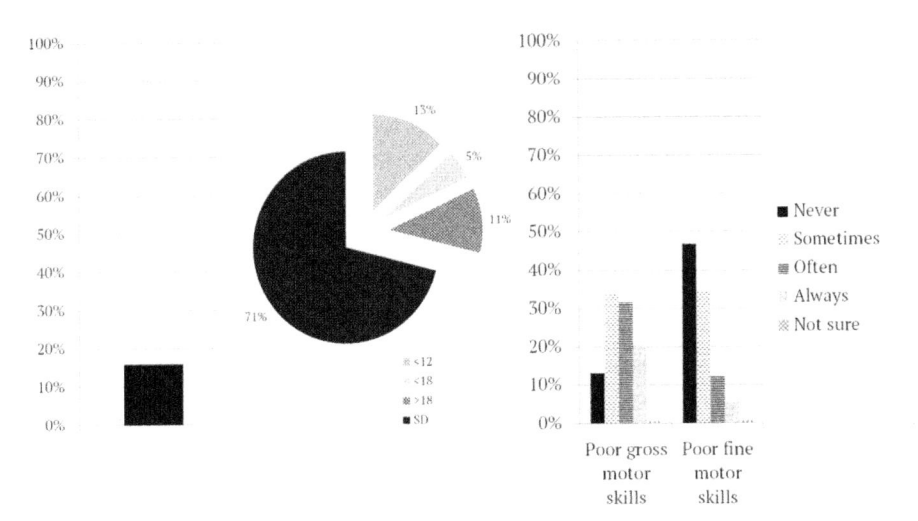

8% of respondents are dyspraxic, of which 46% are self-diagnosed. By contrast, 52% of respondents often or always have poor gross motor skills and 18% have poor fine motor skills. 88% of respondents with poor fine motor skills also have poor gross motor skills.

Unsurprisingly, the best-known neurodivergences have the lowest discrepancies between people with a diagnosis and people who struggle in a certain domain. Depressingly, even the neurodivergence with the smallest discrepancy (dyslexia) was diagnosed under the age of 12 in only 29% of respondents, while 46% are self-diagnosed. For the much less popular dyscalculia, diagnoses under 12 are down to 8%, and 75% of respondents are self-diagnosed.

Discrepancies between people with a diagnosis and people who struggle in a certain domain do not necessarily indicate that we are not diagnosing enough people. As I already discussed, our ability to perform in any of these domains can be influenced by a number of different factors.

However, the results of this survey clearly indicate that too many people are diagnosed too late, if at all. Combined with the discrepancies we discussed, these figures raise some important questions:

- Given the importance of early academic interventions and support, why are less than a third of children diagnosed under the age of 12?
- Are children who already have a diagnosis of neurodivergence more or less likely to receive additional diagnoses? Neurodivergences and learning difficulties often co-occur, but is there a risk that having one diagnosis means that all future struggles are chalked down to that single factor? Is this risk greater for diagnoses that encompass a variety of traits and symptoms? (E.g., "This kid just can't school because ADHD," with no further investigations.)
- For children who have more than one undiagnosed neurodivergence, what exactly happened? Why did the system fail them?
- If there are marked discrepancies between the number of people who have a learning difficulty and the number of people who have difficulties learning, is the current system working?
- Ultimately, is this how we should be doing things? Should kids receive support and accommodations because they have a diagnosis, or because they need some help?

I personally have a very poor opinion of deficit-based diagnoses, but I acknowledge that they can be helpful. Knowing that these neurodivergences exist and that they are affecting us is important. As a minimum, it tells us that we are dealing with problems that the majority of other people do not have to face. The playing field isn't level, and knowing that can help us look for solutions. At the very least, it might stop us from punishing ourselves for things outside of our control. However, the current approach seems to be letting a lot of people down.

The last question is not associated with any neurodivergence I know of. I just asked it because I was curious. A few years ago, I was made aware of the fact that the majority of people can only hear music when music is actually playing. They don't have a mental juke-box that plays music for them. That's why they complain so much when they get "a song stuck in their head:" their heads are normally devoid of music unless they use artificial devices to feed it in there through their ears.

Once I had established that this sad state of affairs is really a thing, and a common thing at that, I became curious as to how many people are affected by it. I don't know enough neurotypical people to find out the prevalence of this condition in their community, but I thought I'd ask here.

"Mental juke-box" that plays a constant soundtrack	
Never	8%
Sometimes	21%
Often	29%
Always	40%
Not sure	2%

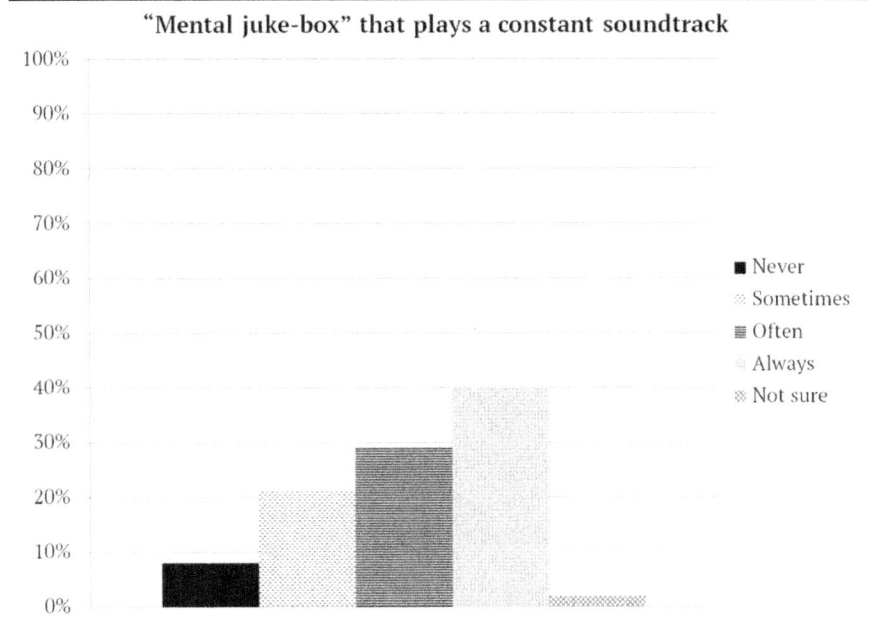

Only 8% of survey respondents lack a mental juke-box, although 21% only hear it sometimes. 2% are not sure. 69% of us hear it often or always.

I don't know what else to say about this. Without knowing the prevalence of mental juke-boxes in the neurotypical community, it's impossible to draw any comparisons.

Exposure to painful stimuli

This section looked at people's exposure to painful stimuli, and at the problems their atypical sensory experiences caused them in childhood and beyond. The questions were:

- When you were a child, did you get into trouble for having "tantrums" when you were trying to avoid painful physical sensations?
- When you were a child, were you forced by your parents or teachers to endure painful physical sensation in order to learn to get over them?
- Are you routinely forced to endure unpleasant or overwhelming physical sensations in order to navigate your environment?

Many NDs have sensory experiences different from those of neurotypical people. Sometimes we are able to pick up stimuli neurotypicals cannot register; for instance, we might hear noises they can't hear. Sometimes our bodies register otherwise harmless stimuli as painful; for instance, people with allodynia experience light touch as painful. Sometimes we are physiologically hypersensitive to certain stimuli; for instance, we might have allergies to certain smells or chemicals. All these responses are physiological, not emotional or psychological.

Unfortunately, this fact is routinely overlooked by parents and teachers who do not understand the issue. When neurodivergent children react to stimuli in ways the adults do not relate to, the common assumption is that the child is over-reacting, rather than showing signs of over-sensitivity. If a child expresses their discomfort through a verbal or physical outburst or any type of "misbehavior," they may be punished for having a "tantrum." That is a double whammy: not only these children are not protected from painful stimuli by the adults responsible for their care, but they are punished for trying to protect themselves.

	Punished for "tantrums"	"Desensitized"	Current exposure
Never	47%	60%	52%
Sometimes	25%	21%	30%
Often	17%	13%	13%
Always	11%	7%	5%
Not sure	16%	12%	5%

Exposure to painful stimuli

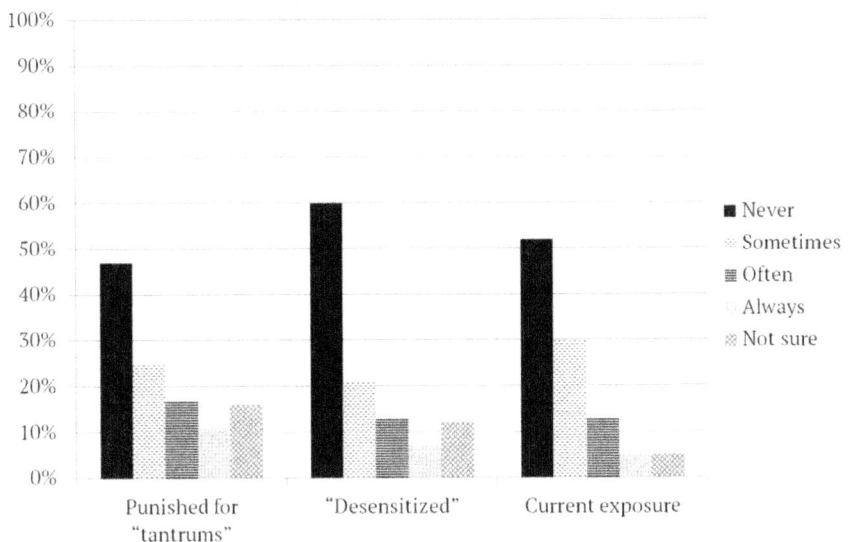

28% of respondents reported that they often or always got into trouble for having "tantrums" when trying to avoid painful physical sensations. I personally find that heartbreaking.

To make matters worse, some parents and teachers try to "help" ND children by exposing them to the stimuli they are "overreacting" to in order to teach them to tolerate them. 11% of survey respondents reported that this happened to them always, and 17% often, giving us a total of 28%. However, I would argue that this is one of those occasions where an answer of "sometimes" is bad enough to warrant inclusion, because it is never OK to force a child to endure unnecessary pain. This would raise the percentage of responders who answered positively to 53%.

This type of "therapy" may have good intentions. The hope is that exposure to unpleasant or painful stimuli will "desensitize" us. However, what is being done here is *not* desensitization.

Desensitization is a technique that aims to diminish responses to a stimulus through repeated exposure, but it has a key prerequisite: the core issue must be overreaction. For instance, I freak out when I see large spiders, even though they are not causing me any pain and I know that spiders in this country are perfectly safe. I am overreacting to a stimulus. A systematic program of gradual exposure to spiders might help me get over this issue. Over time, I might become desensitized to spiders. I might learn to tolerate looking at pictures of spiders, watching them on video, or sitting next to a spider tank. I might even get used to touching them.

Learning to hug my elementary school music teacher was a different process altogether. I avoided her as least as enthusiastically as I avoid spiders, that's true, but that was because she wore so much scent that being within twenty yards of her set off my allergies. If I went anywhere near her, my sinuses would swell up so much and so fast that I felt as if I'd been smacked in the face. Hugging her left me covered in her smell, so my face would hurt more and more until I could change my clothes and wash. The bottom line was that being anywhere near her *hurt*. It didn't just upset me, although the pain was unquestionably upsetting.

Forcing a person to endure a stimulus when their aversive response is the result of a physiological issue is *not* desensitization. If done without that person's consent, it's abuse. Even when the person consents, the process cannot result in "desensitization" in the therapeutic sense of the word. The person isn't learning to manage their emotional responses to a benign stimulus; they are learning to suffer quietly.

Unsurprisingly, there appears to be a correlation between attempts at "desensitization" and people's ability to recognize their feelings. Out of all respondents, 36% reported that they are often or always unable to recognize their feelings. This value goes up to 50% in the "desensitized" group.

It gets worse. The results of this survey showed that respondents who, in childhood, were "desensitized" also have an increased prevalence of interoception problems, dissociative states, and crisis responses such as meltdowns, shutdowns, selective mutism, and burnouts. These issues will be discussed in the relevant sections. While these results cannot prove a causal link, they suggest a connection between attempts at "desensitization" and significant, long-term problems in later life.

Again, from the outside these "therapeutic interventions" might look successful, because the children undergoing them no longer respond negatively to stimuli. However, I would argue that causing serious detrimental long-term consequences in the name of "therapy" is somewhat misguided.

To make matters worse, in the group of "desensitized" children, 73% reported that they were often or always punished for having "tantrums" when they were trying to avoid painful physical sensations. While the people responsible for meting out such punishment may not have realized what they were doing, their actions still have consequences.

Our problems do not always end in childhood. When asked whether they are routinely forced to endure unpleasant or overwhelming physical sensations in order to navigate their environment, 13% of respondents answered often, and 5% always.

Of these, 56% of them reported that they were often or always unable to recognize their own feelings, and 64% reported that they often or always feel disconnected from their thoughts, feelings, memories, and surroundings. The results for the same parameters for survey respondents overall was 36% and 38%. This suggests a correlation between symptoms of alexithymia, symptoms of dissociation, and being forced to routinely endure unpleasant or overwhelming physical sensations.

	Inability to recognize own feelings	Disconnection from thoughts, feelings, memories, and surroundings
Whole survey	36%	38%
"Desensitized"	50%	64%
Currently exposed	56%	64%

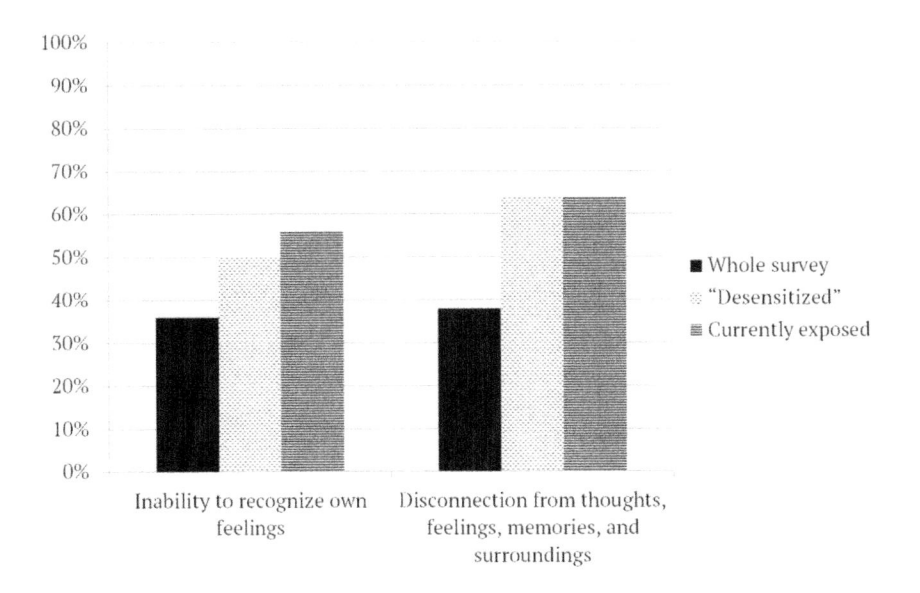

Restlessness, fidgets, and stims.

This section went totally sideways, and I don't fully understand why. The questions were:

- Are you fidgety or restless? (mental restlessness counts!)
- Do you stim?
- Do you make repetitive or unusual movements or noises when you need to calm down?
- Do you make repetitive or unusual movements or noises when you are understimulated?
- Are any of the repetitive behaviors you engage in harmful to yourself?
- Are any of the repetitive behaviors you engage in harmful to others? (annoying them does not count!)
- Do you get told off because of your repetitive behaviors?
- Do you force yourself to stop your repetitive behaviors to avoid getting told off?
- Do you redirect your repetitive behaviors to less noticeable ones to look more "normal"?
- Do you find that your need to make repetitive or unusual movements increases under stress?

Stimming is the abbreviation for "self-stimulating behavior": any repetitive actions or movements designed to help us deal with conditions that aren't quite right for us. Finger-tapping, nail biting, pacing, hair twirling, fidgeting on a chair, chewing your lips or the inside of your mouth, sucking on pens, and humming are all stims. Literally any repetitive action that has no function beyond making us feel better while we deal with something is a stim.

Everyone stims, in various ways and to varying degrees. Neurotypical people stim; they just don't do it so often, for so long, or so obviously. Stimming is perfectly natural, and is not a symptom or trait of any condition. If it indicates anything, is that the current situation is not meeting the needs of the stimming person – or, rather, the stimming *organism*, because animals also stim. A pacing new-parent-to-be and a pacing caged lion are both stimming, even though the underlying emotional causes of their stimming may be very different. Pacing won't help a baby be born and it won't dissolve the bars of the cage, so it doesn't help change their situation. However, it helps them tolerate it.

This is important: stims are *not* useless. They might not have a direct impact on our situation, but they *do* have an impact on our ability to tolerate it, and that is important. And this isn't just a psychological or emotional issue: as we will discuss in the chapter on stress, long-term stress can have serious negative impacts on our health. If stimming can help us manage our stress levels, repressing it could have an adverse impact on our long-term health.

	Fidgety or restless	**Stim**	**Stim to calm down**	**Stim when u/stimulated**
Never	0.5%	6%	18%	15%
Sometimes	8%	26%	37%	32%
Often	37%	40%	27%	31%
Always	54%	17%	14%	16%
Not sure	0.1%	11%	4%	5%

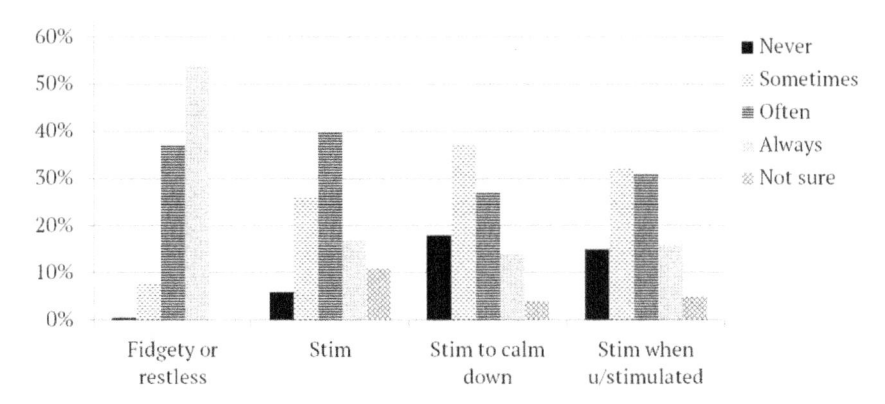

I split this section into separate, overlapping questions because I know that stimming isn't a commonly-known concept, and that different terms are used to describe the phenomenon in different context. When talking about ADHD, for instance, it's more common to hear about "fidgeting" than "stimming," but fidgeting is a form of stimming. I wanted to compare the percentage of people who reported that they stim with the percentage of people who reported that they meet the descriptions of stimming, as I did with other technical terms.

That backfired. A number of people got in touch to say that they would not answer this section because I had used the word "stim," which they believe to be strictly associated with Autism. They are not Autistic, hence they do not stim, hence they refused to report that they engage in behaviors that I might classify as stimming. Some expressed concerns that I was trying to diagnose them with Autism.

An individual also contacted me to explain that they make repetitive movements or noises because of co-occurring conditions. They also stated that they would not be answering these questions as their repetitive behaviors are not stims, and they are absolutely correct. Compulsive repetitive behaviors such as those associated with OCD and tics such as those associated with Tourette's are not stims: they have totally different causes and may not lead to a reduction in overall distress. They should be handled separately, and this survey did not do that.

When formulating this survey, I did not anticipate these issues. I have no way of knowing how much they affected the results. I am still trying to figure out how these issues could be avoided in future surveys. Maybe this section should be split into questions using different terminologies – for instance, asking about compulsive behaviors, tics, fidgets, and stims separately. I can't tell whether this would work without trying it out.

As for the results of the current survey, the problems I have outlined mean that the results may under- or over-represent the prevalence of restlessness and stimming. Under-representation is more likely, but I cannot quantify the problem.

Before we go any further, let's go on a bit of a tangent. I promise you, it's both important in general and significant in this context.

In the last decade or so, a slogan emerged: "all behavior is communication." The intentions behind it are good. The idea is that if, for instance, a child is being disruptive or even destructive, they are not "just having a tantrum." Their behavior means something. The child is expressing unmet needs in the only way they know. Therefore, it is the adults' responsibility to interpret the behavior, work out the unmet needs, and resolve the situation.

This sounds good, right? If adults spent more effort on understanding and helping children and less on punishing them, that would be good. Unfortunately, the slogan ignores the reality of people whose behavior is not under their control, and in doing so, can put them in serious danger.

Not everyone can control their body at all times. For instance, the degree of control people have over their stims can vary hugely. Some people can control most of their stims most of the time, while others can't control them at all. Many people have varying degrees of control depending on the stress they are under. In this sense, stimming tells us something, inasmuch as it indicates that the person is in some kind of distress. However, it isn't a message formulated for and directed to anyone.

A person who is bouncing their leg in a waiting room may be doing so on purpose, because they want onlookers to know how frustrated they are at the wait. However, they might simply be so stressed that they cannot control their stim. To assume that their leg bouncing is a message is incorrect; it means something, to be sure, but that doesn't make it a form of communication. Assuming that it is can lead to misunderstandings.

Mistaking all behaviors as communication is particularly dangerous to people with tic or movement disorders. Some people have very limited control over their actions. For instance, apraxics are unable to perform familiar movements on command, even though they know what they need to do and they want to do it. People with Tourette syndrome may display a variety of tics – repetitive twitches, movements, or sounds outside of their control. These behaviors are not volitional: people are not doing them on purpose. Their body is simply not cooperating.

Interpreting non-volitional behaviors as purposeful communication, or even as a manifestation of people's subconscious intentions, totally misses the point. In doing so, it puts vulnerable people in danger. There are plenty of news stories about people with echolalia and tics being criminally prosecuted, injured, or killed in confrontations with law enforcement because their behaviors were believed to be willful communication. And while this was not the intention of the "all behavior is communication" slogan, it is its unintended result.

NeuroClastic[19], arguably the best Autism self-advocacy organization out there, suggest an alternative approach:

> "**All behavior is an indicator.** Breathing is an indicator of being alive. It's not usually communication. Sneezing a lot can be an indicator of allergies. It's not communication. Seizures, meltdowns, tics, motor loops, and many behaviors disabled

---

[19] https://neuroclastic.com/infographics/

people engage in are not communication. All behaviors are indicators. They all have a reason for happening. Not every behavior is communication."

Stims are indicators. They are not communication. And now that we've got that down, let us return to our regularly scheduled programming.

92% of respondents reported that they are often or always restless and fidgety, 57% that they often or always stim, 41% that they often or always make repetitive or unusual movements or noises when they need to calm down, and 48% that they often or always make repetitive or unusual movements or noises when they are understimulated. These figures seem unremarkable in the context of a survey with a high percentage of ADHDers and Autistic respondents, but I have no official figures to compare them to.

	Harmful to yourself?	**Harmful to others?**
Never	53%	94%
Sometimes	36%	3%
Often	8%	1%
Always	1%	0.3%
Not sure	2%	2%

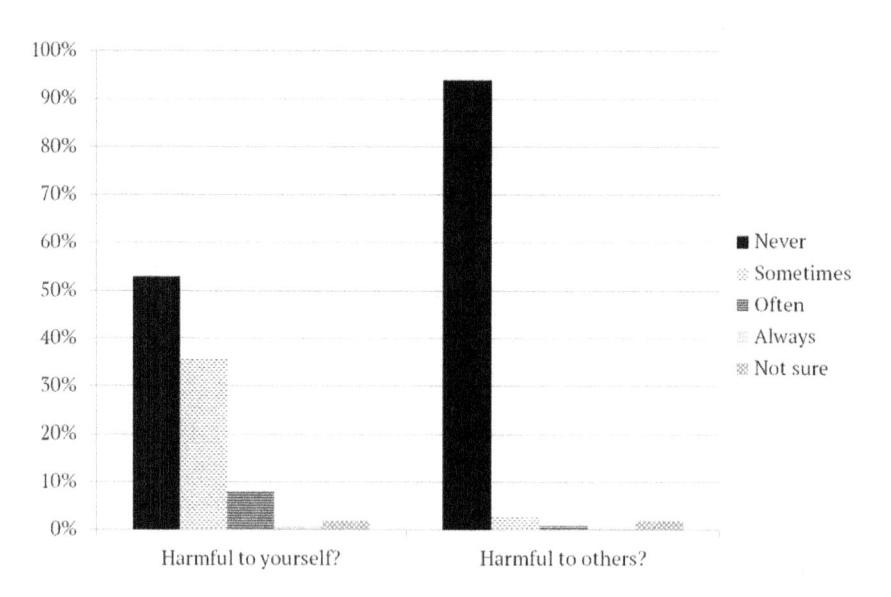

Not all stims are safe or healthy. The thing to remember is that even injurious stims are better than whatever the person doing the stimming is going through at that moment. The discomfort or pain caused by the stimming serves to mask or distract from the discomfort or pain the person is already suffering from. The stim may be bad, but the underlying problem is worse. Also, stims are not always under that person's control. If a person is not in control of their stims, telling them off for stimming is not unlike telling them off for sneezing.

9% of respondents stated that their stims are often or always harmful to them, and 1.3% that their stims are often or always harmful to others. When looking at these numbers, it is important to remember that "harmful" is a very broad concept. Chewing your lip can be harmful, but lumping it together with stims that can cause severe long-term damage, like head banging, is a bit silly.

	Told off for stimming	Need to stim more under stress
Never	36%	12%
Sometimes	47%	20%
Often	13%	29%
Always	3%	33%
Not sure	1%	6%

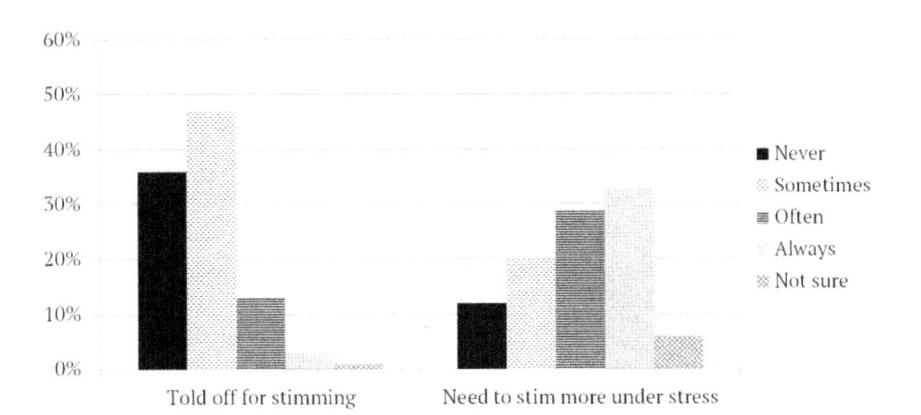

26% of survey respondents reported that they often or always get told off because of their repetitive behaviors. Only 36% never get told off. Of the people who often or always get told off, 17% often or always engage in self-harmful stims, and 3% in stims that are harmful to others. 41% of respondents get told off for stimming even though their stims are never harmful to themselves or others. And, for additional context, 99.4% of survey respondents are adults.

These results should surprise nobody who has ever stimmed in public. I could go off on a rant about why exactly people feel that they have the right to police what we do with our bodies, but I won't. Instead, I will go off on a different rant.

People's need to stim changes depending on their environment. An increase in the intensity or duration of stims typically indicates an increase in distress. This has been studied extensively in animals, for whom self-damaging stims are usually the response to inadequate conditions; confined animals use these stims when they are chronically thwarted from expressing essential behaviors or meeting basic needs. The results of this survey indicate that 62% of respondents often or always need to stim more when they are under stress.

Stimming is both a stress response and a coping mechanism. When trying to reduce stimming , this should be taken into account. A reduction in stimming should be the result of environmental improvements, not of forced repression. Forcing people to stop stimming not only doesn't address the core issue, but creates an extra stressor: not only are we still forced to deal with unfavorable conditions, but we have to do so while repressing our natural responses. This is the opposite of helpful, or logical.

Unfortunately, as we have seen, it isn't uncommon for neurodivergent people to be told to stop stimming. Sometimes this is done offhandedly, when people get annoyed by our stimming and demand that we stop. Sometimes it's part of a more defined behavioral code that may be in force in a certain setting (e.g. in school) or as general "good behavior." Sometimes, it's part of structured, formalized compliance-based "therapies" that aim at "normalizing" our behavior by coercing us into mimicking neurotypical people. If you have heard of "quiet hands" or "whole body listening," they are prime examples of this kind of approach. If you haven't heard of them and decide to look them up, brace yourself for a bumpy ride.

The irony of these interventions is that by forcing our outward behavior into a semblance of neurotypicality, they can reduce our chances of actually *functioning* like neurotypical people. For instance, "whole body listening" is a very good way of ensuring that we look like we are paying attention to a speaker while being completely unable to process what they are saying. Having to tightly monitor our entire body throughout an interaction demands our attention. The stress of behaving unnaturally reduces our ability to focus on the task at hand even further.

When we are forced to behave unnaturally for hours on end, this can have a negative impact on our stress levels, our mental health, and our health in general. And while constant repetition might force us to develop a tolerance for these unnatural behaviors, they don't actually become natural. We just learn that self-repression is our natural state of being.

Stimming is a natural behavior, and repressing it comes at a profound cost. Stims can, however, be redirected to make them safer, less noticeable, or more socially acceptable. For instance, chewable jewelry (chewelry) is a safer alternative to self-biting, or biting hard objects.

	Force self to stop stimming to avoid getting told off	Redirect stims to look more "normal"
Never	30%	19%
Sometimes	36%	28%
Often	26%	34%
Always	6%	15%
Not sure	2%	3%

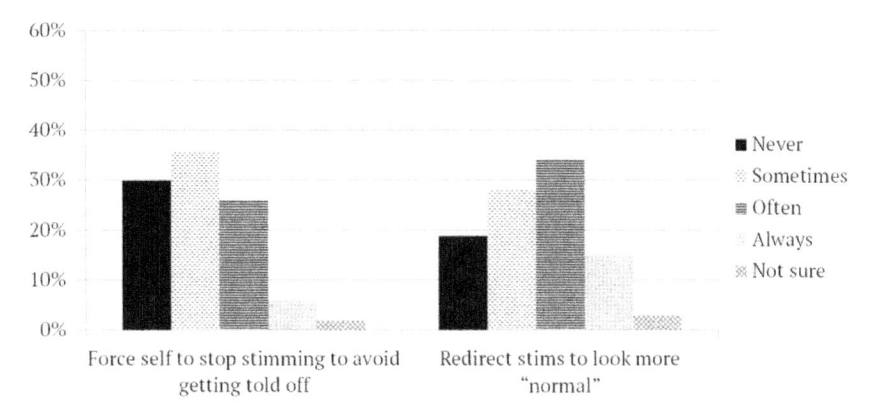

32% of survey respondents often or always force themselves to stop their repetitive behaviors to avoid getting told off, and 49% redirect them to less noticeable ones to look more "normal." While doing so may help us get along with those around us, it isn't without costs. The impact of repressing and redirecting stims on physical and mental health will be discussed in the relevant sections.

Focus and stimulation.

This section looked at people's ability to focus in different situations and at some issues related to understimulation. The questions were:

- Do you find it hard to focus on a task when there is activity or noise around you?
- Do you find it hard to focus on a task if there isn't enough going on around you?
- Do you find it hard to focus on one thing at a time? (e.g., you can only listen to a lecture if you can doodle or fidget.)
- Do you try to avoid situations that require you to wait?
- Do you feel exhausted, drained, or agitated if you are forced to do nothing?
- Do you interrupt during conversations or lectures?
- Do you space out during conversations or lectures?
- Have you engaged in risky or illegal behaviors just "for the buzz"?
- Do you feel depressed or agitated if your life is running too smoothly?

ADHD is fabulously mislabeled inasmuch as ADHDers do not in fact have a deficit of attention. Our apparent "inattention" is usually the result of a combination of factors, including:

1. We might lack the ability to *direct* our attention. We have plenty of attention, but we can't always decide what we are going to be paying attention to. I think of it as the difference between a light with a dim bulb, and a light with a broken stand; I have plenty of attention to give, but I can't always direct it where I want. Or, rather, I can't always direct it where I want to want to direct it, because of the next factor.

2. We have an "interest-based nervous system." Unlike neurotypicals, many ADHDers are not motivated by conventional rewards. In fact, some of us are actually demotivated if we are offered external rewards. The current theory is that this is due to dysfunctions in the brain reward cascade, especially in the dopamine system.

   As I understand it, neurotypical brains are like one of those games where you complete tasks and you get rewards. The NT does a thing, and their brain rewards them with feel-good neurotransmitters. Evidently, the whole "satisfaction of a job well done" is not actually just a string of words. Sounds fake to me, but I'm told that's how they roll.

ADHD brains don't seem to work like that, or don't do it consistently enough. We do a thing and we get nothing for it, because our brain reward system isn't working properly – again, this is only a theory. But if it is correct, it would explain why we might consciously or subconsciously develop an aversion to doing certain things. From an evolutionary standpoint, carrying out rewardless tasks is a potentially lethal waste of energy. Even in less extreme settings, it just sucks. How many of us would go to work every day if we knew that we weren't going to get paid? How many of us could afford to put that much effort into a rewardless activity? And how many of us would do so with a spring in our step and a song in our heart?

3. We may have sensory processing disorders. If we are given information in a way we can't process – for instance, if someone talks to us in a place with too much background noise – any resulting issues won't be caused by a lack of attention on our part. Unfortunately, it might look like that to people who don't understand what's going on. Even more unfortunately, that's most people.

4. We may have memory problems. In particular, we may have working memory problems, either because of our neurodivergence or because of chronic sleep disturbances. If we forget something, it's not because we were not paying enough attention; our brains simply can't hold that amount of information. Unfortunately, as for the point above, many people don't understand this and believe that memory is a function of attention, or even of respect, care, or love.

5. Many of us can't sit still and pay attention. We can do one or the other, but not both. In settings where stillness is enforced, our chances of actually being able to pay attention are therefore greatly reduced.

There are plenty of other factors that may negatively affect our ability to engage our attention; for instance, stress, communication issues, social pressure to regulate our eye contact, or the fact that so many people are so painfully slow, but asking them to speed up a bit is rude and inconsiderate.[20] None of this has anything to do with a deficit of attention, so it's a bit unfortunate that our neurotype should be mislabeled so

---

[20] But asking us to slow down is totally OK, though, because reasons.

incorrectly. Maybe it's not just us who should pay more attention... but I digress.

	Hard to focus with activity or noise	Hard to focus if there isn't enough going on	Hard to focus on one thing at a time
Never	2%	13%	3%
Sometimes	25%	41%	18%
Often	37%	33%	38%
Always	35%	13%	40%
Not sure	0%	1%	1%

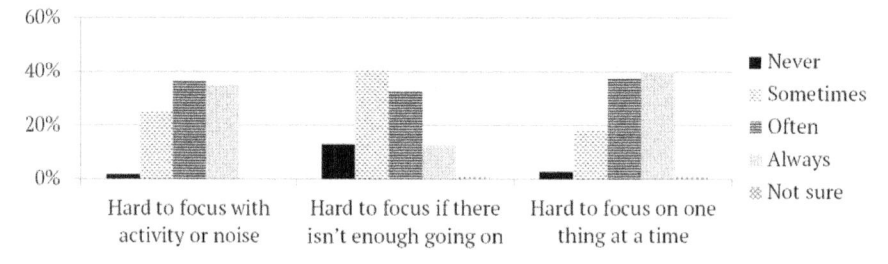

73% of respondents often or always find it hard to focus on a task when there is activity or noise around us. 45% often or always find it hard to focus on a task if there isn't enough going on around us. 79% often or always find it hard to focus on one thing at a time.

These results suggest that relatively simple adaptations that shield us from external disturbances while giving us an extra sensory input – for instance, listening to music with noise-cancelling headphones - could greatly increase our ability to focus on a task. This is probably not news to many of us. Unfortunately, the concept has yet to catch on with many educational "experts," who still insist that the only way to Really Pay Attention is to do the stuff we know doesn't work for us, but harder.

These results also indicate that certain environments are likely to have a serious detrimental impact on our ability to focus. For instance, open offices bombard us with multi-sensory distractions and force us to tightly control our behavior. In a setting of that kind, finding adaptations that work for us is critical.

Situations in which we are required to wait are something many ADHDers struggle with. This is often seen as a sign of impatience, or even of rudeness, selfishness, a sense of superiority, or a lack of empathy. We don't want to wait because we don't care about other people's needs. Furthermore, if we manifest any outward sign of stress, such as fidgeting, we are doing so in order to communicate our displeasure or to hurry people on, which is even ruder.

	Try to avoid waiting	**Exhausted, drained, or agitated if forced to do nothing**
Never	8%	7%
Sometimes	28%	23%
Often	38%	29%
Always	25%	39%
Not sure	1%	2%

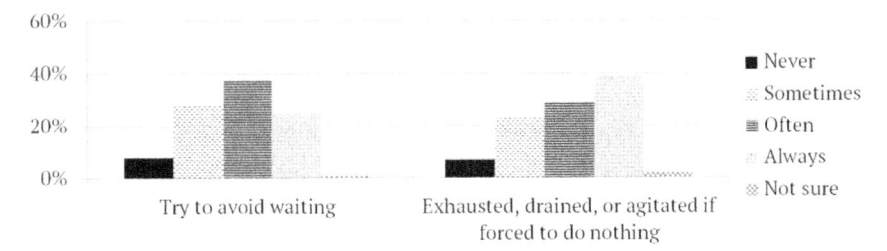

63% of respondents often or always try to avoid situations that require them to wait. 68% often or always feel exhausted, drained, or agitated if they are forced to do nothing. These two issues are connected: 81% of those who avoid waiting also feel exhausted, drained, or agitated if they are forced to do nothing. This suggests that our unwillingness to wait isn't due to any of the commonly-assumed explanations: we do not like to wait because doing nothing makes us feel ill. The real question is why that is.

My first theory was that it might have to do with low blood pressure or dizziness from standing. If standing about makes us feel dizzy or pass out, it's pretty natural that we would avoid doing so. However, those correlations turned out to be quite low: 19% of respondents who avoid waiting also have low blood pressure, and 18% feel dizzy, lightheaded, or faint if they stand up for too long. While these factors are likely to be significant for those affected, they clearly do not explain why waiting is a problem for the rest of us.

Having found out that my theory was largely a dud, I took to trying out different correlations to see what stuck.

36% of those who avoid waiting feel depressed or agitated if their life is running too smoothly. While this percentage may seem relatively low, it is slightly higher than in the survey overall (29%). Also, the fact that this reaction is unusual makes it interesting. I will discuss that issue later on in this chapter.

48% of respondents who avoid waiting also find it hard to focus on a task if there isn't enough going on around them. 83% of them find it hard to focus on one thing at a time. 94% of respondents who avoid waiting are often or always fidgety or restless. While these percentages may seem high, they broadly reflect the percentages for the survey overall, so they are unlikely to be significant.

While the absence of obvious correlations is somewhat disappointing, it doesn't make these results worthless, and it doesn't prevent us from developing theories as to what the core issue might be. I personally suspect that it's an issue of understimulation: if we need a certain amount of stuff going on to keep our brains running smoothly, or to stop them from seizing up, being deprived of enough stimulation can be problematic.

[Personally, doing a minimum of two things at a time keeps my engine running. If I am forced to do nothing, my engine winds down until it eventually stops, and starting it up again is very hard. I have been trying to think of a metaphor, and the nearest I can think of is bird flight. Once a bird is up and soaring, it can keep going without investing much energy.[21] Getting up there, however, takes a lot of energy. That's how my brain and body work: they rely on a kind of momentum to function. If I stop, I never know whether I will be able to start again. And situations where I'm constantly forced to stop and start or to operate at a speed too slow to maintain momentum are absolutely exhausting.]

Another realm in which ADHDers tend to fail is that of interrupting or spacing out while at the receiving end of verbal input – for instance, during conversations of lectures. As with our struggles with waiting, these issues are often interpreted as manifestations of our rudeness, selfishness, sense of superiority, or lack of empathy. How often this happens and how much it will impact our social life will vary depending on our culture, but most English speakers will be affected by this.

---

[21] https://journals.plos.org/plosone/article?id=10.1371/journal.pone.0013956
https://journals.plos.org/plosone/article?id=10.1371/journal.pone.0084887

Cultures and subcultures vary in their customs. However, many Anglophone cultures have been at least partly influenced by British etiquette, which includes a number of customs regulating human interactions. For instance, listening in silence is considered polite and respectful, while interrupting or interjecting are rude and domineering. This isn't a universal truth: there are plenty of cultures and subcultures that favor a more participatory conversational style. However, this fact is often ignored by those who are so used to British-style customs that all alternatives are deemed inappropriate, invalid, or inferior.

That is only the start of our problems. Many Anglophone cultures also have a tendency to assume that breaches of etiquette have an underlying motive, usually a nefarious one. It couldn't be that we interrupted because that is what we are used to where we are from, because we need something repeated or clarified, or because we are so engaged in the conversation that our neurotypical mask slipped. Each interruption is a message at best; at worst, it is a move in a power play.

Here is what an etiquette expert has to say on the subject:

> "When you interrupt someone it says to the person talking that what you have to say is more important than what they are sharing. It shows disregard for the person and what they are saying."[22]

According to this particular expert and to a myriad of her colleagues interrupting is "rude, arrogant and selfish," and we should all just cut it out. This is an interesting approach, to put it mildly, as it entirely ignores the existence of people with auditory sensory processing or short-term memory problems. We often need to interrupt a flow of words to ask for repetitions, reminders, or clarifications just to follow the conversation. The alternative is to let people ramble on way past the point where we can follow them, wait for them to come to a natural stop, and then ask them to repeat themselves, which can waste a lot of time and cause a lot of frustration. I am unclear as to whether the expert I quoted is unaware of our existence or simply doesn't care. I am very clear, however, about the impact of opinions like hers on the neurodivergent community, and it isn't good.

---

[22] https://www.cliseetiquette.com/tag/why-interrupting-is-rude/

	Interrupt during conversations or lectures	Space out during conversations or lectures
Never	8%	1%
Sometimes	35%	15%
Often	37%	50%
Always	19%	34%
Not sure	0.3%	0%

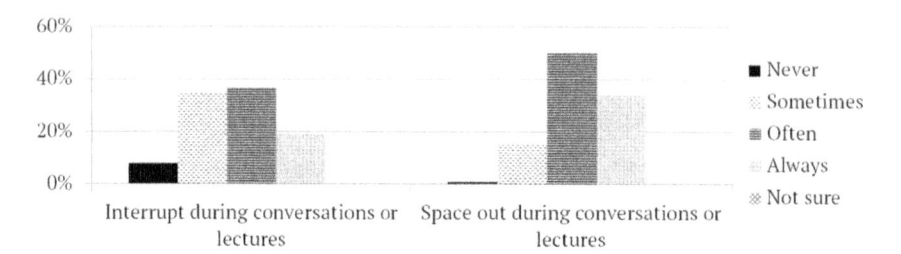

56% of survey respondents often or always interrupt during conversations or lectures, and 84% often or always space out during conversations or lectures. Now, one could just look at the percentage of ADHDers in the mix and chalk that down to that – which, sadly, is what many experts do – but I'm not going to. As far as I am concerned, "because ADHD" is not an insightful or helpful answer.

If you hark back to the section on learning styles, only 10% of respondents selected auditory learning as one of their preferred learning styles, and only 2% selected it as their main learning style. Of the people who are not auditory learners, 57% often or always interrupt, and 84% often or always space out. Again, we could shrug off these results as just ADHDers ADHDing, but I won't.

If we dig a little bit deeper, we find that 38% of respondents who always or often interrupt have Auditory Processing Disorder (APD), as do 39% of those who always or often space out. Conversely, 56% of respondents with APD always or often interrupt, and 86% always or often space out. That should come as no surprise whatsoever, given that APD makes it hard for people to process auditory input. The only surprising thing is how infrequently children who routinely interrupt or space out are investigated for APD, given how severely it can impact their ability to function in school.

The correlation between working memory problems and interrupting or spacing out should be even less surprising. 76% of respondents who always or often interrupt have working memory problems, as do 77% of those who always or often space out. Conversely, 58% of respondents with working memory problems always or often interrupt, and 87% always or often space out. It's almost as if the fact that our working memory has suboptimal storage could be a factor here. Whoddathunkit.

So, yeah, many of us struggle to process what we hear and when we do, we struggle to retain it. Many of us can't sit still and listen, but we could listen if we didn't have to sit still. Many of us are aware that auditory input doesn't really work for us, and that we can work much better with other media. But by all means, let us carry on insisting that when we fail to "pay attention" when people are talking at us, we are doing so as part of a subtle and complex secret strategy designed to undermine them. Because subtle, complex, and secret stuff is totally up our street.

This survey did not cover every issue that might have an influence on whether we interrupt or space out. In particular, the speed of speech is likely to be significant– or, at the very least, that's the case for me. It's incredibly hard to "pay attention" to people who are talkingtoofast or t o o s l o w l y . If you don't believe me, just pick a video on YouTube, fiddleabout withtheplaybackspeed, and s e e h o w w e l l y o u f a r e .

The same issues arise if people are talking at a perfectly regular speed, but our brain processes things slower or faster. Personally, I find it much easier to listen to most recordings at speeds of 1.25 to 1.50. Unfortunately, humans lack that setting. They also lack subtitles. It's like they're not even trying, really.

The last part of this section looked at issues that may be linked with understimulation, which may be linked with the theorized dysfunctions in the brain reward system that may be linked to ADHD.

Dopamine is a hormone responsible for feelings of pleasure and reward. It allows us to regulate emotional responses and take action to achieve specific goals. When the brain reward system does not function as intended, it may fail to release enough dopamine in response to "normal" positive stimuli, resulting in what has been dubbed Reward Deficiency Syndrome (RDS).

Reward deficiency issues may explain why so many of us feel awful when we are forced to engage in repetitive, boring tasks or to live repetitive, boring lives: the resulting understimulation makes our brain chemistry go out of whack. This is a physiological, not psychological response. If the situation persists, it might cause us to develop dysthymia, a persistent form of depression.

Consciously or unconsciously, we may try to fix our understimulation by making our environment more stimulating. Some of us do that by working in high-intensity, high-risk careers, or by engaging in extreme sports. Some of us, however, use coping strategies that can have profound negative impacts on our life.

This is where stuff gets depressing. Statistically, ADHDers are more prone to engaging in a number of risky, addictive, impulsive, and compulsive behaviors. These include compulsive shopping, substance use, alcoholism, risky sex, gambling, carbohydrate bingeing, aggressive behavior, and other high-risk activities. These behaviors are, effectively, coping mechanisms: they stimulate the production of the brain chemicals we lack, which allows us to feel "normal." We use over-arousal to compensate for our biochemical inability to derive reward from ordinary, everyday activities.

These coping strategies carry serious costs. Research indicates that between 25% and 40% of people in prison are ADHDers, many of whom are undiagnosed or untreated. Untreated ADHD is also associated with higher rates of substance abuse, traffic violations, and motor vehicle accidents. ADHDers are more than twice as likely to die prematurely compared with their neurotypical counterparts, and mortality rates are highest among people diagnosed in adulthood. Children with ADHD, adolescents in particular, have a suicide rate three times higher than the national average. Estimates vary, but current studies suggest that ADHDers can expect an 11- to 25-year reduction in life expectancy.

Our neurochemical deficiencies may also predispose us to entering and staying in troubled relationships. Dopamine levels shoot up in the early parts of a relationship, and peter off over time as the relationship stabilizes. Alas, dopamine levels also increase in response to stress. My hypothesis is that when we have a crush on a Bad Boy/Girl/Person, we may get a greater dose of dopamine than we would by falling for someone who makes us feel safe and secure. Even if that's not the case, in the early stages of a relationship it can be hard to tell whether we are getting the lovestruck dopamine, the stress variety, or a bit of both.

	Engaged in risky or illegal behaviors "for the buzz"	Depressed or agitated if life runs too smoothly
Never	37%	30%
Sometimes	38%	34%
Often	17%	19%
Always	7%	9%
Not sure	1%	8%

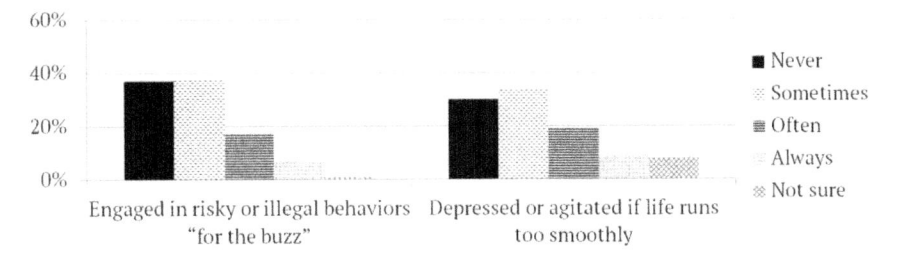

24% of respondents reported that they often or always engage in risky or illegal behaviors just "for the buzz." A further 38% reported that they "only" do it sometimes, but as doing this kind of thing *once* can be enough to wreck a life, or end it, this result is still significant. That leaves 37% of respondents who have never done this, and 1% who are not sure.

29% of respondents reported that they feel depressed or agitated if their life is running too smoothly, while a further 34% reported that they do it sometimes. That leaves only 30% of us who don't feel depressed or agitated, and 8% who are not sure, some of whom got in touch with me to point out that they could not answer the question because they have never experienced a smooth-running life. In future surveys, this question should be reworded to take this fact into account.

Of those who reported engaging in risky or illegal behaviors just "for the buzz," 97% are ADHDers, as are 96% of those who feel depressed or agitated if their life is running too smoothly. In future surveys, it would be interesting to investigate whether these issues are lessened by the use of medication, and to which extent.

I want to stress that these issues are neurochemical, not moral or ethical. Despite Sir George Still's original qualification of ADHD as an "abnormal defect of moral control in children" back in 1902, these issues are physiological. While we are responsible for our actions, we have no control over our brain chemistry. The fact that we are statistically likely to resort to potentially self-damaging coping mechanisms in order to compensate for our neurochemical issues should reinforce the importance of early diagnosis and adequate support.

We should remember that the risks associated with this type of behavior are not distributed evenly throughout the population. Studies have shown that biases contribute to disciplinary disparities in educational institutions, in law enforcement, and in the legal system. Members of discriminated groups are punished more often and more severely than those of non-discriminated groups for the same misbehaviors. They are also more likely to be punished in response to subjective categories of misbehavior (e.g., "defiance"). This disciplinary disparity is associated with negative long-term outcomes, including lower chances of academic success, difficulties in finding employment, involvement in the criminal justice system, and incarceration.

Unfortunately, the chances of getting a diagnosis of ADHD are also lower for marginalized groups. As a result, societal biases may determine whether people's mistakes result in them getting diagnosed and treated, or end up wrecking their life.

Memory.

This section looked at a variety of memory problems and some of the tactics we use to compensate for them. The questions were:

- Do you forget important appointments or obligations?
- Do you use multiple reminders to remember important appointments or obligations?
- Do you frequently misplace things or have difficulty finding them?
- Do you use a strict storage system to avoid losing things?
- Do you perform repeated checks to make sure that you have not lost or forgotten things?
- Do you forget that you own things if you put them out of sight?
- Do you have problems with your working memory? (e.g., if you needed to pick up five ingredients for a recipe, could you remember them without a written list?)
- Do you have problems storing information in your long-term memory? (e.g., you have to go over the same bit of information a number of times before it is stored, or you fail to store chunks of your life.)
- Do you have problems accessing your long-term memory? (e.g., you know that you know something, but you cannot access that specific bit of information at will.)

"Memory" refers to the process of encoding, storing, and recalling information. It's a complicated and somewhat contentious subject we don't fully understand yet. I will attempt to summarize the key points, but if you want a comprehensive introduction, I recommend you check out the "Memory" section of the Queensland Brain Institute website.[23]

Encoding refers to the way in which we absorb information and convert it for storage. Many people find it easier to process certain types of information – for instance, they may prefer visual, auditory, or kinesthetic inputs. When we form memories, we convert inputs into the type of information that works best for our storage system, so to speak. For instance, if we are visual learners and thinkers, we may memorize how a

---

[23] https://qbi.uq.edu.au/brain-basics/memory

picture looks. If we are verbal learners and thinkers, on the other hand, we might memorize our mental description of the picture, rather than the picture itself.

There are two main types of memory storage: short-term and long-term memory. Information is first stored in our short-term memory, and then transferred to our long-term memory if necessary. Short-term memory is limited both in duration and the amount of items it can hold. For instance, working memory, the shortest type of short-term memory, lasts only 15 to 30 seconds and can hold between five and nine items, seven on average. Long-term memory, on the other hand, has a much greater storage capacity and can hold information indefinitely.

Recall refers to the process through which we access stored information. During memory recall, the brain replicates the neural activity that took place while the memory was formed. Memories aren't just retrieved from storage, like books from a shelf; they are recreated from information scattered throughout the brain.

Any part of this process can fail, temporarily or permanently. Some people struggle to commit information to memory, but once it's in there, it's safe and easily accessible. Some people find it easy to memorize information, but bits of it seem to disappear in storage. Some people know that they know something, but they can't recall the information at will. These issues can affect all types of information, or be restricted to specific types. For instance, "lethologica" is the inability to remember the right word, while "lethonomia" is the inability to remember a name.

Memory problems, in particular working memory problems, are one of the banes of many ADHDers – or, rather, we suffer partly because our memory doesn't always work terribly well, and partly because people often fail to accept that. Memory problems are not always easily identifiable from the outside, and can be mistaken for a lack of attention, interest, respect, or intelligence. People may get frustrated because we lost track of what they were saying, or because they have told us the same thing already, perhaps several times. They might conclude that we are deliberately slighting them; if we actually gave a damn, we would have listened the first time! Alternatively, they might conclude that we are just not smart enough to understand them or to carry out certain tasks, when the actual issue is that we cannot hold a list of instructions in our head. This is blatant ableism, and explaining to people that we actually have a memory problem does not always resolve it.

	Forget important appointments or obligations	**Use multiple reminders**
Never	7%	3%
Sometimes	42%	13%
Often	41%	32%
Always	9%	51%
Not sure	0.1%	0.1%

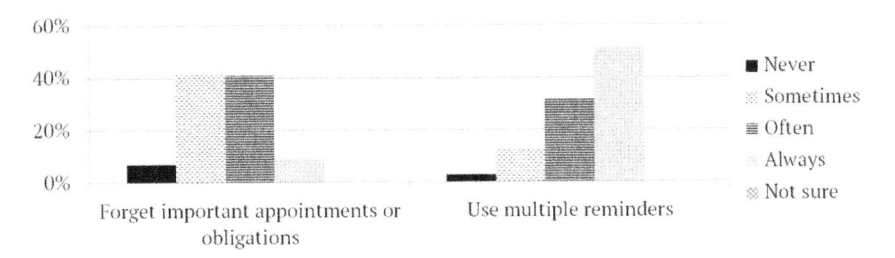

Diagnostic criteria for ADHD vary between countries and have changed over time, but they generally include one or more questions about forgetfulness, which is classed under "Inattention." This is problematic for two main reasons.

First of all, memory problems can exist independently of inattention, and psychiatrists, of all people, should be aware of that. The idea that 'if we were paying enough attention we would not forget' does not reflect the modern scientific understanding of how memory works, and why it may fail. It also doesn't reflect recent studies that suggest that forgetfulness may have a genetic basis.

Unless a person's memory is tested and found to work correctly, assumptions should not be made as to *why* they forget things. There are numerous reasons that may cause a person's memory to underperform or malfunction; based on my experience of the ADHD community, it would not surprise me at all if ADHD was eventually found to be one of them.

Secondly, this type of question ignores the impact of coping mechanisms. Most adult ADHDers are aware of the fact that we have a tendency to forget things and have had plenty of opportunities to suffer through the consequences. As we don't actually enjoy messing up our lives, we take steps to try and avoid these issues. Anecdotally, one of the most common strategies is to use multiple reminders, especially if we need to remember something important. The reminders allow us to outsource the task of remembering: instead of holding the memory in our brain, we hold it in our diary, in our computer calendar, in the alarms in our phone, on a sticky note on the fridge, and so on and so forth. This strategy is not guaranteed to succeed, particularly as we have a tendency to stop seeing reminders that are under our nose for too long and forget those that are out of sight, but it can help, at least some of the time. However, it's not cost-free; aside from the extra work required in maintaining our platoon of 'external memory banks', living like this can be stressful.

51% of respondents said that they often or always forget important appointments or obligations, and 84% often or always use multiple reminders to help them remember. 90% of respondents who forget appointments or obligations use multiple reminders, and 55% of those who use multiple reminders still forget. This indicates two things: first of all, we are aware of our forgetfulness and we are trying to overcome it, which sinks a hole in the theory that our forgetfulness is due to "inattention." Secondly, using multiple reminders is definitely not an infallible strategy.

Many of us have developed additional coping strategies over time. Anecdotally, many ADHDers report having a "waiting mode": for instance, if we know that we have a commitment in the evening, we spend the entire day unable to do much of anything, because our brain is stuck in this weird zone in which all we can do is wait for The Thing to happen. This phenomenon is sometimes attributed to anxiety; we can't do anything because we are ruminating about the incoming commitment, and we are ruminating because we feel anxious about it. Although there is no argument that anxiety can lead to rumination, and rumination can suck our ability to do stuff, I believe that the ADHD Waiting Mode is something else entirely. I think it's either a coping mechanism or a trauma response stemming from past experiences around forgetting commitments.

Most of us have had plenty of occasions to experience the consequences of forgetting something. Most of us know how easy it can be for us to fall out of time if we become engrossed in a task, or if we just space out. I think we enter Waiting Mode to prevent this from happening. For me, Waiting Mode it's like having a giant pop-up on my computer screen: I can sort of see around it, and I know that there's stuff behind it that I should or could be looking at instead, but I don't dare close it because I know how likely I am to forget all about it if it's not right in my face. It's less like rumination, and more like a temporary shutdown of all normal functions, because those functions may get in the way of remembering The Thing. And none of this has anything to do with whether I feel anxious about The Thing – if anything, it's my anxiety about forgetting it that is at play.

As a result, common suggestions for how to overcome Waiting Mode, such as stimulating the senses or picking a healthy distraction, are totally useless for me. I *know* that if I get engrossed in something, anything, then I will forget that I am waiting for The Thing and be able to get on with my day. But I also know how likely I am to forget about The Thing if I do that, and I know how costly my forgetfulness can be. I can either waste a day waiting for The Thing, or risk forgetting about The Thing and deal with the consequences – not a choice my Rejection Sensitive Dysphoria is likely to allow. Over time, going into Waiting Mode has become a mental habit, and now I do it even for things that wouldn't cause me any grief if I forget about them. This is just my experience, though, and people mileage may vary. Unfortunately, this survey did not ask about Waiting Mode. I think future surveys should cover this issue, as it isn't very well known and it seems to affect a lot of people.

Psychologists have demonstrated that losing things can be associated with a failure in memory encoding: if our memory does not register that we have just put something somewhere, we will not know where that item is. This issue has been shown to be worsened by stress, sleep deprivation, or multitasking. Physical coordination and poor sensory responses can also play a part: for instance, if we try to put something in our pocket, miss, and don't feel it, then we will easily lose it. Despite of all this, losing things is still routinely treated as a symptom of inattention at best, lack of care at worst. I don't know about you, but I find this vexing.

	Frequently lose things	Use a strict storage system to avoid losing things	Perform repeated checks not to lose things	Forget things if you put them out of sight
Never	3%	20%	7%	5%
Sometimes	18%	34%	23%	19%
Often	36%	24%	34%	35%
Always	43%	21%	36%	40%
Not sure	0%	1%	0%	1%

[Bar chart showing responses (Never, Sometimes, Often, Always, Not sure) for: Frequently lose things; Use a strict storage system to avoid losing things; Perform repeated checks not to lose things; Forget things if you put them out of sight]

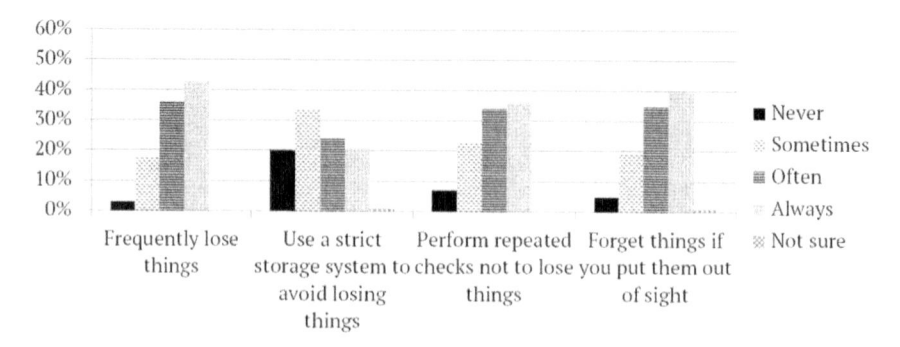

79% of respondents often or always lose things. 45% of respondents use a strict storage system to try and avoid this problem, but 75% of them still lose things. 70% of respondents perform repeated checks to make sure that they have not lost or forgotten things, but 81% of them still lose things.

75% of respondents often or always forget that they own things if they put them out of sight. For us, "Out of sight, out of mind" is all too literal a concept. In popular parlance, this is often referred to as "poor object permanence," but that is not the correct term for the problem. Object permanence refers to the understanding that an object continues to exist even though we can no longer see it. A true lack of object permanence past babyhood is the sign of severe neurological issues, and is not the problem described here. This is strictly a memory issue, not a cognitive issue.

84% of respondents who forget they own things if they put them out of sight also forget important appointments and obligations, and 85% of them frequently lose things. But yeah, let's just keep harping on about how we just need to pay more attention.

	Working memory problems	**Problems storing information in long-term memory**	**Problems accessing long-term memory**
Never	4%	11%	7%
Sometimes	22%	29%	33%
Often	30%	29%	35%
Always	44%	29%	24%
Not sure	0%	3%	1%

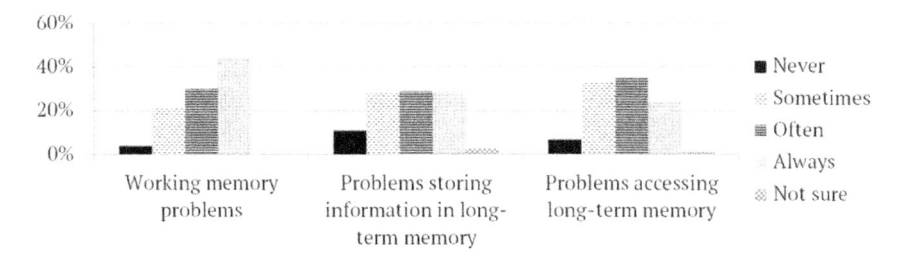

[Bar chart showing survey responses for "Working memory problems", "Problems storing information in long-term memory", and "Problems accessing long-term memory" with categories Never, Sometimes, Often, Always, Not sure]

74% of respondents stated that they often or always have working memory problems, 58% of respondents stated that they often or always have problems storing information in their long-term memory, and 59% of respondents stated that they often or always have problems accessing their long-term memory. So, yeah, it looks like memory might be a bit of an issue for us, which will come as no surprise to anyone who has spent any time around us.

The only surprising thing is that our memory isn't tested as a matter of course. Memory, particularly working memory, can be tested cheaply and easily. For instance, the General Practitioner Assessment of Cognition (GPCOG) tests a patient's working memory by asking them to memorize a name and address and recall it a few minutes later. If this test indicates that a patient's working memory may not be actually be working (pun intended), further tests may be indicated. These tests are just as simple and easy to administer. They are used when dementia is suspected, but working memory problems can be the result of a number of conditions, including depression, trauma, and sleep deprivation. Evidence suggests that it may also be a common feature in neurodivergence.

A poor working memory can have a profound impact on a person's life, because we use our working memory all the time without realizing it: to carry out mental arithmetic, follow instructions, prioritize tasks, solve problems, and generally just to get on with our day. Not being able to rely on those mental sticky notes can make it very hard for us to create a smooth work flow. It can turn simple tasks into complicated processes, and complicated tasks into unmanageable messes.

Working memory is not a stable feature. It is negatively affected by a number of factors, including various medical conditions, sleep deprivation, and negative emotional states. Some people with poor working memory show improvements from brain training programs, although the mechanism underlying the improvement has not been established yet.

Time management and decision-making.

This section looked at two elements that contribute to executive functioning: time management and decision making. The questions were:

- Are you able to correctly gauge the passing of time (e.g. what time it is, how long a routine task takes) without checking a watch?
- Do you find it hard to organize your time effectively?
- Do you stick to a strict schedule because it's the only way you can get everything done?
- Do you stick to a strict schedule because you find it comforting?
- Do you try to stick to a schedule, but you just can't?
- Do you find living under a strict schedule suffocating?
- Do you struggle to make small decisions when you have too many options? (e.g., you spend an unreasonable amount of time reading reviews before buying a cheap item.)
- Do you make big decisions too quickly? (You don't "look before you leap.")
- Do you struggle to make decisions if you do not have enough information to work out the possible risks and effects?

Executive function is a complex of skills that allow us to get things done. These skills can be grouped under two main categories:

- Organizational. They enable us to gather, organize, and use information.
- Regulatory. They enable us to assess our environment and respond appropriately to situations.

When we have the required executive functioning skills, we are able to manage our time, plan, organize, switch between tasks, multitask, and emotionally self-regulate in the face of changing circumstances. When we don't, we will experience a degree of executive dysfunction.

Executive dysfunction is not currently recognized as an official condition, although there are tests to measure it. However, it is anecdotally known to be a serious and pervasive issue within the neurodivergent community.

One of the essential components of executive function is **time management**: the conscious management of time spent on activities, often with the goal of maximizing efficiency and productivity. Like executive functioning, effective time management is the result of a constellation of skills all working together: goal-setting, prioritizing, scheduling, and so on. Achieving all of that can be hard enough, but for many of us, time management involves an extra hurdle: that of working around our time agnosia, or time blindness.

Time blindness is also not a recognized condition; it is a label used to describe the inability to feel the passing of time that is a common feature of neurodivergence. It is wholly unrelated to the ability to tell the time, which is a learned skill. Time-blind individuals lack the ability to feel time passing, or feel it very differently depending on context. Time spent doing something engrossing flies, while time spent in boredom seems to last forever; and this happens on a wholly different scale from the neurotypical "time flies when you are having fun." Time-blind individuals simply cannot judge how long a task has taken, or estimate how long it might take. We get lost in the clock and in the calendar. This can cause us great difficulties in planning both long- and short-term goals, and makes time management extremely difficult. It's hard to manage a resource if we don't know how much of it we have, or how quickly we are spending it.

	Able to gauge the passing of time	**Find it hard to organize time effectively**
Never	50%	1%
Sometimes	36%	15%
Often	10%	41%
Always	5%	43%
Not sure	0.4%	0.1%

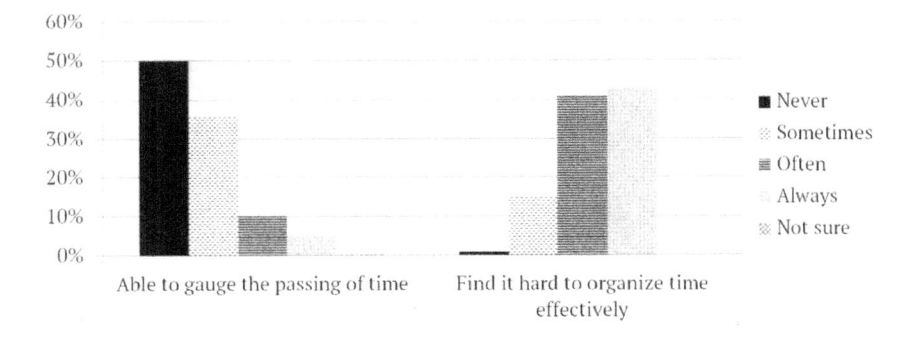

50% of respondents are never able to gauge the passing of time, and 35% can only do it sometimes. That gives us a total of 85% of respondents who experience a degree of time blindness. The percentage of respondents who often or always find it hard to organize their time effectively is similar – 84%. For ADHDers, these percentages are slightly higher – 86% for both.

87% of respondents with symptoms of time blindness find it hard to organize their time effectively, and 87% of respondents who find it hard to organize their time effectively have symptoms of time blindness. (Yes, those are two different values, which just happen to be the same. Isn't math fun?)

There is no cure for time blindness; there are, however, a number of strategies that might reduce its impact. Most of them work by bypassing our need to feel the passage of time by using external cues and reminders. These may include:

- Watches or clocks, particularly those that visualize the passage of time rather than just giving us a figure.
- Timers or stopwatches to enable us to stop activities on time.
- Alarms to warn us of where we are in the day, or whether we need to task switch.
- Music or video playlists timed to give us a sense of how much time has passed, and to cue us about the impending need to task switch. (I like to think of this as the modern equivalent of keeping time by listening to the church bells; instead of counting dings and dongs, we are prompted by a shift from Enya to At The Drive In, or whatever floats our boat.)
- Keeping records of how long routine tasks take, so we can schedule them realistically in the future.
- Schedules, which may include both routine and non-routine tasks.

None of these methods are guaranteed to work perfectly all of the time, but they can all help. Scheduling, however, can be both a blessing and a curse. It can allow us to plan our days efficiently, particularly if we go through the process of measuring how long routine tasks actually take us.

However, scheduling greatly reduces our ability to be spontaneous and to do what interests us most in any particular moment. This can be especially hard on ADHDers, as our brains tend to shortchange us in the feel-good chemicals department if we don't keep them suitably entertained. Sticking to routines and schedules is *not* entertaining, and can feel positively restrictive. The tighter the scheduling, the more restrictive it can feel, even if we schedule plenty of free time.

Scheduling can be comforting, though. Some of us need schedules because we need a high level of stability and predictability in our life. Schedules allow us to know what to expect and when to expect it. They also allow us to hope that we won't forget anything important, run late, and generally mess up. This can greatly reduce our stress levels.

When our needs come into conflict, it can be very hard for us to balance them. We may need schedules, but feel frustrated or depressed if we are forced to follow them. These conflicting needs can be particularly hard to balance for people who are both ADHD and Autistic.

When examining the result of this survey, we need to bear in mind that the vast majority of respondents are ADHDers. 91% of Autistic respondents are also ADHDers. Only 39 responders – less than 3% of the total – are Autistic but not ADHDers. This is a reflection of the audience of the social media page where we advertised the survey, not of the neurodivergent community at large. This fact should be taken into account when looking at the answers of Autistic respondents.

	Strict schedule because it's the only way to get everything done	**Strict schedule for comfort**
Never	24%	42%
Sometimes	45%	34%
Often	23%	16%
Always	8%	7%
Not sure	0.9%	2.0%

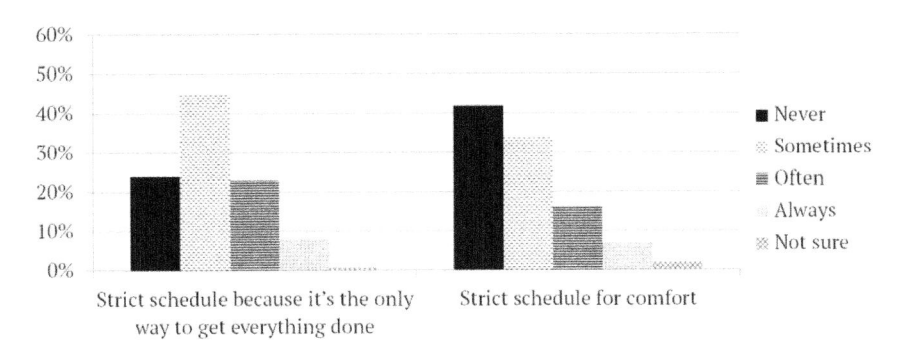

31% of respondents said that they often or always stick to a strict schedule because it's the only way they can get everything done. This percentage is slightly higher for Autistics (33%) than ADHDers (30%).

23% of respondents said that they often or always stick to a strict schedule because they find it comforting. This percentage is higher for Autistics (30%) than for ADHDers (22%).

	Try to stick to a schedule, but can't	Find strict schedules suffocating
Never	4%	12%
Sometimes	26%	33%
Often	38%	27%
Always	33%	26%
Not sure	0.4%	2.8%

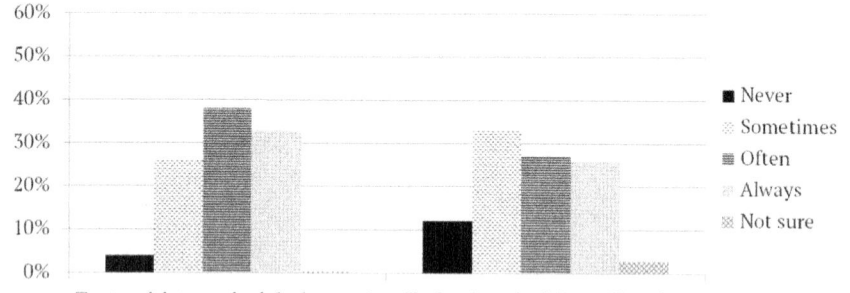

70% of respondents often or always try to stick to a schedule, but just can't. This percentage is slightly higher for ADHDers (71%) than for Autistics (68%). 53% of respondents often or always find living under a strict schedule suffocating. This percentage is slightly higher for ADHDers (54%) than for Autistics (50%).

All in all, these differences aren't huge and might not be significant, aside from a higher percentage of Autistic people finding comfort in strict scheduling.

33% of respondents who stick to a strict schedule because it's the only way they can get everything done find living under a strict schedule suffocating, as do 23% of respondents who stick to a strict schedule because they find it comforting. Needless to say, this is suboptimal.

Having to trade our mental well-being for efficiency is bad. I'd argue that having to trade one kind of mental well-being for another is even worse.

Time management is not the only key aspect of executive function. Decision-making is also very important, and is another domain in which ADHDers don't always excel. One aspect of the issue, impulsivity, is part of the current diagnostic criteria. However, making decisions without thinking them through isn't the only decision-making issues affecting ADHDers, nor is always the one with the greatest impact on our life. Other issues include:

- Difficulties comparing numerous options, particularly when multiple factors are involved. This may be linked to working memory issues, which are a common feature of neurodivergence. A poor working memory can make it difficult for us to hold and manipulate the information we require to make a decision. The more information we need to consider, the more we will struggle. (This is where it can pay to make a pros and cons list: instead of relying on our memory, we can use a piece of paper.)
- Difficulties in finalizing a decision if we do not have enough information to work out the best option. Sometimes this is due to lack of information, or the availability of conflicting information. Sometimes, though, it's just life; every decision is an experiment, and we cannot always anticipate what the results are going to be. If we cannot accept this uncertainty, we will struggle to decide.
- Lack of trust in our decision-making processes. Experience might have taught us to mistrust the decisions we make, which can make us reluctant to finalize any decision. Alternatively, we might mistrust our ability to come to a decision, which can cause to push ourselves into deciding without thinking things through.
- Risky decision making. This is often taken to be a result of our inability to stop and think, or to evaluate potential risks and outcomes. However, that's not always the case. Sometimes we make risky decisions precisely *because* we know that they are risky. Taking risks can activate the release of neurochemicals we are short of, which makes us feel good. This type of activity, however, isn't always cost-free, and the associated costs can be very high indeed. Untreated ADHD is associated with higher rates of substance abuse, traffic violations, motor vehicle accidents, criminality, imprisonment, suicide, and premature death.

These decision-making difficulties can cause us to oscillate wildly between impulsivity and decision paralysis. Sometimes we make decisions without thinking, because we know that if we start thinking we'll never stop. Sometimes we end up spending so long evaluating all the pros and cons that the opportunity to make a decision passes us by. And we don't necessarily spend the most time working on the most significant decisions, either; on the contrary, we might make huge decisions on the fly but get bogged down working out all the pros and cons of something utterly insignificant. That might seem nonsensical, but there is a kind of logic to it. We might have a chance to think through small decisions without succumbing to decision paralysis. For big decisions, however, the only possible course of action is to charge forth without thinking at all.

	Struggle to make small decisions if too many options	Make big decisions too quickly	Struggle to make decisions if can't work out risks and effects
Never	4%	17%	4%
Sometimes	14%	36%	22%
Often	31%	32%	35%
Always	50%	14%	38%
Not sure	0.4%	0.6%	1.1%

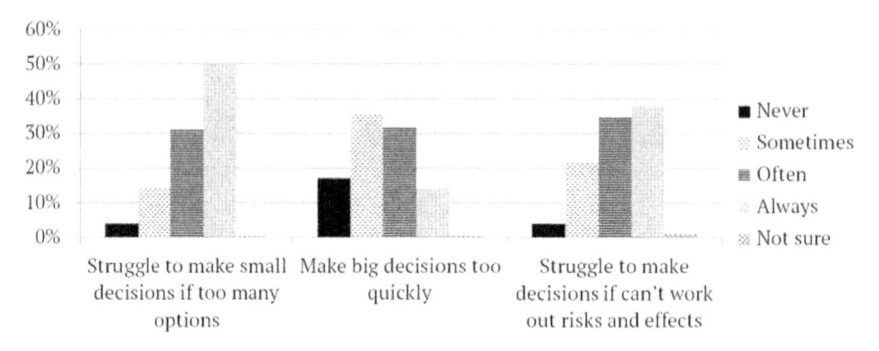

81% of respondents often or always struggle to make small decisions when they have too many options. This percentage is slightly higher for Autistics (85%) than for ADHDers (82%).

46% of respondents often or always make big decisions too quickly. This percentage is the same for ADHDers and Autistics (47%).

73% of respondents struggle to make decisions if they do not have enough information to work out the possible risks and effects. This percentage is higher for Autistics (83%) than for ADHDers (73%).

Again, these differences aren't huge and might not be significant, aside from a higher percentage of Autistic people struggling to make decisions if they do not have enough information to work out the possible risks and effects.

I want to reiterate that the majority of Autistic respondents of this survey are also ADHDers, which is likely to have had a significant impact on these results. Future surveys should be advertised in order to facilitate the participation of a greater number of Autistic non-ADHDers, which would allow a more informative comparison of the impact of various traits and issues on different neurotypes.

Interest and hyperfocus.

This section looked at some of the factors that affect our interest, attention, and motivation, and at what happens when we become too engrossed in a subject or task. The questions were:

- Do you find daily tasks boring or repetitive?
- Do you find it hard to stay focused on tasks you find boring or repetitive, even when they are important to you?
- Do you tend to avoid or delay starting tasks that are new, complicated, or important?
- Do you abandon tasks if they turn up to be too complicated?
- Do you find it hard to complete tasks once you know you can do them?
- Do you pick up new hobbies only to abandon them if you don't get good at them fast enough?
- Do you pick up new hobbies only to abandon them once you get good at them?
- Do you have an interest or passion that captures the majority of your interest?
- Is that interest or passion common for people of your age/gender/socioeconomic status?
- Do you make money from your interest or passion?
- Do you get into trouble with the people around you for getting too sucked in into your passion or interest?
- Do you feel upset or agitated if you are pulled away from being engaged in your tasks or passion?

One of the features of neurodivergences is that our attention, focus, interest, and motivation tend to operate in non-standard fashions.

ADHD brains are said to be motivated by four things: interest, challenge, novelty, and urgency. Is it something we are interested in? Is it going to challenge our abilities? Is it new? Is it about to smack us with a deadline? If a task meets at least one of those four criteria, we're good: not only we can start it, but we might even finish it! If not, it's a thankless chore, and even thinking of starting it might suck our will to live. This can lead to the not-yet-official phenomenon known as "ADHD Fainting Goat Syndrome." This term was coined by Jennifer Seal Martin, who observed that our brains disengage when forced to do something boring, and may shut down altogether when confronted by an unavoidable but dull task.

I posit that there are two additional motivators. The first one is procrastination: if working on a task means that we can avoid another, less desirable task, then the first task is suddenly doable, even though we might have been avoiding it for ages. Those of us who learn to game their procrastination often achieve spectacular amounts; while they're always doing anything but what they should be doing, they are always doing *some*thing. That kind of productivity can add up.

The second extra motivator is being a contrarian. If we are told that we can't or shouldn't do something, many of us just *have* to do it. I could try and pass it off as an aspect of challenge, but I'm not that good a liar.

And then there's hyperfocus – highly focused attention that lasts a long time. Not all of us get it, but for those of us who do, all normal functions go out the window.

During a hyperfocus, we become so immersed in a thought or activity that we lose track of everything else going on around us. We might forget or neglect to drink, eat, and sleep. Children may have toileting accidents because they are so focused on what they are doing that they don't notice that they need to go until it's too late. Some adults do that, too.

When we are hyperfocused, we may spend hours or days on our interest without noticing it. Time becomes wholly untethered from the clock, and even from the calendar. If a hyperfocused person tells you that they'll be "just five more minutes" and shows up five hours later, they weren't necessarily lying: those five hours may have felt like five minutes to them, so they might be just as surprised by their lateness as you are.

All of these are drawbacks, but there are even bigger ones. Firstly, hyperfocus cannot be turned on and off at will. We can't just engage our hyperfocus because we have an urgent deadline. Secondly, hyperfocus cannot be directed, or re-directed. It's like a prize wheel: you get what you get, and hope that it won't suck. Thirdly, while we are in the middle of a hyperfocus, trying to pay attention to anything else can be very difficult. However hard we try to focus on whatever else is going on, we might be unable to do so, or to do so well enough to meet the demands of those around us.

These issues combine, and the result is that many of us can't get into things unless we are genuinely interested in them, and can't get out of the things we are interested in. This can give us the ability to enjoy ourselves immensely while we are working on something we love, but it can render us incapable of doing much of anything else. Unfortunately, a lot of adulting falls outside of our "interest tunnel." That presents us with a problem: if we fail to meet our basic obligations, there will be consequences; if we force ourselves to meet them, we might literally make ourselves sick by causing our neurochemistry to get out of whack.

	Find daily tasks boring or repetitive	Hard to stay focused on boring or repetitive tasks
Never	2%	1%
Sometimes	27%	12%
Often	42%	40%
Always	29%	47%
Not sure	0.1%	0.1%

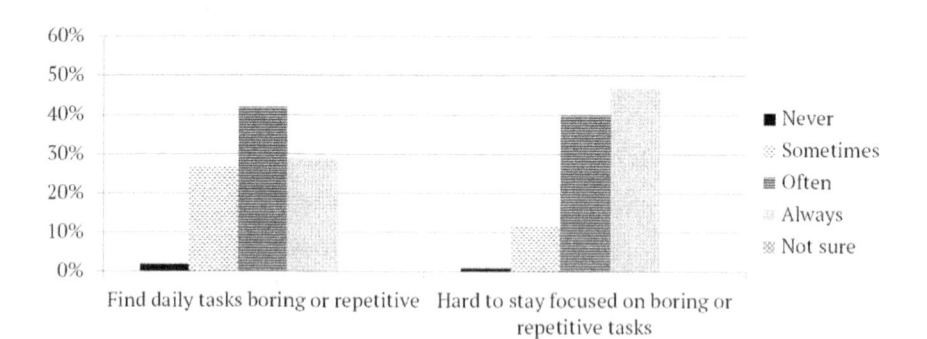

71% of respondents often or always find daily tasks boring and repetitive, and 87% find it hard to stay focused on tasks they find boring or repetitive, even when those tasks are important to them. This is important: the issue isn't that we don't care about these tasks, but that our neurochemistry makes it very difficult for us to engage with them.

97% of respondents who find daily tasks boring and repetitive also find it hard to stay focused on boring or repetitive tasks. (If you resemble these remarks, your housekeeping style may resemble mine. You're still not allowed to enter my house without wearing a blindfold, though.)

The next set of questions covers two related issue, that of starting and finishing tasks. ADHDers have a tendency to struggle with either or both, depending on the circumstances. Sometimes we delay starting on a task we consciously or unconsciously classified as difficult until it's unavoidable... and then realize that we spent way more time and energy avoiding the task than it took to complete it. Sometimes we start working on a task, but abandon it as soon as it turns out to be difficult.

As a result of these issues, many of us have been told that we are lazy, that we lack motivation or dedication, and so on. Sometimes we say that to ourselves. There are two problems with this. Firstly, calling someone lazy (or worse) has never stopped anyone from being lazy. You can't exorcise personal shortcomings by calling them out. And anyway, if years of getting told off by our parents, teachers, bosses, partners, and so on haven't managed to purge us of that pesky laziness, is the next self-berating session really likely to work?

Secondly, lazy people don't spend half their life metaphorically kicking themselves in the backside because of the stuff they aren't doing. That's not how laziness works. If we desperately want to do something but just can't, our problem is not laziness.

I am going to borrow the words of Autistic social psychologist, professor, and author Devon Price:

> "For decades, psychological research has been able to explain procrastination as a functioning problem, not a consequence of laziness. When a person fails to begin a project that they care about, it's typically due to either a) anxiety about their attempts not being "good enough" or b) confusion about what the first steps of the task are. Not laziness. In fact, procrastination is more likely when the task is meaningful and the individual cares about doing it well.
>
> When you're paralyzed with fear of failure, or you don't even know how to begin a massive, complicated undertaking, it's damn hard to get shit done. It has nothing to do with desire, motivation, or moral upstandingness. Procrastinators can will themselves to work for hours; they can sit in front of a blank word document, doing nothing else, and torture themselves; they can pile on the guilt again and again — none of it makes initiating the task any easier. In fact, their desire to get the damn thing done may worsen their stress and make starting the

task harder."[24]

If we freeze in the face of a complex task, there are two likely reasons: we fear we won't be able to do it, or we just don't know how to do it. Granted, there may be other factors in play, but if we're sitting there seething with frustration and self-loathing at our inability to get something done, laziness isn't one of them.

	Avoid or delay starting new, complicated, or important tasks	**Abandon tasks if they are too complicated**	**Find it hard to complete tasks if you can do them**
Never	1%	3%	10%
Sometimes	10%	31%	39%
Often	36%	45%	32%
Always	52%	20%	17%
Not sure	0.4%	0.1%	1.8%

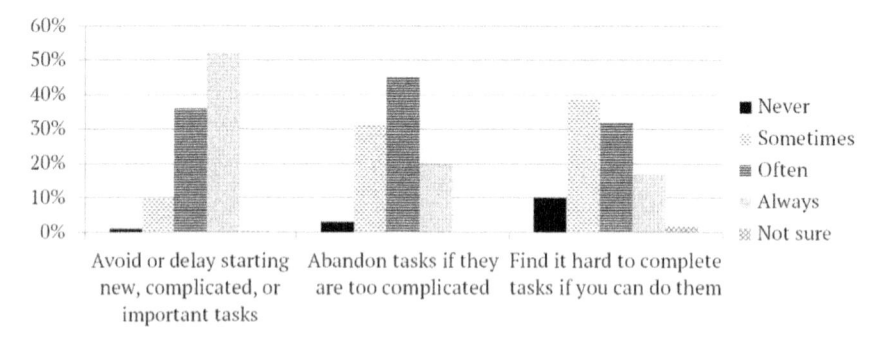

88% of respondents often or always tend to avoid or delay starting tasks that are new, complicated, or important. 66% of respondents often or always you abandon tasks if they turn up to be too complicated. Of the latter, 95% also avoid or delay starting tasks that are too complicated. Obviously, I can't draw any conclusions as to why we are getting these numbers, but Devon Price's theory of performance anxiety and executive dysfunction could explain them.

It doesn't explain another phenomenon, however: sometimes we start

---

[24] https://humanparts.medium.com/laziness-does-not-exist-3af27e312d01
CW: mentions of ableism, mental health stigmas, sexual abuse, and institutional asshattery.

working on a task, and abandon it as soon as we realize that we *can* finish it. This may sound absurd, but it is quite common – 49% of respondents often or always find it hard to complete tasks once they know they can do them. This issue is better explained by the interest theory of ADHD: once we have familiarized ourselves with a task, it loses its novelty, and once we know that we can definitely do it, it is no longer a challenge. That only leaves us with two possible motivators, interest and urgency. Alas, we can't will ourselves to be interested in something, and not all tasks are important enough to ever become urgent.

Hobbies have a tendency to fit in the never-quite-urgent category. As a result, ADHDers have a tendency to have short-lived but passionate relationships with our hobbies. We fall head over heels in love with a subject or activity, invest considerable amounts of our time and energy into it... and then we drop it, fall in love with something else, and do it all over again. Rinse and repeat. This can frustrate the heck out of the people around us, particularly if they harbored hopes of us becoming subject matter experts. It can also frustrate the heck out of us, unless we learn to roll with it. And then there are the financial implications, the storage issues, and the guilt we might feel every time we are reminded of how much time and energy we "wasted" by being joyfully engaged in a since-abandoned hobby.

	Drop hobbies if you don't get good fast enough	**Drop hobbies once you get good at them**
Never	5%	14%
Sometimes	25%	34%
Often	38%	31%
Always	31%	17%
Not sure	1%	3%

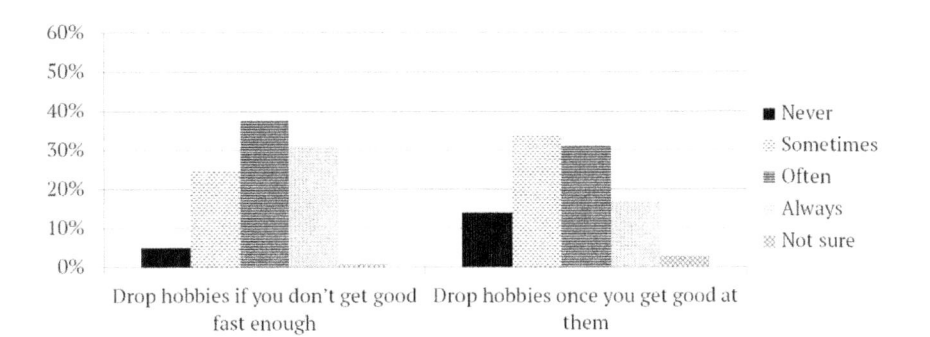

69% of respondents often or always abandon new hobbies if they don't get good at them fast enough. 49% of respondents often or always abandon new hobbies once they get good at them. 87% of those who abandon hobbies when they get good at them also abandon them if they don't get good fast enough. Again, this is pure conjecture, but the combination of performance anxiety, executive dysfunction, and ADHD motivation requirements could explain these numbers.

The Autistic interest system is believed to be rather different. Autistics are said to have a "monotropic interest system" or a "monotropic mind." The primary characteristic of monotropism is focus on a small number of interests at any time, combined with the tendency to ignore or forget things outside of those interests. It's mental tunnel vision, so to speak, and it allows people to immerse themselves into topics or experiences, thinking deeply and accessing the kind of flow state that takes other people years of meditation training to master. However, the positive aspects of monotropism are generally ignored. Being a common feature of Autism, it can't possibly be good, after all.

Our society all but worships neurotypicals whose one-track-mind makes them solely dedicated to a single field – scientists, artists, athletes, entrepreneurs, you name it. Autistic monotropism, however, is habitually pathologized, especially in people with complex support needs. At its worst, it is a barrier to human connections and communication. At its best, it is just a "splinter skill" – an ability disconnected from its context or purpose, which renders it basically useless. The fact that it can be a source of immense joy to the Autistic people in question is obviously of no importance.

Yes, I think this is bullshit, but it is officially-sanctioned bullshit. We might disagree with it, but we can't ignore it, because it affects how Autistic people are treated by "experts" and by our society in general.

	Have a main interest or passion	**Upset if pulled away from special interest**
Never	10%	8%
Sometimes	26%	27%
Often	30%	31%
Always	30%	32%
Not sure	4%	2%

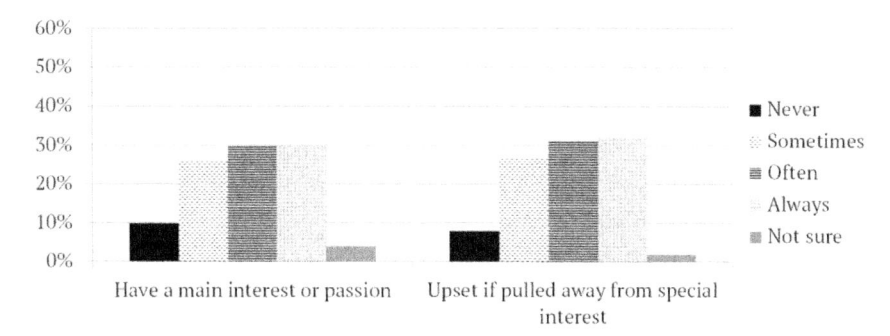

[Bar chart: Have a main interest or passion; Upset if pulled away from special interest — Never, Sometimes, Often, Always, Not sure]

60% of respondents often or always have an interest or passion that captures the majority of their interest, and 63% of them feel upset or agitated if they are pulled away from being engaged in that interest. Given that only 30% of survey participants were Autistic, this is clearly not just an Autistic issue.

	Special interest is "normal"	Monetized special interest	Get into trouble for special interest
Never	19%	64%	30%
Sometimes	41%	23%	39%
Often	17%	7%	19%
Always	5%	5%	8%
Not sure	19%	2%	4%

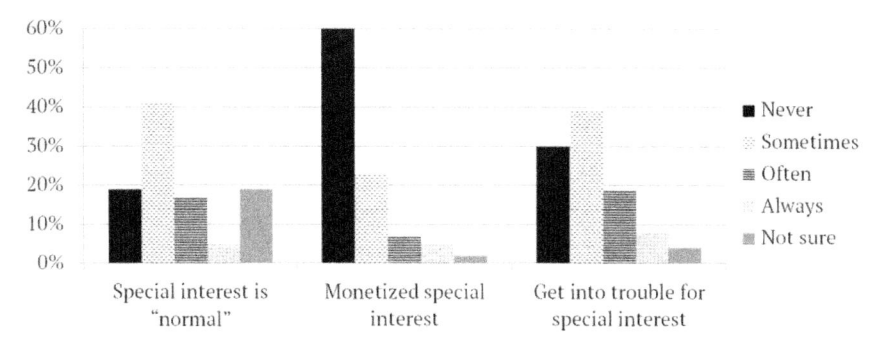

[Bar chart: Special interest is "normal"; Monetized special interest; Get into trouble for special interest — Never, Sometimes, Often, Always, Not sure]

21% of respondents often or always have interests or passions that are common for people of their age/gender/socioeconomic status.

11% of respondents often or always make money from their interest or passion, and another 23% make money sometimes.

28% of respondents often or always get in trouble with the people around them for getting too sucked in into their passion or interest.

The reason I asked the last three questions is that I had a theory. From what I've seen, "special interests" tend to be more tolerated or even accepted if they are considered "normal" for the person in question, or if they bring in money. So, for instance, my neighbor's passion for football is perfectly fine because he's a boy and that's what boys do, and his passion for drums is also fine because he plays in a band that gets paying gigs. When I got into the Kalevala in elementary school, however, that made me a weirdo, as did trying to learn to play the psaltery a few years back (fear not, I failed).

The results of this survey sank my theory. 41% of those whose interest is monetized get into trouble for getting too sucked in into them, as do 34% of those whose interest is "normal." As those figures are higher than those for survey respondents as a whole, neither monetization nor normalcy brings tolerance for our passions.

My guess is that other factors must be in play here – for instance, those who have monetized their passion may be spending more time on it. Why those of us whose passions are "normal" should be more likely to get in trouble over them is beyond me, though.

Communication.

This section looked at communication difficulties that are common within the neurodivergent community. The questions were:

- Do you have a passion for learning new words or languages?
- Do you have to translate your thoughts into simpler language to communicate with those around you?
- Do you get into trouble for using words that are "too complicated"?
- Do you struggle to notice or interpret non-verbal communication cues (e.g., body language, facial expressions, tone of voice)?
- Do you struggle to give out socially appropriate non-verbal communication cues (e.g., body language or facial expressions)?
- Have you been told that your body language, facial expression, or tone of voice are inappropriate?
- Do people misinterpret what you are saying or make incorrect assumptions as to the intentions behind your words?
- Are you uncomfortable with "small talk"• ? (i.e., social pleasantries designed for politeness rather than the transfer of information.)

It might seem weird that I'm asking whether people are into language in the context of communication difficulties, but there is a reason for that. If you hark back at the section on "Types of Neurodivergence," one of the questions was about hyperlexia. I haven't discussed it earlier because, although it sounds like it belongs with dyslexia, it's a very different neurodivergence with very different implications.

Hyperlexia derives its name from Greek terms 'hyper' (overmuch) and 'lexis' (word – the root of "lexicon"). Contrary to popular opinion, the term does not literally mean "too much reading;" if anything, it would be better translated as "too much wording." While that's not good English, it's a damn good explanation of the nature of hyperlexia and the problems it can cause.

Unpacking the issues around hyperlexia is complicated and unpleasant for one simple reason: the current diagnostic criteria are so imbued with anti-Autistic ableism that it's hard to look at them without feeling nauseous. One might look at the diagnostic criteria for Autism itself and think that medical ableism peaked there and couldn't possibly get any worse, but one would be wrong. It can get worse, and the clusterfuck around hyperlexia is a good example of what happens when it does.

Different medical systems use different diagnostic criteria, but the broad outline is similar. Hyperlexia can be good, bad, or indifferent. This doesn't depend on how hyperlexic we are, or whether our hyperlexia is causing us difficulties, but on whether we are Autistic and, if we are, on the extent of our support needs.

If we are neurotypical or neurodivergent but not Autistic, then hyperlexia is either going to make us gifted, or kind of fizzle out as other children catch up with us. If we are Autistic and have low support needs, our hyperlexia may help us in some specific and often narrow settings. If it doesn't, then it's just a "splinter skill" – an ability disconnected from its context or purpose, which renders it basically useless. If we have complex support needs, however, our hyperlexia is a barrier to human connection and communication. If this reminds you of the issues around monotropism (narrow interest range), it's because it is the same approach, applied to a different domain.

As a hyperlexic adult who once used to be a hyperlexic child, my experience of this issue is rather different. Hyperlexia in children is sometimes associated with learning to read early and to an abnormally advanced level, but that's not always the case. Hyperlexia and dyslexia can coexist,[25] so a person may struggle with the physical act of reading and still be hyperlexic. I think the reading side of hyperlexia attracts most of the focus because it is easy to spot and measure, but this distracts from the most impactful aspect of hyperlexia: that it is a passion for language that, when it isn't shared, can end up causing profound communication and socialization difficulties.

There are two reasons for this. Firstly, when a person uses words other people cannot understand, that creates a communication barrier. It's as simple as that. It is no different to speaking a different language, or speaking with an accent so different as to be incomprehensible. People just can't understand what you are saying.

In childhood, that can lead to socialization issues. Young children may become frustrated with us, and us with them. Children old enough to group themselves into cliques are also old enough to classify us as weird,

---

[25] And in case you're wondering, yes, I am both dyslexic and hyperlexic.

though, and that can lead to social exclusion and even bullying.

As one grows up, however, a second issue arises: it isn't uncommon for people to use overcomplicated language as a tool for establishing one's superiority, or asserting someone else's inferiority. As a result, when one uses a word someone else doesn't understand, this is often assumed to be a deliberate attack: I am choosing to use words you don't know in order to make you feel st@pid, or to make you look st@pid in public. This is patently absurd, because we cannot know whether other people know a word until we use it. However, from personal experience, explaining this only aggravates people further.

As a result of these communication and socialization issues, hyperlexia can cause severe social friction in multiple settings. It can also lead to academic difficulties, especially for young children, for three main reasons. Firstly, if we are spending our evening reading adult fiction, it is incredibly hard to pay attention to lessons about how Spot The Dog found his ball. If you've ever been asked by a toddler to watch their favorite show, you know the feeling. As a result, children may overperform in their learning while underperforming in their academic achievements. You can end up with children who read "Moby-Dick" in their spare time,[26] but repeatedly fail their tests because trace, copy, and recall exercises are just too boring to keep their attention.

The disconnect between what children know and what they are supposed to learn can also cause behavioral issues. Bored and frustrated children aren't generally good students. If teachers cannot find a way to keep their hyperlexic students focused and busy – or, at the very least, to let them carry out their own learning at their own pace, regardless of what the rest of the class is doing – disciplinary difficulties can ensue.

The last reason is less wholesome. Not all teachers are comfortable dealing with children who know too much. Sometimes this is purely because of the extra work involved – managing advanced learners can require an extra set of activities, and teachers have enough on their plates already. However, some teachers' ego is wrapped in being the smartest or most knowledgeable person in their classroom. When children reveal that they know as much or more than them – or, heaven forfend, prove them wrong about something – this can result in an emotional knee-jerk

---

[26] Or is that just me? In fairness, nobody told me that "Moby-Dick" wasn't meant for children. It had an animal in it, after all. I thought all animal books were children books.

reaction. If they are irked enough, this can affect their ability to remain professional, which may cause them to behave unfairly towards their advanced students. Other students may imitate these teachers' behavior, or escalate it into social ostracism and bullying. After all, if a teacher is doing it, it must be the right thing to do!

So, while learning to read early and to an abnormally advanced level are common signs of hyperlexia, they aren't the crux of the matter. Hyperlexia can cause serious communication, socialization, and academic performance issues. This is particularly true for undiagnosed hyperlexics, who might not know what is causing their problems. Unfortunately, as hyperlexia is poorly known and even more poorly treated, many of us fall into this camp.

Hyperlexia			Passion for words or languages	Translate into simpler language	Use words that are "too complicated"
% total	10.5	Never	14%	12%	24%
<12	24%	Sometimes	35%	37%	40%
<18	2%	Often	28%	34%	24%
>18	1%	Always	23%	15%	10%
SD	73%	Not sure	1%	2%	1%

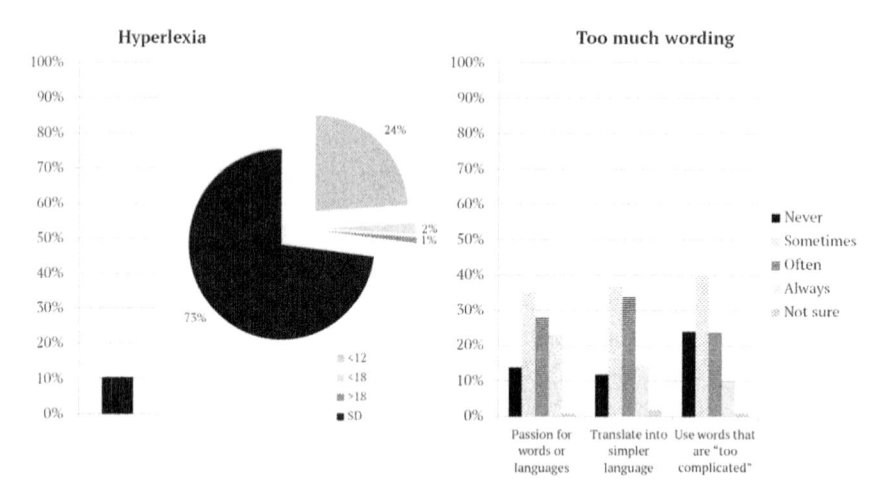

10% of survey respondents are hyperlexic. Of these, only 24% of them were diagnosed under the age of 12, while 73% are self-diagnosed. 17.5% of respondents are not sure whether they are hyperlexic. 61% of hyperlexics are also Autistic, and 13% are also dyslexic.

Traits and issues commonly associated with hyperlexia affect a much greater proportion of respondents. 50% of respondents often or always have a passion for learning new words or languages. 49% of them often or always have to translate their thoughts into simpler language to communicate with those around them. 35% often or always get in trouble for using words that are "too complicated."

56% of those who get in trouble for using words that are "too complicated" translate their thoughts into simpler language. Unfortunately, the limitations of this survey do not allow us to clarify whether they translate their thoughts because they get into trouble, or get into trouble even though they translate their thoughts.

In many cultures, language conventions are a gendered affair, so I ran correlations between assigned gender and these communication difficulties. This showed minor differences in the frequency with which people are told off for using words that are "too complicated," but a noticeable difference in the percentage of people who always translate their thoughts into simpler language: 24% of AMAB individuals do this, compared to 13% of AFABs.

	Use words that are "too complicated"		Translate into simpler language	
	AFAB	AMAB	AFAB	AMAB
Never	26%	20%	13%	8%
Sometimes	40%	41%	39%	31%
Often	24%	29%	35%	37%
Always	10%	11%	13%	24%

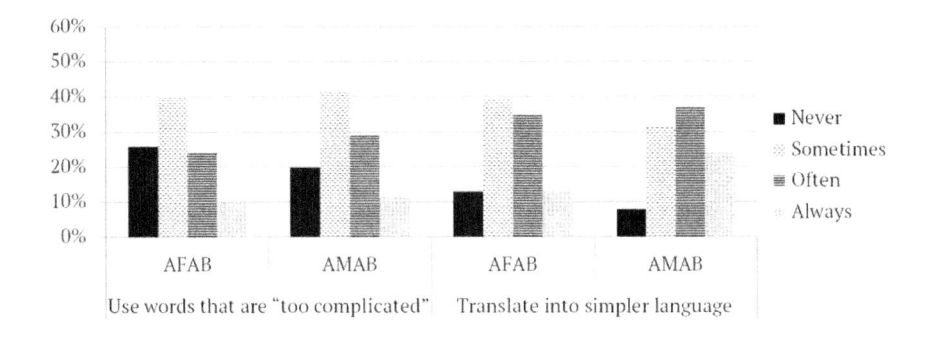

It's not just verbal communication that can cause us difficulties. Non-verbal communication – the combination of facial expressions, gestures, loudness and tone of voice, body language, proxemics or personal space, eye contact, and touch - can also be a challenge. We might struggle to give out the right signals, and/or to correctly interpret the signals we receive. This can result in corrections, complaints, or passive-aggressive friction.

	Struggle to notice or interpret non-verbal communication cues	Struggle to give out socially appropriate non-verbal communication cues	Told that body language, facial expression, or tone of voice are inappropriate
Never	32%	24%	22%
Sometimes	39%	35%	35%
Often	19%	25%	29%
Always	9%	12%	12%
Not sure	1%	3%	1%

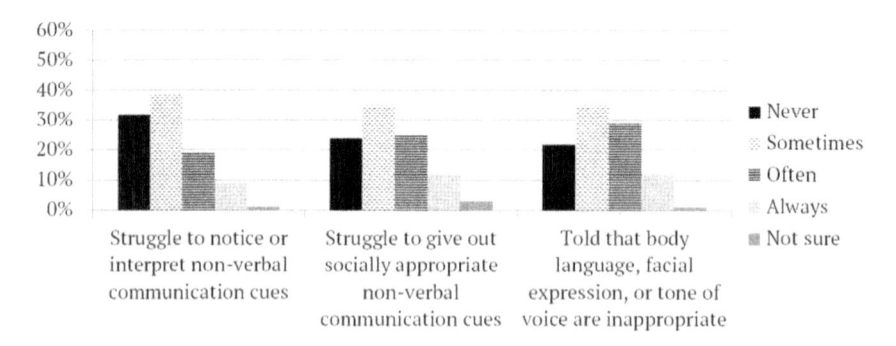

28% of respondents often or always struggle to notice or interpret non-verbal communication cues. This issue is more prevalent in AMABs (36%) than in AFABs (26%).

37% of respondents often or always struggle to give out socially appropriate non-verbal communication cues. The difference between AMABs and AFABs is smaller here – 41% for AMABs and 36% for AFABs – but it might indicate that the gender in which we are socialized might be a factor.

Our ability to recognize our emotions and those of others may also be a factor. 51% of respondents who struggle to notice or interpret non-verbal communication cues also struggle to recognize their feelings, and 43% struggle to recognize other people's feelings. 55% of respondents who struggle to give out socially appropriate non-verbal communication cues also struggle to recognize their feelings, and 55% struggle to recognize other people's feelings. These results are not surprising, given that interpreting and expressing the right emotions in the right way is an important part of non-verbal communication.

These issues do not go unnoticed. 41% of respondents are often or always told that their body language, facial expression, or tone of voice are inappropriate. I was genuinely surprised to find virtually no difference here between AMABs (42%) and AFABs (41%). Given the tendency of randos to volunteer comments about the appearance and behavior of people they perceive as women ("resting b!tch face," anyone?), I assumed that AFAB individuals would be more affected by this issue unless they transition. Clearly, my experience and assumptions do not reflect reality. I would be genuinely interested to know the context in which AMAB individuals receive this type of feedback and how it is worded.

	Misinterpreted or incorrectly assumed intentions
Never	7%
Sometimes	33%
Often	40%
Always	18%
Not sure	2%

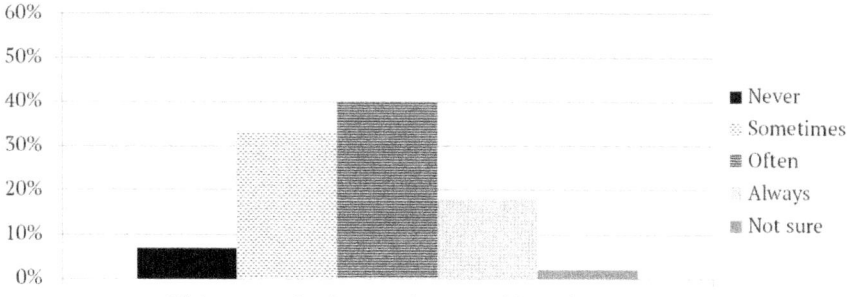

Misinterpreted or incorrectly assumed intentions

These communication difficulties, unsurprisingly, can lead to miscommunications. 58% of respondents often or always find that people misinterpret what they are saying or make incorrect assumptions as to the intentions behind their words. Again, this is a problem that affects AMABs more than AFABs (62% and 57%, respectively). However, our ability to interpret and give out non-verbal communication cues is a much more significant factor. 79% of those who struggle to notice or interpret non-verbal communication cues struggle with being misinterpreted, as do 77% of those who struggle to give out socially appropriate non-verbal communication cues. While these results are utterly unsurprising, they highlight the importance of non-verbal communication to how our statements and intentions are perceived.

And then there is small talk, aka "phatic communication." Phatic communication is ~~hell~~ communication that serves to establish or maintain social relationships rather than to exchange information. Information is exchanged, in a way, but that exchange happens around the words, rather than through them. If we met at a bus stop and started chatting about the weather, that exchange would be ~~hell~~ not about giving one of us the opportunity to inform the other of what the weather is. We would both be experiencing the same weather, after all. The information we would actually be exchanging is our mutual good will towards each other. We would be talking to show that we are willing to communicate and connect with each other, rather than to exchange information or compare data.

By contrast, if we met at a bus stop and one of us started to talk about how the approaching clouds are nimbostratus rather than stratocumulus, and therefore an umbrella may be a good investment, we would be exchanging actual information. We might also be manifesting our mutual good will by sharing interesting and useful facts, but that intention might not always come across, particularly if our interlocutor is neurotypical. Generally speaking, neurotypicals prefer to form social connections by chatting. By contrast, some neurodivergents prefer to connect by "infodumping" – providing copious information about a subject they hold dear. It's the communication equivalent of bringing someone a shiny thing, but it is often misinterpreted.[27]

Phatic communication can be misinterpreted, too, particularly as it's not consistent across all cultures. For instance, in some cultures people

---

[27] I don't personally believe that the current label is helping in this respect. I appreciate that reclaiming slurs is important, and I understand that "infodumping" is term beloved by the neurodivergent community. However, I am not convinced that it helps when trying to explain to neurotypicals what is going on. "Infodumping" is already in common usage, and it has negative connotations. Hoping that the people who object to our communication style will go through the bother of re-learning the meaning of the term seems a tad optimistic.

ask you out for food or drinks because they actually want to go out with you for food or drinks, while in other cultures it's just a gesture of general good will. Responding in the affirmative may mean that you have accepted a social obligation, or that you also feel general good will towards the person who asked you. And unless you know how that particular culture operates, you might have no idea what just happened and what you are expected to do next.

Phatic communication only works if both parties understand which parts should be taken literally and how they should be interpreted. That it should be the norm for establishing social connections baffles me – unless the fact that it can so easily fail is a feature, rather than a bug. Outsiders may be able to learn our language well enough to go unnoticed, but picking up all socially appropriate phatic cues is far harder, particularly as they are not usually taught formally. Phatic communication failures could make outsiders easier to spot, so we can throw pointy rocks at them or chase them out of our cave. This is just my current pet theory, though, so don't take it as gospel.

What's hard to disagree with is that many of us struggle with small talk, and that this can have an impact on our ability to function in some social settings. 62% of respondents are often or always uncomfortable with small talk. Of these, 58% struggle to function in group situations that do not center around a defined activity.

	Uncomfortable with "small talk"
Never	12%
Sometimes	26%
Often	28%
Always	34%
Not sure	0.1%

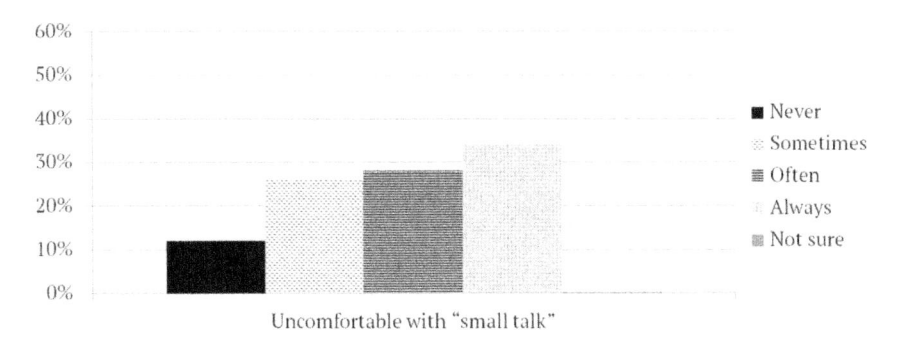

These results are interesting for an additional reason: communication difficulties, and in particular struggles with non-verbal and phatic communications, are usually considered a feature of Autism. However, only 30.5% of survey respondents are Autistic, while 94% of them are ADHDers. There is plenty of research out there indicating that ADHDers struggle to navigate short-term interactions and to establish long-term connections, and the overall result is what the experts refer to as "poorer social function outcomes." However, the assumed wisdom is that our social problems are the result of our inattention, impulsivity and hyperactivity. We exhibit inappropriate behaviors, mess up during social interactions, and struggle to modulate our actions and reactions. It's small wonder that we end up straining our relationships, often to breaking point.

Aside from the ableism and intercultural incompetence inherent in these theories, the result of this survey suggest that ADHDers are affected by a host of communication difficulties that have nothing to do with the current diagnostic criteria for our neurodivergence. This could mean that we might benefit from communication therapy and support, particularly at an early age; however, having seen the kind of "therapy" and "support" Autistic children are so often forced through, I wonder whether we're better off without.

Eye contact and facial recognition.

This section lumps together two issues that may seem unrelated, but are connected, although somehow tangentially. The questions were:

- Do you find direct eye contact unpleasant?
- Do you have to consciously regulate the amount of eye contact you make in order to appear "normal"• ?
- Do you pretend to make eye contact in order to appear "normal,"• but you are actually focusing on something else?
- Do you have prosopagnosia?
- Do you struggle to recognize people out of context?
- Do you struggle to recognize people if they change their hair or clothes?
- Do you worry about the possibility of not recognizing someone or not remembering their name?

Eye contact is a subject that fascinates me because it is a Western obsession. There are plenty of cultures which recognize that people can listen to and respect others without linking eyeballs with them – in fact, there are plenty of cultures which consider direct eye contact rude.[28] There is also plenty of evidence that eye contact isn't essential to verbal communication; anyone who ever used a telephone can attest to that. Yet many Western cultures deem eye contact so important that neurodivergent children are put through grueling training regimes to force them to "do it right" – i.e., to maintain the neurotypically-approved amount of eye contact, regardless of the costs.

And there are costs. Maintaining eye contact isn't "just" unpleasant for many of us; it can create a barrier to learning and interpersonal connection. Having to constantly think about and manually adjust the amount of eye contact we give out takes up mental resources we could otherwise use for listening and learning. Having to constantly worry about whether we are doing eye contact right is stressful, and can prevent us

---

[28] Yet even those whose business it is to know that, seem to forget it with remarkable frequency. This was the first sentence of a scientific article about cross-cultural differences in eye contact: "The eyes have a universal language."
Your own study contradicts that, good sirs. But hey, you're the experts.

from being truly present in our interactions.

And that's for those of us who are not naturally wired for neurotypical-style eye contact, but find it merely bothersome. For some of us, eye contact is so overwhelming that all other functions go out the window. Enforced eye contact makes some of us totally incapable of processing verbal input and can be a trigger for meltdowns, shutdowns, and selective mutism. But hey, eye contact is critical for the comfort of the neurotypicals around us, so it has to take priority, right?

	Find direct eye contact unpleasant	Consciously regulate the amount of eye contact to appear "normal"	Pretend to make eye contact in order to appear "normal"
Never	14%	15%	25%
Sometimes	39%	25%	27%
Often	28%	31%	28%
Always	18%	26%	18%
Not sure	1%	3%	2%

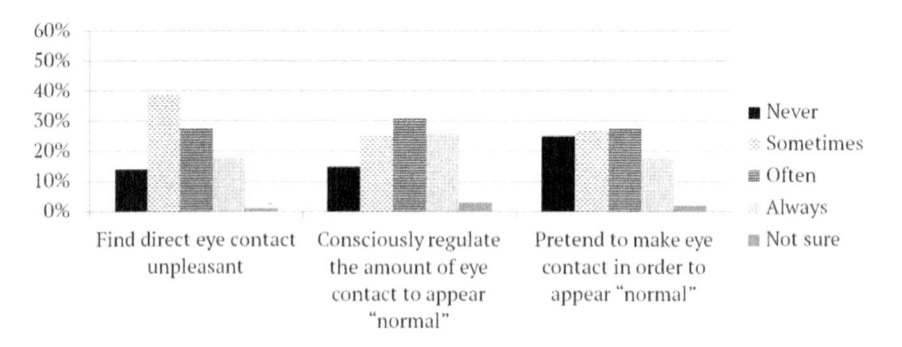

46% of respondents often or always find direct eye contact unpleasant. Of these, 46% are Autistic. 68% of Autistic respondents find direct eye contact unpleasant.

57% of respondents often or always have to consciously regulate the amount of eye contact they make in order to appear "normal." Of these, 41% are Autistic. 77% of Autistic respondents have to consciously regulate the amount of eye contact they make in order to appear "normal."

57% of respondents often or always pretend to make eye contact in order to appear "normal,"• but they are actually focusing on something else. Of these, 42% are Autistic. 63% of Autistic respondents pretend to make eye contact in order to appear "normal,"• but they are actually focusing on something else.

These results suggest that Autism is a factor here. However, they also indicate that it isn't the only factor, as more than half of respondents who are affected by these issues are not Autistic. While these proportions may be very different in surveys with a higher proportion of Autistic respondents, that does not detract from the fact that plenty of non-Autistic neurodivergents have issues around eye contact.

83% of those who find direct eye contact unpleasant have to consciously regulate the amount of eye contact they make in order to appear "normal." As this requires conscious, sustained effort and is a potential cause of stress, it is not inconceivable that it would have a detrimental impact on our ability to function in those circumstances.

69% of those who have to consciously regulate the amount of eye contact they make in order to appear "normal" pretend to make eye contact, but they are actually focusing on something else.[29] That's just one of the coping mechanisms we can use to appease the neurotypicals instead of making actual eye contact. I wonder how many therapists are aware of these tricks, and teach them to their patients.

Of course, it would also be theoretically feasible to teach neurotypicals to cope without eye contact from us, but that would require a rather large shift in perspective. If we start asking those who aren't affected by an issue to make minor adaptations to their expectations so that issue stops being an issue, where are we going to end up? Gaining actual acceptance??

Facial recognition is another issue that wouldn't be that big of a deal if people could only accept that it is a real problem for some of us. Facial recognition isn't just a technological challenge; for some neurodivergent people, it's an everyday struggle.

Prosopagnosia or face blindness is a condition that prevents people from recognizing faces. Problems in facial recognition can arise from a variety of causes, including visual processing issues, memory issues, neurological disorders, and anxiety. Different people are affected to different degrees; some people struggle to recognize faces they aren't

---

[29] My trick is to look at a person's face without focusing my eyes, so their features are a blur.

overly familiar with. Other people can't recognize any faces, including those of loved ones and even their own.

People with mild prosopagnosia may not be aware that they have an issue, for two simple reasons. Firstly, this condition isn't commonly known or mentioned. Unless we stumble upon it by chance, or by reading neurodivergent content, we might never hear of it.

Secondly, even if we do hear of it, we might not realize that it applies to us. We may be vaguely aware of the fact that we struggle to recognize faces in the wild, but we have no idea of knowing how easy other people find it. As with any chronic condition, because it's all we know, we might not realize that it is a condition at all.

Over time, some of us develop coping mechanisms that allow us to recognize people using other markers – their hairstyle, their clothes, their voice, their posture or gait, and so on. Alas, these strategies only work if those markers are reliable. If we are dealing with an extremely homogeneous population – for instance, the students at a school that enforces a strict dress and hairstyle code – we might struggle to tell people apart. Also, people are often sneaky, and may change their clothes and hairstyle without warning us in advance.

	Prosopa-gnosia	Struggle to recognize people out of context	Struggle to recognize people if they change hair or clothes
Never	29%	24%	42%
Sometimes	4%	37%	34%
Often	4%	22%	15%
Always	3%	14%	9%
Not sure	60%	3%	1%

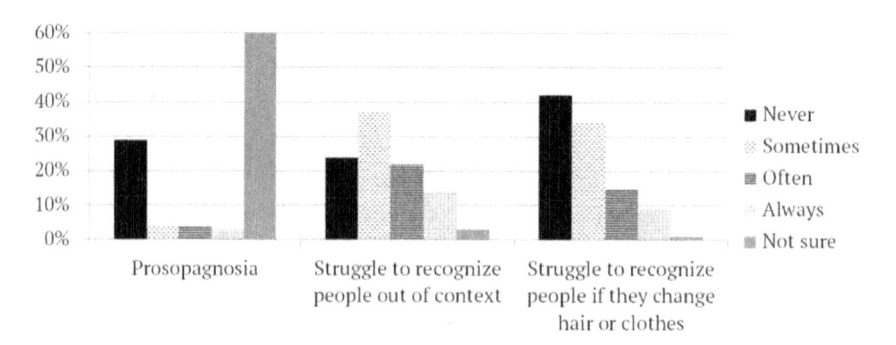

7% of respondents often or always have prosopagnosia, while 60%

aren't sure. These results are unsurprising; given how rarely this condition is mentioned, this survey might have been the first place many respondents heard of it.

Looking at the symptoms of prosopagnosia paints a rather different picture. 37% of respondents often or always struggle to recognize people out of context, and 23% struggle to recognize people if they change their hair or clothes. These two issues overlap: 92% of those who struggle to recognize people if they change their hair or clothes also struggle to recognize people out of context.

These issues may seem trivial, but they can cause severe social difficulties. Many people are hurt or offended when we cannot recognize them – do we care so little about them that we don't even notice them? Are we trying to slight them by deliberately ignoring them in public?

Similar issues are caused when we forget people's names. It has been amply demonstrated that memory is a function that works or fails independently of how we feel about the data in question. The inability to remember names is also a known memory problem with a posh name and everything – lethonomia. However, it is still common for people to believe that forgetting a name indicates lack of care or respect. There are also people out there who believe that we might pretend to have forgotten a name just to score a point; the slight felt by the forgotten person is clearly more significant than any shame we may feel.

	Worry about not recognizing people or not remembering names
Never	14%
Sometimes	28%
Often	30%
Always	28%
Not sure	0%

Worry about not recognizing people or not remembering names

58% of respondents often or always worry about the possibility of not recognizing someone or not remembering their name. The prevalence of this worry is much higher amongst those who have traits associated with prosopagnosia: 86% of those who struggle to recognize people out of context worry about the possibility of not recognizing someone or nor remembering their name, as do 92% of those who struggle to recognize people if they change their hair or clothes.

Current studies indicate that social anxiety affects our ability to recognize faces; there is a marked correlation between those two issues, and the latter is considered to be the result of the former. I harbor the hope that researchers may one day consider the possibility that they are looking at the issue from the wrong angle; that they might accept that real, congenital difficulties in recognizing faces may be a cause of social anxiety due to the social difficulties they create.

Functioning in groups.

This section looked at people's ability to function within groups, and at some of the factors that determine whether they enjoy doing so. The questions were:

- Do you struggle to function in group situations, even though you would enjoy the company of the same people one-to-one?
- Do you struggle to function in group situations that do not center around a defined activity? (e.g., working, playing a board game or a sport, etc.)
- Do you enjoy informal, unstructured group situations? (e.g., a party at someone's house.)
- Do you enjoy formal, unstructured group situations? (e.g., a formal social function.)
- Do you avoid social events because you find them unpleasant?
- Do you attend social events even though you find them unpleasant?
- Do you find yourself drained after attending social events, even when they went well?
- Do you struggle to identify or negotiate social hierarchies?
- Are you able to follow a conversation in a room with background noise?

Problems with functioning in groups are often thought of as an Autistic issue, but anecdotal evidence suggests that they also affect other neurotypes. However, that's not to say that every neurotype struggles in groups because of the same issues, or that neurodivergence is the primary cause of these issues. There are plenty of factors that affect our ability to function in groups, and not all of them are a direct result of our neurodivergence.

There are also plenty of factors that affect our ability to enjoy ourselves in a group setting. This is important: it is possible for people to be able to function in groups, but to hate it, or to like it only in very specific circumstances. The issues of ability and enjoyment are rather separate, and too many specialists seem to forget that. Some people do not like socializing or working in groups, and that's not a symptom that needs treatment. Heck, some people do not like interacting with people, full stop; and if that's not causing them any problems, then it isn't a problem.

Assuming that we don't just loathe the presence of humans in general, one of the key factors to establish is whether we struggle being in groups, or we struggle with the individuals who form the groups we are in. If a group is composed solely of people we don't get along with, then any problems we have may be due to that. Engaging with several asshats at the same time is no less unpleasant than engaging with them individually, and can be far worse. On the other hand, if we absolutely love to hang out with some people one-on-one but we can't stand to hang out with them in a group, this suggests that our issues are with groups per se.

This isn't necessarily an issue of neurodivergence. People's behavior often changes when they are in a group: they might do different things, display different sides of their personality, or even display a completely different personality. They might also display very different attitudes towards us, particularly if our presence within the group is contentious. The people we enjoy deep and meaningful private conversations with might behave very differently if we meet them at a rave, so the setting of our group activities matters. However, if we consistently enjoy the company of individuals but struggle whenever two or three of them come together, this suggests that functioning in groups may be an issue for us.

Another factor is whether we prefer to get together with people to carry out a defined activity, rather than for some free-form socialization. Carrying out an activity reduces the need for small talk, gives us a sense of purpose, and sometimes can even provide a set of clearly-defined rules for social intercourse. Also, the activity itself can be a source of enjoyment; we might suffer through being in a group so we can do it, rather than do it to have a reason to meet people.

	Struggle to function in group situations, even though you would enjoy the company of the same people one-to-one	**Struggle to function in group situations that do not center around a defined activity**
Never	9%	11%
Sometimes	32%	29%
Often	36%	32%
Always	23%	26%
Not sure	0.006%	0.013 %

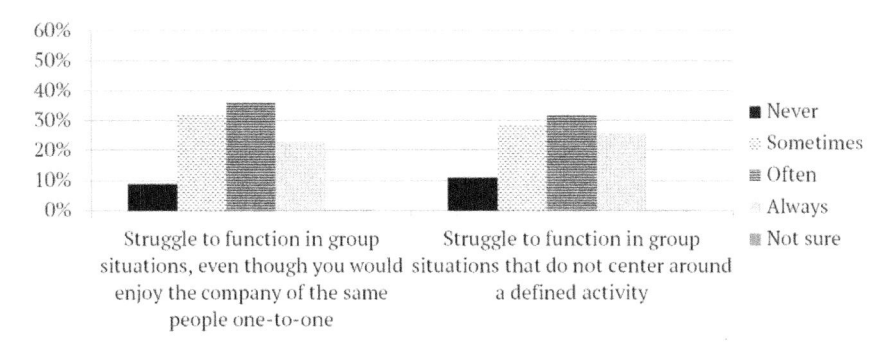

59% of respondents often or always struggle to function in group situations, even though they would enjoy the company of the same people one-to-one. Of these, 41% are Autistic. 58% of respondents often or always struggle to function in group situations that do not center around a defined activity. Of these, 41% are Autistic. There is a significant overlap between these two groups: 80% of respondents who struggle with one issue also struggle with the other. Of these, 35% are Autistic.

As only 30.5% of survey respondents are Autistic, this suggests that Autism may be a factor here. However, it clearly cannot be the only factor, or even the main one, as the majority of respondents who struggle with these issues are not Autistic.

Different group situations can involve different degree of formality, and this can have an impact on our ability to enjoy ourselves. For instance, the requirements and expectations involved with attending an informal house party are rather different from those involved with a formal reception at the local County Club (or so I hear: truth be told, you'd have to physically drag me to the latter, and I'd fight you all the way there). This can affect our ability to enjoy ourselves in different situations.

	Enjoy informal, unstructured group situations	Enjoy formal, unstructured group situations
Never	17%	37%
Sometimes	53%	48%
Often	22%	11%
Always	7%	2%
Not sure	0.005%	0.014%

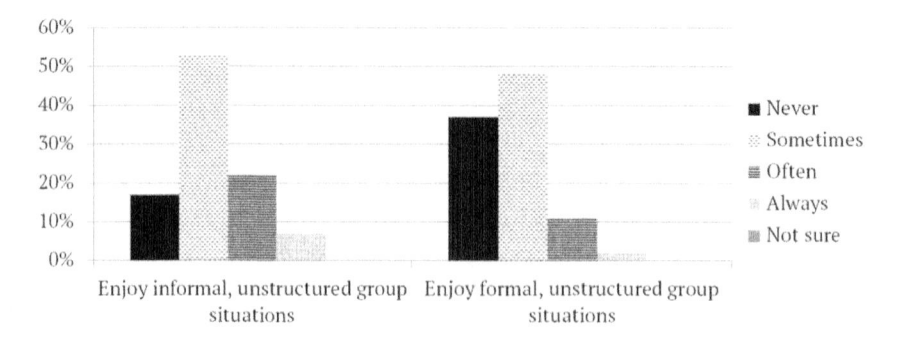

17% of respondents never enjoy informal, unstructured group situations, and 53% of them enjoy them sometimes. By contrast, 37% of participants never enjoy formal, unstructured group situations, and 48% enjoy them sometimes. So, informal group situations are a bit meh for 70% of respondents, while formal situations are a bit meh for 85%.

There is an overlap between these two groups: 94% of those who never enjoy informal situations also don't enjoy formal ones. However, of the 7% of respondent who always enjoy informal situations, only 31% also always enjoy formal ones.

These results seem unsurprising to me, because they match my likes and dislikes. If I like some individuals, I *might* enjoy spending time with them as a group in an informal setting, but I would loathe spending time with them in a formal setting; that's because I am not overly fond of being in groups, but I absolutely abhor the demands and restrictions posed by formal situations.[30] However, my experience is far from universal. In future surveys, it would be interesting to investigate why exactly people dislike formal setting more than informal ones.

Disliking social situations can lead to avoidance. This is not necessarily a problem, let alone a symptom requiring therapeutic interventions. It really depends on what the person in question actually wants to do.

Alternatively, people may dislike social situations but not avoid them, either due to choice or to lack thereof. (Personally, it took a pandemic to make me realize that people attend social events because *they actually like them*. I thought that social events were just unavoidable chores that everyone suffered through because of some unspoken social rule. You have to attend funerals or run the risk of falling foul with your social

---

[30] It's why I will never be an international superspy à la James Bond. It's tragic, really, because I'd be so good at it otherwise.

group; I genuinely thought the same was true of parties.)

	Avoid social events because you find them unpleasant	Attend social events even though you find them unpleasant	Drained after attending social events, even when they went well
Never	11%	11%	4%
Sometimes	43%	58%	15%
Often	32%	26%	28%
Always	13%	4%	52%
Not sure	0.006%	0.013%	0.008%

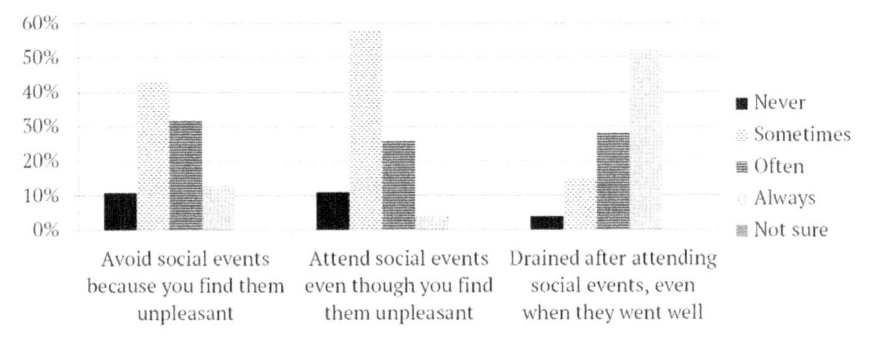

45% of respondents often or always avoid social events because they find them unpleasant. Of these, 40% are Autistic.

30% of respondents often or always attend social events even though they find them unpleasant. Of these, 32% are Autistic.

80% of respondents often or always feel drained after attending social events, even when they went well. Of these, 65% are Autistic.

These results suggest that Autistic people may be slightly more likely to avoid social events because they don't like them, and are definitely more likely to feel drained after social events. However, Autism cannot be the only factor here, as it leaves too many respondents unaccounted for.

There are countless factors that may have an impact on whether we enjoy certain social situations, and many of them don't have anything to do with our liking for people. For instance, if we have environmental sensitivities, we are unlikely to look forward to situations in which we will be exposed to triggers. If we struggle with our interoception, we might be worried about failing to respond to our body's signals until it's too late. If our blood pressure or blood sugar levels aren't up to snuff, we might be worried about becoming faint or dizzy, or even passing out. If we have anything that causes us chronic pain or fatigue, we might worry about doing anything that could aggravate our symptoms, or we might simply not be up for a shindig. It's all about pros and cons, really: if the pros don't balance out the cons, we will probably not enjoy ourselves, or not enjoy ourselves enough to justify our attendance. After all, the time we spend at any social event is time we could have spent doing something else; and if that something else is something we'd like better, then why shouldn't we do that instead?

Some aspects of neurodivergence present particular challenges independent of physical factors. This survey looked at issues in two domains: identifying and negotiating social hierarchies, and the ability to follow a conversation in a room with background noise.

	Struggle to identify or negotiate social hierarchies	**Able to follow a conversation in a room with background noise**
Never	16%	18%
Sometimes	36%	53%
Often	31%	24%
Always	13%	5%
Not sure	0.046%	0.004%

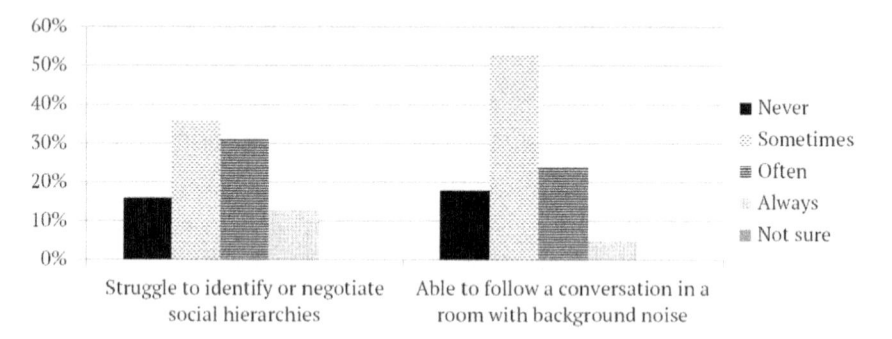

I don't think there is a word as yet for the neurodivergent struggle to respect social hierarchies, and maybe that is a good thing, because this issue can have different causes. Some of us genuinely cannot discern the hierarchy within a group unless it is clearly stated. Some may be able to perceive it, but as it makes no sense, we do not let it guide our behavior. Some understand and respect local hierarchies, but struggle to give out the neurotypical markers of respect; for instance, we might not stay still enough while we listen, not give enough eye contact, or have a participatory conversational style. Any of these issues can land us in the soup in situations where observing the conventions set by hierarchies is crucial.

52% of participants often or always struggle to identify or negotiate social hierarchies. Of these, 92% dislike formal, unstructured group situations. This is hardly surprising, given the importance of respecting social hierarchies in formal settings.

Hearing difficulties and Auditory Processing Disorder are another potential cause of accidental social faux pas. People with APD may have normal hearing, but experience impaired sound processing in the central auditory nervous system. For instance, a person may have perfect hearing, but might be unable to follow a conversation in a room with background noise. Their ears can pick up the sounds in the room, but their nervous system cannot pick out the relevant ones. APD can also present with other symptoms, such as auditory memory problems (difficulties recalling verbal information), auditory discrimination problems (difficulties hearing the difference between similar words or sounds), auditory attention problems (difficulties maintaining focus on auditory input), and auditory cohesion problems (difficulties putting together or processing complex auditory information).

38% of survey respondents have APD. However, 18% of respondents are never able to follow a conversation in a room with background noise, and 53% can do it sometimes. This gives us 71% of respondents who struggle with this. Unfortunately, the limitations of this survey prevent us from knowing whether this is due to hearing difficulties, undiagnosed APD, or some other factor.

77% of respondents who struggle to function in group situations, even though they would enjoy the company of the same people one-to-one, struggle to follow conversations in a room with background noise. It's not unconceivable that the fact that they struggle to hear what's going on might have some bearing on their ability to function in that setting.

Emotional regulation.

This section looked at emotional volatility, self-regulation, and rejection-sensitive dysphoria. The questions were:

- Do you have mood lability?
- Do you experience rapid, pronounced changes in mood with very little reason?
- Do you struggle to control your behavior when you are experiencing strong emotions?
- Do you get in trouble for behaving impulsively when you feel emotional?
- Do you have Rejection-Sensitive Dysphoria?
- Do you tend to anxiously expect social rejection?
- Do you believe that people are going to reject you even though they haven't done anything concrete to show that?
- Do you find rejection very painful, even when it comes from people you do not really like or care for?
- Do you do things you'd rather not so people will like you?
- Do you pretend to be someone else so people will like you?

Mood lability is the technical name for the tendency to experience unpredictable, uncontrollable, and rapid shifts in mood. It isn't the same as moodiness, because the shifts in mood do not always have an apparent or specific trigger. Mood lability can be a symptom of mood disorders, personality disorders, or PTSD/cPTSD. It can also occur as the result of traumatic brain damage or neurological illnesses, or as a side effect from the use of certain medications or substances.

Some neurodivergents experience rapid and dramatic shifts in mood that, while they might not meet the diagnostic criteria for mood lability, can still cause them significant problems. For instance, many ADHDers struggle with emotional self-regulation, both in childhood and as adults. We might struggle to control our reactions to negative stimuli, to calm ourselves down after experiencing intense emotions, to respond appropriately to changes in situations or expectations, and to manage our responses to frustration and upsets. This can have a pervasive negative impact on our life. Poor emotional self-regulation not only causes problems in the moment, such as the interpersonal, disciplinary, or legal consequences of inappropriate reactions to situations; it is also linked to the establishment and persistence of longer-term issues, including depression, addictions, and suicidal ideation.

There is an ongoing debate about emotionality in ADHD. The core issue is whether ADHDers feel more intensely than their neurotypical counterparts, or are just less able to handle their feelings. This issue may affect the efficacy of therapeutic interventions. Many of the current strategies for self-regulation are designed for neurotypical individuals, and might be of limited use to neurodivergent people who are dealing with a completely different emotional situation. If I may use a ludicrous analogy, a cat cage is perfectly suited to its intended purpose, but it won't hold a tiger.

	Mood lability	Rapid, pronounced mood changes w/o reason	Struggle to control behavior when emotional	Get in trouble for behaving impulsively when emotional
Never	9%	16%	12%	21%
Sometimes	24%	48%	39%	38%
Often	15%	27%	32%	26%
Always	4%	8%	17%	13%
Not sure	48%	1%	1%	1%

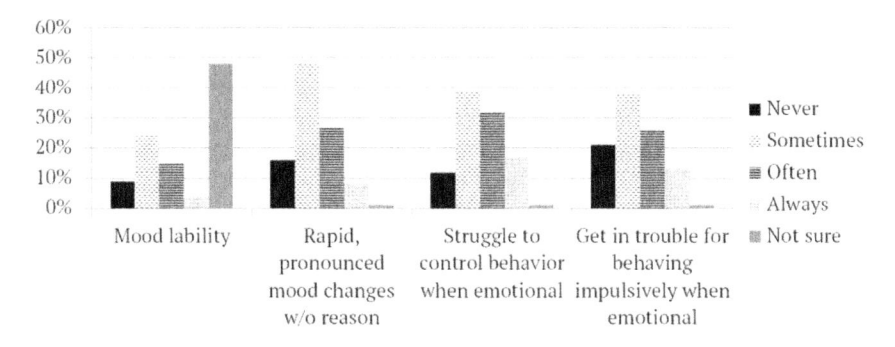

19% of respondents said that they often or always have mood lability. However, that doesn't mean that the rest of the respondents do not struggle with emotional regulation. 35% often or always experience rapid, pronounced changes in mood with very little reason. 49% often or always struggle to control their behavior when they are experiencing strong emotions. 39% often or always get in trouble for behaving impulsively when they feel emotional.

There is another potential aspect of emotional self-regulation in neurodivergence. Many neurodivergent adults are survivors of trauma, or are forced to live in environments that traumatize them. This isn't necessarily due to deliberate neglect or abuse (although those happen), but to a chronic and critical mismatch between our abilities and the demands placed upon us. As childhood trauma is proven to have a long-lasting detrimental impact on emotional self-regulation, a discussion of trauma is critical to a discussion of self-regulation, and any intervention aimed at improving self-regulation should be trauma-informed.

The results of this survey bear this out. The prevalence of emotional self-regulation issues is higher in people who have symptoms caused by exposure to a traumatic event or by exposure to long-term trauma, abuse, or neglect. However, it is even higher in people who, when children, were forced by their parents or teachers to endure painful physical sensation in order to learn to get over them. It looks as if these attempts at "desensitization" therapies might have a worse impact on our emotional self-regulation than trauma, abuse, or neglect.

	Rapid, pronounced mood changes w/o reason	Struggle to control behavior when emotional	Get in trouble for behaving impulsively when emotional
Whole survey	35%	45%	39%
PTSD	43%	55%	45%
cPTSD	42%	58%	46%
"Desensitized"	53%	63%	56%

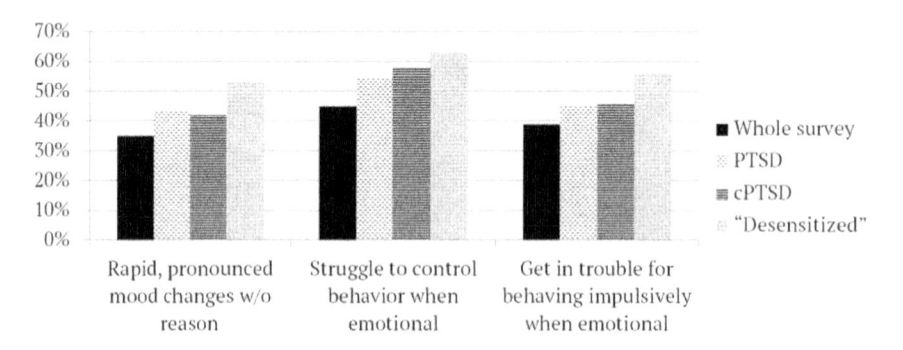

These result matter, because therapeutic interventions aimed at helping us develop emotional self-regulation skills should take into account the underlying causes of our issues. Therapies that fail to account for the impact of trauma – and, in particular, therapies that fail to account for the impact of trauma caused by other therapies – might fail to give us the right tools. This issue may explain while current therapies and strategies designed to help children and adults improve their emotional self-regulation tend to have a limited impact on people's lives, as any improvements tend to be specific to a particular setting.

The next issue may also be linked to trauma, abuse, or neglect. **Rejection-Sensitive dysphoria (RSD)** is the disposition to anxiously expect, readily perceive, and intensely react to rejection. Up to 99% of teens and adults with ADHD are more sensitive than their neurotypical peers to rejection, and nearly 1 in 3 say it's the hardest part of living with ADHD. RSD can have a profound impact on our ability and willingness to engage in social interactions. We may "adapt" by becoming hostile, socially withdrawn, or over-accommodating of others.

RSD is not a currently recognized condition. It might also not be a condition in its own right, or a symptom of neurodivergence, but a reaction to maltreatment or attachment failures in childhood. In essence, RSD may be a response to the trauma of being neurodivergent in a neurotypical world and the attendant social difficulties, rather than a feature of our neurodivergence.

An adult's ability to emotionally handle rejection is a skill learnt in childhood, and is dependent on several factors including:

- Secure attachments with one's care giver(s).
- Self-confidence in one's ability to handle situations.
- Self-worth independent of achievements.

In order to foster children's trust in their own abilities, it is essential not to face them with demands they cannot meet. Children's self-worth can be encouraged by validating their concerns and experiences. Both may be issues for neurodivergent children. Our families, schools, and society do not consistently validate our experiences or accommodate our needs. We might have unmet physical needs and unrecognized oversensitivities that cause our caregiver(s) to suppress or punish our natural responses to our environment. Furthermore, as our development doesn't match that of our neurotypical peers, we are constantly measured against inappropriate milestones, and found wanting. For those of us who did not get diagnosed in childhood, this effect may be particularly severe, as our poor performance and behavior were often seen as the signs of personal failings, rather than as symptoms. Not knowing that our peers are not dealing with the same issues can also make us profoundly dissatisfied with ourselves.

When we consider these facts, it's unsurprising that untreated ADHD is associated with poorer long-term self-esteem and social function outcomes, or that we should grow to fear rejection. Quite simply, it is a much more common feature of our social landscape than most neurotypical people could ever guess.

	Have RSD	Tend to anxiously expect social rejection	Believe that people are going to reject you with no proof	Find rejection very painful, even when it comes from people you do not really like or care for
Never	6%	6%	8%	6%
Sometimes	12%	21%	20%	21%
Often	24%	33%	35%	27%
Always	41%	39%	36%	45%
Not sure	17%	1%	1%	1%

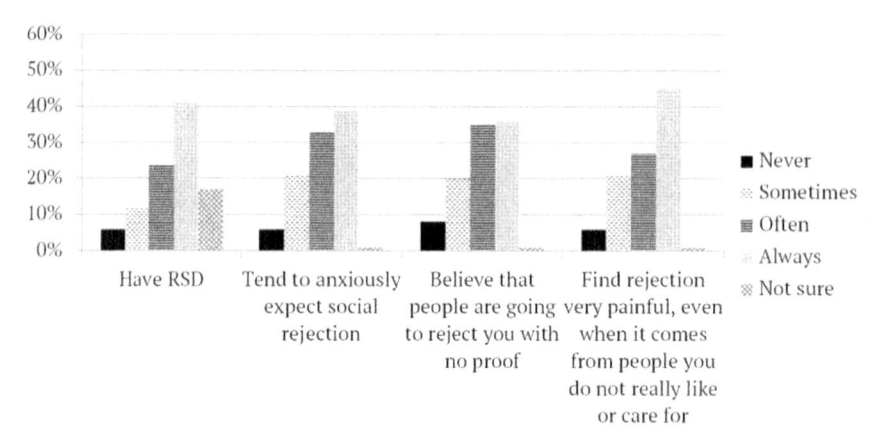

65% of respondents often or always have RSD. Bearing in mind that this condition isn't widely known, this is quite a result.

72% of respondents often or always tend to anxiously expect social rejection. 71% of respondents often or always believe that people are going to reject them, even though they haven't done anything concrete to show that. 72% of respondents often or always find rejection very painful, even when it comes from people they do not really like or care for.

These results do not imply that we are a paranoid bunch. If we look at the results about relationships, they indicate that our struggles are real. 72% of respondents struggle to make new friends, 68% struggle to keep their friends, and 70% struggle in relationships with partners and relatives.

RSD isn't just unpleasant; it can push us to take up unhealthy and even dangerous behavioral patterns in order to avoid rejection. We might become people-pleasers, trying to make up for our perceived shortcomings by doing whatever it takes to make people like us. We might bury our personality and create a character we believe to be more likeable. We might learn to be tolerant of harmful behaviors from those around us, and to accept them as the price of admission in a relationship. When our social world is hurting us, we try to change ourselves instead of protecting ourselves. If part of that hurt is caused by being in a relationship with an abuser, that can take us to very bad places.

	Do things you'd rather not so people will like you	**Pretend to be someone else so people will like you**
Never	15%	28%
Sometimes	43%	38%
Often	26%	22%
Always	14%	10%
Not sure	1%	2%

41% of respondents often or always do things they'd rather not so people will like them. Of these, 91% find rejection very painful, even when it comes from people they do not really like or care for. 32% of respondents often or always pretend to be someone else so people will like them. Of these, 88% find rejection very painful, even when it comes from people they do not really like or care for. These results support the theory that RSD may be a factor in people-pleasing and masking.

Interoception.

This section looked at interoception – the collection of senses that help us know what is going on inside our bodies. Interoception allows us to know when we are hungry, full, thirsty, hot, cold, in need of a pee or poo, and so on. The questions were:

- Do you have poor interoception?
- Do you struggle to read your body's hunger signals, so you forget to eat until you feel sick from hunger?
- Do you struggle to read your body's thirst signals, so you forget to drink?
- Do you struggle to know when you need to pee or poo until you are desperate, or have an accident?

(I neglected to ask about pain signals. This is an oversight that should be rectified in future surveys.)

Interoception is not a well-known concept, and the results of this survey support this. 15% of respondents reported that they often or always have poor interoception, but 40% reported that they often or always struggle to read their hunger signals, 48% their thirst signals, and 18% their pee/poo signals.

	Poor interoception	Hunger signals problems	Thirst signals problems	Pee/poo signals problem
Never	29%	22%	19%	48%
Sometimes	43%	37%	32%	33%
Often	18%	30%	33%	13%
Always	10%	11%	16%	6%
Not sure	44%	0.4%	0.4%	0.4%

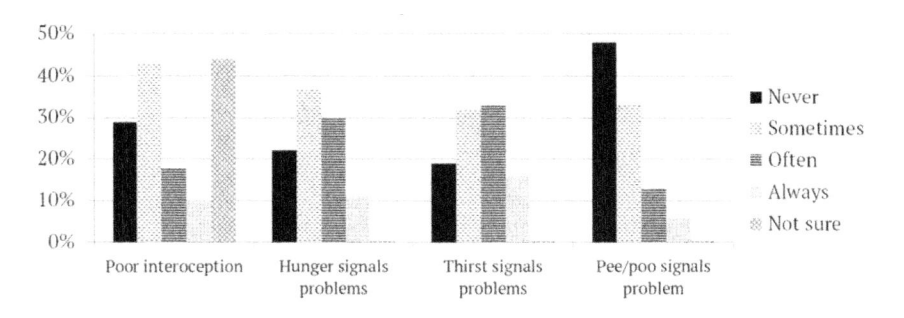

Poor interoception can make self-care a challenge, as we may have unmet physical needs we cannot perceive. For instance, we might feel vaguely unwell, but not be able to work out that we need to eat or drink.

Poor interoception can also have damaging long-term impacts on our health. For instance, not registering thirst can cause us to be dehydrated so often that we develop urinary tract infections, kidney stones, or even kidney failure.

While interoception is an innate ability, our life experiences can affect the degree with which we can connect with our bodies. We can be trained to disconnect from our bodies in order to cope with our environment, either by accident or as part of misplaced and uninformed attempts at "desensitization" – why this kind of intervention is not desensitization is explained in details in the section about exposure to painful stimuli

If we compare the results for interoception from the group as a whole and from those who in childhood, were forced by parents or teachers to endure painful physical sensation in order to learn to get over them, there are marked differences. 28% of "desensitized" respondents reported poor interoception, 68% poor hunger signals, 68% poor thirst signals, and 36% poor pee/poo signals.

	Poor interoception	Poor hunger signals	Poor thirst signals	Poor pee/poo signals
Whole survey	15%	40%	48%	18%
"Desensitized"	28%	68%	68%	36%

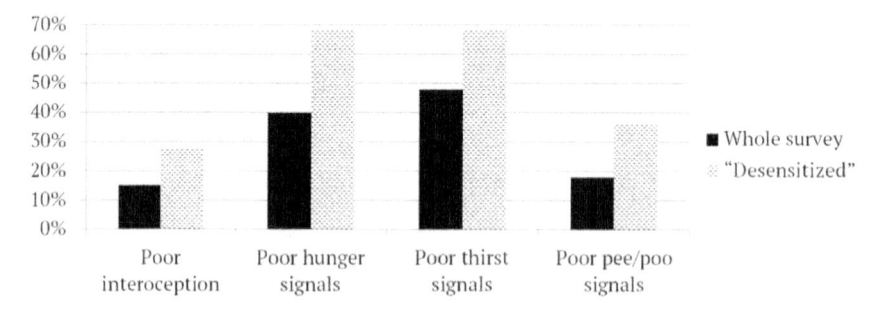

While these results cannot prove a causal link, they suggest a correlation between attempts at "desensitization" and suboptimal interoception. It is possible that these "therapies" do not affect our

reactions to stimuli, but our ability to feel our bodies. From the outside, these therapies might look successful, because when we lose their ability to feel sensations we also lose the urge to react to them. However, what is going on is much more pervasive, and much less benign.

Sleep.

This section looked at sleep disorders that seem to be more prevalent in the neurodivergent community, both anecdotally and according to scientific studies. The questions were:

- Are you able to sleep at least 7 hours every night?
- Does it take you longer than 20 minutes to fall asleep after you go to bed?
- Do you have delayed sleep phase syndrome?
- Are you unable to fall asleep at a socially acceptable time even though you get to bed on time?
- Do you wake up in the middle of the night for no reason?
- Do you have long spells of insomnia in the winter?
- Do you have long spells on insomnia in the summer?
- Do you wake up tired, even when you get enough sleep?
- Do you have sleep apnea?
- Do you have narcolepsy?
- Do you have restless legs syndrome?
- Do you have an overwhelming urge to move your legs, particularly in the evening or at night?

I did not ask sleep hygiene questions because, unlike many medical professionals, I don't believe that the majority of sleep-deprived people choose insomnia because they get a kick out of it, or because they do not understand how sleep works. However, I should have asked about circumstances outside of a person's control that might prevent them from sleeping long enough or well enough – young babies, loud neighbors, pets bent on nighttime destruction, irregular work shift patterns, the lack of a comfortable or safe place to sleep, and so on. Future surveys should clarify that the answers should reflect an ideal situation, sleep-wise, as many people's normal is far from optimal.

I also did not ask whether people are already medicated for sleep disorders. That was a gross oversight, as many sleep disorders are easily treatable. People who are being treated effectively may not show any symptoms, but that does not mean that they no longer have a sleep disorder. This particularly true of disorders linked to problems with melatonin production, which we will discuss at length.

The last issue I neglected to cover was latitude. Daylight exposure increases nocturnal melatonin secretion. At higher latitudes, day length variations between the seasons are greater. While these changes may not be significant enough to affect the sleep of those whose melatonin secretion is "normal," they can have a significant impact on susceptible individuals, who may suffer worse symptoms at higher latitudes.

Sleep disorders are a critically important issue for neurodivergent people, for two main reasons: their prevalence, and their impact.

Studies show that as many as 70% of ADHDers and 80% of Autistics suffer from sleep disturbances. Some of these sleep disturbances are quantity issues; quite simply, we do not get enough sleep. This can be caused by a variety of reasons, the most common being that we struggle to fall asleep when we need to, to stay asleep through the night, or to go back to sleep quickly enough if we do wake up in the night. Other sleep disturbances are quality issues; we may sleep long enough, or even longer than "normal", but we wake up still tired because our sleep quality isn't up to snuff. Anecdotal evidence suggests that we may also be more prone to rarer sleep disorders, such as narcolepsy – a condition that causes attacks of drowsiness during the day.

	Sleep 7hrs hours	**>20 mins to fall asleep**	**Delayed sleep phase syndrome**	**Unable to fall asleep at an acceptable time**
Never	14%	4%	13%	12%
Sometimes	54%	24%	8%	31%
Often	26%	31%	11%	32%
Always	6%	41%	18%	24%
Not sure	0.3%	1%	51%	1%

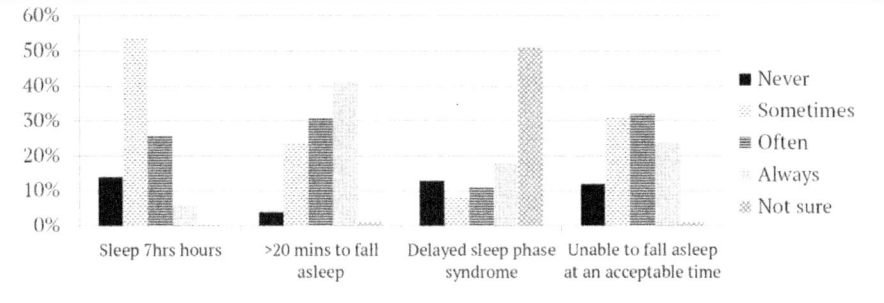

In the context of what we know about neurodivergence and sleep, the results of this survey are utterly unsurprising. Seven hours of sleep is the minimum recommended amount for the average adult – and that means seven hours *every day*. According to this survey, only 6% of us manage that. That's... really not great. The 26% of us who often manage to get sever hours of sleep may be getting enough sleep on average, and as a result may only be sleep deprived some of the time, but that's still suboptimal.

The second question is not a typo: under normal circumstances, most people take between 10 and 20 minutes to fall asleep at night. We are clearly not most people, because only 4% of us manage that. While this may sound like it's not a big deal, it can be, depending on two factors.

The first factor is how long it actually takes us to fall asleep. Time spent waiting to fall asleep is time spent not sleeping. If it takes us two hours of lying in bed to fall asleep, that means that we need to allocate an extra two hours of our day to our sleep. That isn't always feasible and it's almost never consequence-free, particularly if we cannot control when we have to wake up.

For instance, a person who has to wake up at 6am needs to fall asleep at 11pm in order to get 7 hours of sleep (which, again, is the *minimum* recommended amount; many people need more). If it takes them two hours to fall asleep, that means that they will have to get to bed at 9pm or they will be sleep deprived. While some people may be able to schedule their life in order to achieve that, not everyone can. And for those who can, having the bedtime of the average 12 year old can make for a fairly miserable social life, or lack thereof.

The second factor is whether the problem is that we can't fall asleep quickly enough, or that we just cannot fall asleep at the bedtime we set (or, most often, the bedtime our obligations set for us). For some of us, the issue isn't that we cannot move from rest to sleep quickly enough, but that our bodies aren't wired to go to sleep at a "normal" bedtime. Our internal clock and the actual clock are not in sync. The resulting sleep disorders are called **Circadian Rhythm Sleep Disorders** (CRSD).

Circadian rhythm is the name given to the body's internal clock. Its mechanism is very complicated and trying to summarize it here would test my skills and many of my readers' patience. The TL/DR version is that light tells a control center in our brain what time it is, and the control center regulates the production of various hormones. One of these hormones is melatonin, a key player in the sleep-wake cycle.

Melatonin is linked to the onset, duration, and quality of sleep. Its production increases soon after the onset of darkness, peaks in the middle of the night, and decreases during the second half of the night. During the day, melatonin levels are at their lowest. If the system works as intended, these chemical shifts sync our internal clock with the actual clock. If something goes awry, this synchronization does not happen, and we can end up suffering from a circadian mismatch. If that mismatch causes us to lose sleep, we have a circadian rhythm sleep disorder.

There are several types of CRSDs. Anecdotal evidence suggests that the most common within the ADHD community is **Delayed Sleep Phase Syndrome** (DSPS), a disorder in which a person's sleep is delayed by two hours or more beyond what is considered an acceptable bedtime. This happens regardless of the implementation of good sleep hygiene practices.

For instance, let's say that our hypothetical person who needs to wake up at 6am goes to bed at 11pm, but try as they might, they can't fall asleep until 1am. This causes them to be sleep deprived, because they can't cram 7 hours of sleep in 5 hours. In order to fix that, they decide to go to bed at 9pm; factoring in 2 hours to fall asleep, that should guarantee that they will be asleep at 11pm, which will give them 7 hours of sleep. If what happens instead is that day after day they go to bed at 9pm and then lay awake until 1am, then there is a good chance that they might have Delayed Sleep Phase Syndrome. The clock may say that it's bedtime, they might want it to be bedtime, they might have done everything in their power to make it bedtime, but their body has other plans.

As most people are not able to schedule their obligations around their idiosyncratic sleep schedule, Delayed Sleep Phase Syndrome can result in chronic sleep deprivation. Estimates of prevalence vary between studies and between age groups, but 0.2-1.7% of adults in the general population are believed to be affected by DSPS. Unfortunately, this low prevalence means that DSPS isn't widely known, even within the medical community. As a result, it is often undiagnosed and untreated.

The results of this survey support this lack of information and medical support. Out of our respondents, "only" 29% reported that they often or always have DPSP, but 56% are often or always unable to fall asleep at a socially acceptable time even though they get to bed on time. 51% were not sure whether they have DSPS.

While answering a question on an amateur survey is not sufficient to diagnose a sleep disorder, any sleep problem that causes chronic sleep deprivation should be taken seriously and investigated by medical professionals. This is important for anyone, because all humans need sleep, but it can be particularly critical for neurodivergents. Remember earlier in this chapter, when I said that sleep disorders are a critically important issue for neurodivergent people because of their impact? There was a reason for that.

Sleep disturbances can have serious impacts on people's health and quality of life. Short-term sleep deprivation can cause difficulties getting up in the morning, daytime drowsiness, and a general decline in mood and performance. Children, particularly young children, may be unusually hyperactive or bad-tempered. That's unpleasant enough for all involved, but the effects of chronic sleep deprivation are where things get really interesting for us, as they include:

- Decline in executive function.
- Impaired sustained attention.
- Increased tendency to make errors, particularly under time pressure.
- Difficulties in performing long tasks.
- Slower or impaired information processing.
- Slower response time.
- Working memory decline.
- Reduced memory formation.
- Difficulties in decision-making.
- Poor judgment.
- Increased risk-taking behavior.
- Decline in motor control.
- Increased emotional reactivity.
- Difficulties in modulating behavior.
- Anxiety.
- Depression.

Does this all sound familiar? If so, it's because it's basically the carbon copy of the most common ADHD traits and co-occurring conditions.

What this means is that if you take the most neurotypical person on the planet and you deprive them of sleep for long enough, they will start showing the same performance and behavioral issues ADHDers deal with on a daily basis. And these effects are cumulative: the longer the sleep deprivation goes on, the worse its effects get. Also, its impact will be greater on those who already suffer from certain symptoms. For instance, sleep deprived people who normally have a fantastic working memory may notice that it has declined, but people whose working memory is already poor may be rendered virtually non-functional.

Traits associated with Autism, including stimming, communication difficulties, and socialization problems have also been found to be exacerbated by sleep deprivation; in a nutshell, stimming goes up, and communication and socialization go down. This should surprise no one, because sleep deprivation makes everything harder for everyone. If anything is surprising, it's the fact that researchers are still busy trying to work out whether Autistic traits cause sleep deprivation or sleep deprivation causes Autistic traits, instead of focusing their efforts on treating sleep deprivation in Autistic patients.

The failure to treat sleep disturbances is particularly significant for children, whose brains are still developing. There is increasing evidence that chronic sleep loss can lead to neuronal and cognitive loss in children. This can impact not only their cognitive development, but the physical development of their brains. Over time, untreated sleep disorders may lead to impaired brain development, neuronal damage, and permanent loss of developmental potentials.

Delayed Sleep Phase Syndrome is not the only circadian rhythm sleep disorder affecting our community. We may also suffer from:

- **Advanced Sleep Phase Disorder** (ASPD), a condition in which people naturally fall asleep and wake up too early. It's basically the opposite of DSPS – we are out of sync by running early instead of late.

- **Non-24-hour sleep-wake disorder** (N24), a condition in which the biological clock does not synchronize to a 24-hour day. This results in chronic, daily delays in sleep onset and wake times. The length of these delays will depend on the length of day as set by the biological clock.

As with DPSP, these mismatches between a person's internal clock and the actual clock can cause sleep deprivation and social problems. At the very least, they cause us to go through life permanently jet-lagged.

There are also plenty of sleep disturbances that are not linked to the circadian rhythm – insomnias, parasomnias, all kinds of stuff. Looking at them all is beyond the scope of this book, but we will look at some now.

	Waking up in the night	Winter insomnia	Summer insomnia
Never	12%	32%	33%
Sometimes	41%	29%	30%
Often	31%	20%	20%
Always	15%	10%	9%
Not sure	0%	9%	8%

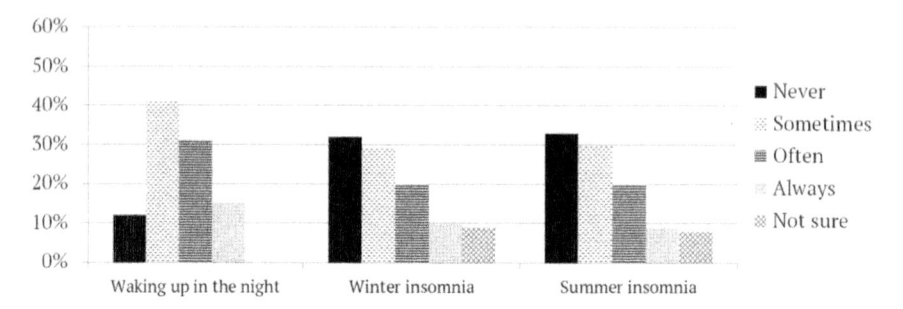

Waking up during the night is fairly common; over 35% of people in the general population wake up during the night at least three times per week. This issue can be caused by environmental factors (e.g. noise, changes in room temperature, etc.), physiological factors (e.g. needing to pee, pains and aches, etc.), psychoemotional factors (e.g. stress, anxiety, depression, etc.), or a number of sleep disorders.

The results of this survey suggest that that this issue may be more prevalent in our community, with 46% of respondents indicating that they wake up in the middle of the night often or always. However, this does not necessarily mean that we will be sleep deprived as a result. As long as we can fall back asleep easily and quickly after waking, the overall impact on our sleep and health can be negligible.

Unfortunately, many of us can't fall asleep quickly or easily. If we go back to our hypothetical person,[31] if every time they wake up it takes them two hours go to back to sleep, then waking up once will mean that instead of getting their seven hours of sleep, they'll only get five. Waking up twice

---

[31] Who am I kidding? It's me. I have been a very sleep-deprived goblin.

will mean that they'll only be asleep 3 hours out of seven. This kind of impact can soon build up and result in serious sleep deprivation.

If the pattern of sleeping and waking is consistent, is not caused by external disturbances, and is not under a person's control, that person may have a **biphasic**, **segmented**, or **polyphasic sleep pattern** – i.e., instead of getting their sleep in a single chunk (monophasic sleep pattern), they get it in two or more chunks.

These sleep patterns may be unfamiliar to us, but they are not unnatural or abnormal. In some cultures, biphasic sleep patterns are the norm; people have a long sleep at night and a shorter sleep during the day, often after lunch. Some historians theorize that prior to industrialization, it was normal for people to have a segmented sleep pattern; they slept in two segments of time during the night – first and second sleep – with a waking period of about one to two hours in between. Some argue that biphasic and segmented sleep may be more natural and healthier. This is no help at all for people whose bodies will only sleep in chunks, but whose lifestyle doesn't allow them to do so.

A siesta may be good for us, but only if we are allowed to take it, and most workplaces do not accommodate that. Segmented sleep might be more natural, but finding an extra two hours a day for our sleep routine may not be practical. This is particularly true for those of us who have to deal with sleep disorders on top of an unusual sleep pattern.

If our hypothetical person who takes two hours to fall asleep had a segmented sleep pattern, they would have to go to bed at 7pm in order to fall asleep at 9pm. They would then wake at 1am and start going back to sleep at 3am. Alas, they would only manage to actually fall asleep at around 5am. If they woke up on time, at 6am, they would spend 11 hours in bed to get 5 hours of actual sleep, and be chronically sleep deprived. If they followed their body's demands and slept until 9am, they would get a glorious 8 hours of sleep over a 13 hour period, and be chronically late for work. I don't know about you, but neither option works for me.

Anecdotal evidence suggests that segmented sleep may be a common feature in winter insomnia. Seasonal variations in the length of the sleep period are normal. These changes are linked to the effect of daylight exposure on the production of melatonin. Remember melatonin, one of the hormones involved in the circadian rhythm? Its production does not only vary depending on the time of day, but also on the time of year.

In the summer, the shorter nights result in shorter periods of melatonin production. In the winter, the opposite happens. What this means is that, if the system works as intended, people will tend to sleep for a slightly longer period in the winter and a slightly shorter period in the summer. If the system does not work as intended, however, people may experience protracted periods of insomnia during the summer, during the winter, or during both seasons.

Winter and summer insomnia can manifest in different ways. Summer insomnia seems to be largely a case of people falling asleep too late and waking up too early, which might be caused by the period of melatonin production being too short due to the days being too long. Winter insomnia, however, can be a much messier affair. Some people have the urge to fall asleep quite early in the evening, but cannot do so due to life getting in the way. When they finally go to bed, they might find themselves unable to stay asleep longer than 3-4 hours, or unable to fall asleep until way past their bedtime. This could be linked to a shift from a monophasic to a segmented sleep pattern; their bodies want to have two sleep periods, but their life only allows them to actually sleep during one of them.

Unfortunately, we only have anecdotal evidence to support this. Seasonal sleep disturbances are poorly studied and even more poorly explained. That's a damn shame, because they have a serious impact on our community. Survey results indicate that 30% of us often or always experience winter insomnia, and 29% experience summer insomnia. These results are even more interesting when we start to look at the correlations between them. 70% of respondents who experience winter insomnia also experience summer insomnia. This could mean that they're just year-round insomniac – I neglected to ask about insomnia in the spring and autumn, so I can't rule that out. However, it could also indicate that there is a glitch in melatonin production that results in sleep disturbances at both ends of the day length spectrum.

This hypothesis is given more credence by another correlation. 40% of the respondents who reported symptoms of Delayed Sleep Phase Symptoms also reported winter or summer insomnia, and 30% reported both. We know that DSPS is a circadian rhythm sleep disorder. The fact that it should co-occur so frequently with seasonal sleep disorder invites further investigations – or, at the very least, it invites treatment.

This is the most frustrating aspect of all of these sleep disorders: they are often easily, safely, and cheaply treatable, yet they often go untreated.

Many people suffering from circadian and seasonal sleep disorders respond well to melatonin supplements. This is hardly surprising, given the role melatonin plays in circadian and seasonal rhythms. It's even less surprising given that one of the effects of sleep deprivation is... a drop in melatonin production. So, even if the root cause of our sleep disturbance isn't a melatonin deficiency, the fact that we are sleep deprived likely means that our melatonin production will be insufficient. Less melatonin, less sleep. Less sleep, less melatonin. Isn't that just great?

Unfortunately, many doctors are reluctant to prescribe melatonin supplements for long-term use, if at all. Melatonin does not just influence the sleep-wake cycle; it has a number of other important roles in the body. Most notably, it affects the timing and release of female reproductive hormones. Long-term use of melatonin supplements can therefore have an impact on the female reproductive system. Interestingly, this impact isn't always negative; it all depends on whether a person's hormone levels are actually what they should be. This issue will be discussed in the relevant section of this book, but it boils down to "if it ain't broke, don't fix it; but if it is broke, trying to fix it might be a good idea."

Please note that I am not advocating for self-medication with melatonin supplements, or with any other substance. Aside from its far-reaching effects on the human body, melatonin has a number of potential side effects and interactions with other drugs. Also, not all melatonin supplements are equivalent, and the issue isn't just their strength. The quality of over-the-counter products is not always as advertised. Studies have shown that the actual amount of melatonin in OTC supplements can vary hugely not only between brands, but even within lots of the same product. Also, more than a quarter of OTC melatonin products have been found to contain serotonin, which can have serious health impacts. Even good quality OTC supplements usually fail to mimic the prolonged release of melatonin during the night. As a result, they might help people fall asleep, but they might not help them stay asleep. Encapsulated and prolonged-release supplements are much more effective in this regard, but they are usually only available with a prescription.

If you believe you have a sleep disturbance and you have access to a medical professional, badger them relentlessly until they do something about it. If you get no joy through regular consultations, it might help to write them a letter including:

- The exact details of your sleep disturbance (e.g., you can't fall asleep,

you can't stay asleep, etc.) including times, dates, and any patterns.
- When it started and how often it happens.
- What you are already doing to try and resolve it (e.g., regular bedtime routine, your sleep environment, any sleep aids, etc.).
- Its impact on your daily life (e.g., tiredness, memory problems, etc.).
- The known prevalence of sleep disturbances in people with your neurotype.

Until your sleep deprivation is resolved, you will be less productive, less functional, and more accident-prone. You will also be at an increased risk of developing serious medical conditions, including heart disease, diabetes, depression, anxiety, infertility, metabolic disorders, immune system impairment, and substance abuse. If you have any existing health conditions, their symptoms may worsen. Your life expectancy will be shorter, and your quality of life lower.

If you can't get help from medical professionals and you decide to try over-the-counter remedies, please research your options carefully – and from PubMed, not YouTube. Sleep is critical to our health and should not be treated like an optional extra, but some sleep aids are downright dangerous, and all medications have side effects and interactions.

Alas, there is more to sleep than quantity. If we get enough sleep and still wake up tired, this indicates that our sleep quality isn't up to snuff.

	Wake up tired	**Sleep apnea**	**Narcolepsy**
Never	2%	54%	81%
Sometimes	20%	6%	3%
Often	36%	3%	0.4%
Always	42%	6%	1%
Not sure	1%	31%	16%

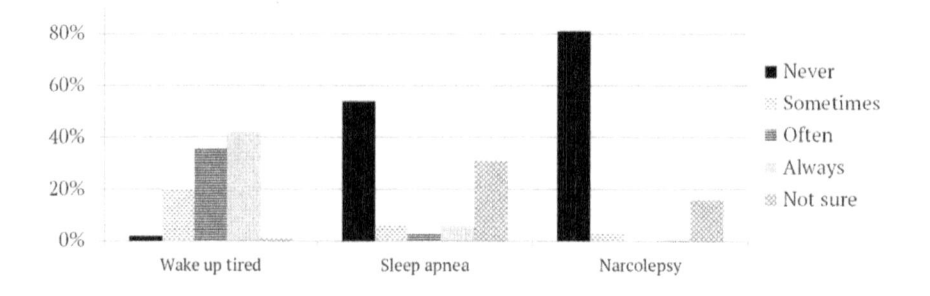

A whopping 78% of our respondents often or always wake up tired, even when they get enough sleep. This could be caused by a variety of reasons, and should really be investigated via a sleep study (polysomnography), a non-invasive, overnight exam that allows doctors to monitor us while we sleep to see what's happening in our brain and body. Unfortunately, due to their complexity and cost, sleep studies are not available to all who need them.

If you cannot afford or are struggling to get referred for a sleep study, you might want to consider investing in a sleep-staging wearable fitness monitors, such as one of the newer Fitbit models. While they are not a substitute for a sleep study, they are a convenient and relatively cheap way to obtain gross estimates of sleep parameters and time spent in different sleep stages. The information generated is not as accurate or reliable as that from a sleep study, but it may give you an idea as to what is going on. Also, relaying this information to your doctor may facilitate a referral to a sleep specialist.

A common cause of poor sleep quality is **Sleep-Disordered Breathing** (SDB, e.g., **sleep apnea**). The prevalence of SDB in the ADHD population is still a matter of controversy, largely due to how SDBs and ADHD are measured, but it is believed to be higher than in the neurotypical community. Current estimates for sleep apnea in the general population are 3 to 7% for adult men and 2 to 5% for adult women. The result of this survey indicate that 6% of respondents have sleep apnea sometimes, 3% often, and 6% always, but these results might underestimate the actual prevalence of sleep apnea in our community due to the inaccessibility of diagnosis.

This might not matter, anyway, because one doesn't need to have sleep apnea for their breathing to affect their sleep quality. Subclinical breathing difficulties, such as those caused by allergies, may have a similar impact on a person's quality of sleep and the resulting daytime symptoms.

The results of this study support this theory. Out of the respondents who reported that they often or always have allergies to smells or chemicals, 84% also reported that they wake up tired. Out of those who have asthma attacks in response to certain smells, 91% also wake up tired. Given how crucial sleep is to our health in general and to our brain development in particular, it is possible that our environmental sensitivities might have a far greater impact than they are currently believed to have, particularly during our childhood.

Narcolepsy is a whole different beast. Unlike other sleep disorders, it is believed to be an autoimmune disorder – a disorder caused when the body's immune system mistakenly attacks healthy tissue or cells. In narcolepsy, the immune system destroys brain cells that produce a peptide called hypocretin. This results in chronic attacks of drowsiness during the day, sometimes called excessive daytime sleepiness (EDS). Attacks of drowsiness may persist for only a few seconds or several minutes. These episodes vary in frequency from a few incidents to several during a single day. Nighttime sleep patterns may also be disrupted.

I included narcolepsy in the survey because I know a handful of NDs who have it. I originally thought I had drawn a blank, because only 4.4% of respondents reported it. As it turns out, the incidence of narcolepsy in the general population is believed to be <<drumroll>> 0.025 to 0.05%. So, huh, that's A Thing. Bearing in mind that 16% of respondents were not sure whether they have narcolepsy, it could be even more of a thing.

Restless legs syndrome (RLS) is another thing, again. Strictly speaking, it isn't a sleep disorder, but a condition that causes an uncontrollable urge to move the legs. This urge is usually most intense in the evening or at night, when sitting or lying down.

	Restless legs syndrome	**Overwhelming urge to move legs in the evening or at night**
Yes	26%	43%
No	55%	47%
Not Sure	18%	9%
N/A	2%	1%

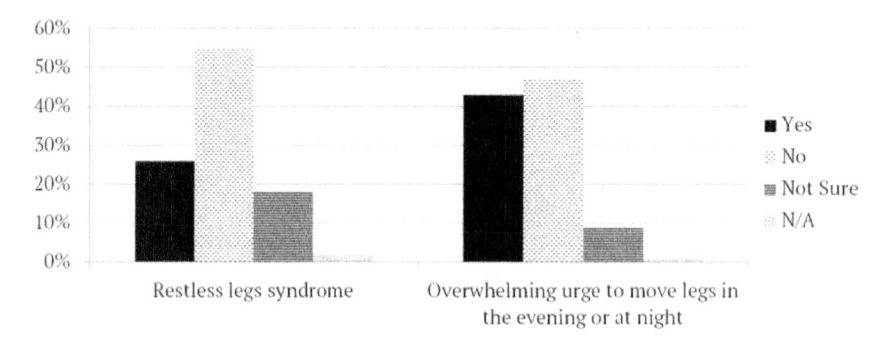

RLS is a relatively rare condition, with a prevalence estimated between 3.9% and 14.3% of the general population. As a result, it is not well-known, and the results of this survey confirm this. "Only" 26% of respondents reported having RLS, but 43% reported symptoms that suggest RLS.

The cause of RLS is as yet unknown, but it is suspected to be linked to an imbalance of the brain chemical dopamine, which sends messages to control muscle movement. Dopamine is also suspected to be a factor in ADHD, so the prevalence of RLS in ADHDers should come as no surprise. Like ADHD, RLS can run in families, but its genetic cause is not yet known.

This is not a comprehensive list of every sleep disturbance that is over-represented in the neurodivergent community, but this is all I've got for now. I spent four days writing this chapter, and now I feel like screaming. None of this is new. Everything I have "discovered" is already out there. We know that most neurodivergents are chronically sleep deprived. We know that our sleep deprivation cannot be resolved by implementing better sleep hygiene practices. We know that short-term sleep deprivation affects performance, cognition, sociability, communication, mood lability, and a ton of other critical functions. We know that long-term sleep deprivation is associated with a wide range of serious health problems, including hypertension, diabetes, obesity, depression, anxiety, heart attack, and stroke. We know that chronic sleep deprivation is particularly damaging in childhood, where it can impair brain development and permanently reduce developmental potentials. So why the hell is treating sleep disturbances in neurodivergents not a priority?

It might be fascinating for researchers to work out why we can't sleep. But that this should be a priority while neurodivergent adults and children are forced to live (or die) with the consequences of treatable sleep disorders fills me with fury.

Food.

This section is a little bit different for the simple reason that I did not specifically address this issue in the survey. Back when I was trying to put the survey together, I was struggling to find information about common gastrointestinal issues in the ND community, and I straight-up forgot about dietary and nutritional issues. This omission should be rectified in future surveys.

I did, however, ask questions about food intolerances and sensory issues, namely:

- Do you have food allergies or intolerances?
- Do you have food sensory issues? (e.g., you cannot eat certain foods because of their texture.)
- Do you get headaches if you consume certain foods or drinks?

	Food allergies or intolerances	**Food sensory issues**	**Headaches after certain foods or drinks**
Never	41%	22%	47%
Sometimes	25%	38%	25%
Often	10%	19%	12%
Always	19%	21%	10%
Not sure	5%	1%	6%

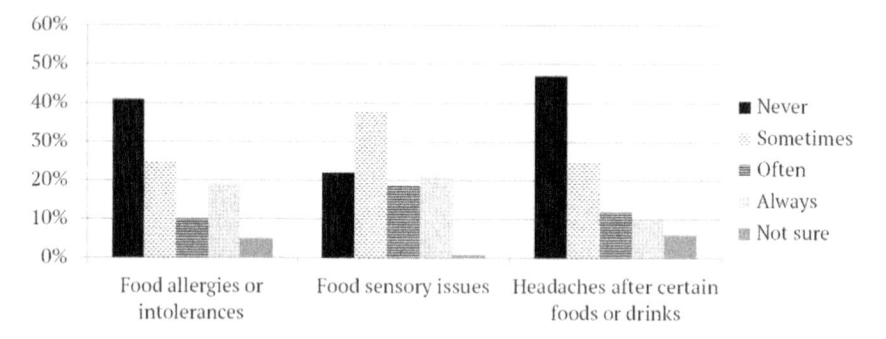

Anecdotal evidence suggests the presence of links between diet, gastrointestinal issues, nutrition, and neurodivergence. However, the most likely links are not what a lot of popular "information" suggests.

Neurodivergences are not caused by diet, and they cannot be cured by diet. However, dietary, gastrointestinal, and nutritional issues seem to be more prevalent within our community. Addressing those issues can improve our general health, and that can have a beneficial impact on every aspect of our life, including the most disruptive traits associated with our neurodivergence. That isn't because we are neurodivergent; it's because we are humans, and humans are usually capable of doing better when they are in better health.

The three main food-related issues affecting us can be classified as:

- Dietary issues; these relate to the food we ingest. Not all neurodivergent people have atypical diets, but many of us do. The reasons for this include:
  - We may have allergies or intolerances that make us ill if we eat certain foods. In this survey, 29% of respondents reported that they often or always have allergies or intolerances.
  - We may have sensory issues around food. These can relate to taste, smell, texture, and so on. In this survey, 40% of respondents reported that they often or always have sensory issues.

    Food sensory issues can be unconnected to allergies or sensitivities. However, it is not unheard of for ND children to be assumed to have food sensory issues when they actually have sensitivities they cannot adequately describe, or are not believed by their parents.

  - We may have anxiety around food that may prevent us from trying foods we cannot trust. This anxiety can have no known causes, but sometimes it is linked to the two issues mentioned above. If we cannot predict how a certain food will taste, smell, or feel, or whether ingesting it will make us ill, we might be reluctant to eat it.
  - We may lack the executive function required to establish and maintain a decent eating plan. Before we eat a healthy meal, we have to decide what it's going to be, work out a list of ingredients, purchase them, and store them – that's four whole steps, and we're not even close to eating yet. On the day of the meal, we have to start cooking well before we are hungry, or our food won't be ready on time. For people with time blindness, that can be a major issue. In order to make food that doesn't suck, we have to follow a set of instructions – which, for some of us, is a struggle. We might have to wait for the food to cook (a.k.a. purgatory), or tend to it while it is

cooking (a.k.a. hell). If we get distracted, we might ruin our meal. It's no wonder that many of us struggle, or just give up and end up living on last-minute snacks while stacks of healthy ingredients turn to mulch in our fridges.

- o Our neurodivergence can make it difficult for us to buy healthy food. Sometimes our neurodivergence is a direct obstacle; for instance, our symptoms may make it difficult for us to go to the relevant shops. We will discuss this in greater detail later on, but, 40% of survey respondents reported that they often or always get headaches in response to certain smells, and 38% in response to bright lights. Supermarkets are almost guaranteed to have both.

  Sometimes our neurodivergence can cause us to experience other obstacles that can prevent us from being able to buy healthy food; for instance, we might be financially disadvantaged because our neurodivergence makes it hard for us to find well-paid employment or work consistently. Sadly, healthy food is rarely cheap.

- Gastrointestinal (GI) issues; these are issues that affect the function of the gastrointestinal tract, which runs from the mouth to the anus. Some GI issues seem to be more common within our community. These include:
  - o Irritable bowel syndrome (IBS), where colon muscles contract more or less often than "normal." IBS can manifest as abdominal pain and cramps, gas, bloating, harder or looser stools, and alternating constipation and diarrhea.
  - o Crohn's disease, a type of colitis (inflammation of the bowel). Common symptoms include diarrhea, intestinal aches and cramps, blood in the stools, fatigue, and weight loss.
  - o Gastroesophageal reflux disease (GERD). A condition where stomach content flows back into the esophagus – like chronic acid reflux, basically. As stomach content is very acidic, it can cause severe discomfort and even permanent damage.
  - o Laryngopharyngeal reflux (LPR).). Like GERD, but the stomach content flows through the esophagus and spills into the throat.

- Nutritional issues; these occur when the food we are ingesting does not meet our nutritional requirements. This could be because the food in question does not contain all of the necessary substances. For instance, chicken nuggets are very low in Vit A, Vit D, and calcium. Hence, if we live on chicken nuggets, our diet will be lacking in Vit A, Vit D, and calcium. Sometimes, nutritional issues arise because our body cannot adequately digest and absorb the food we eat. For instance, Crohn's disease can cause malabsorption of nutrients.

Gastrointestinal, dietary, and nutritional issues often interact. For instance, eating foods we are intolerant to can trigger IBS. Celiac disease (an intolerance to gluten) can cause damage to the small intestine, which can lead to malabsorption, which can lead to malnutrition. However, these issues can also exist in isolation. For instance, a person may have a model diet and still suffer from IBS, GERD, or Crohn's. Conversely, a person may have a restricted diet, but have no resulting gastrointestinal or nutritional issues because their diet provides them with all the fiber and nutrients they need.

I am going to say this very clearly, because it's important: there is nothing inherently wrong in having a restricted diet if it meets our nutritional needs. What we eat might look nothing like a neurotypical diet, or even what most NDs would choose, but if it gives us the right amount of fiber and nutrients, it is not a nutritional issue. In fact, it might prevent us from developing nutritional issues by preventing us from ingesting foods we are intolerant or allergic to. And even when that's not an issue, what we put into our mouths is nobody's business but our own.

However, having a restricted diet can cause us social issues. It can single us out, particularly as children. It can make it difficult for us to attend social events, because it isn't uncommon for people to try and force us to eat foods we do not want, or to become offended if we refuse. This is especially true for those of us whose diets are restricted because of sensory issues rather than intolerances or allergies; the average person is more likely to insist that we try foods we do not like than foods that could kill us. However, it isn't unheard of for people to sneak known allergens into meals to teach an allergic person that their allergies are just in their head.

This is not an issue of neurodivergence, because our neurodivergence doesn't cause people to believe that what we eat is somehow their business. However, it is a problem many of us have to deal with. I could tell you exactly how many if I had put the relevant questions in the survey, but I didn't. Sorry.

The survey did include a question about **eczema**:

- Do you have eczema? *Yes / No / Not sure / Not applicable*

Although it is a skin condition, I think eczema belongs in this section for a simple reason: I don't know anyone with chronic eczema who doesn't have to avoid certain foods because they trigger flare-ups. Therefore, when researching eczema I expected to find a body of research about common intolerances, how to safely carry out elimination diets, that kind of stuff. Boy, was I wrong.

Eczema is an inflammatory skin condition that causes dry skin, itchy skin, rashes, scaly patches, and blisters. If untreated, it can lead to skin infections. There are seven different types of eczema. The most common is atopic dermatitis (aka "allergic eczema"), which is caused by a combination of immune system activation, genetics, environmental triggers, and stress. The condition runs in families with a history of dermatitis, hay fever, or asthma. People with asthma or allergies are at high risk of atopic dermatitis.

Atopic dermatitis affects up to 3% of the adult population. The condition is far more prevalent in children, affecting up to 20% of them, of which 30% also have food allergies. Children with both atopic dermatitis and food allergy have been found to have structural and molecular differences in the top layers of their skin – in a nutshell, their skin reacts differently because it *is* different, even if it looks perfectly "normal."

There is no cure for eczema, but there are treatments. For atopic dermatitis, the goal is to limit and manage flare-ups by:

- Identifying and avoiding triggers;
- Implementing a suitable skin-care routine;
- Using any treatment creams consistently and as prescribed.

So, yeah, knowing which triggers to avoid is pretty important here. Which is why the official medical advice is full of gems like this:

> "Do food allergies cause eczema?
>
> Very rarely. Although some children with eczema also have a food allergy, less than 2 out of 10 children with eczema develop a food allergy."[32]

There is so much wrong with this that it's hard to know where to start. There is the fact that food *intolerances* are completely ignored, even

---

[32] https://www.ouh.nhs.uk/patient-guide/leaflets/files/14460Peczema.pdf

though food triggers are a common cause of flare-ups. There is the fact that when you're asked if A can cause B, replying that B doesn't cause A does not answer the question. More importantly, though, anyone who believes that a 20% chance of something happening is "very rare" lives in a strange world indeed.

Anyhoo, that's what we know: if you have allergies or intolerances, you have a higher chance of also having eczema. And if your eczema flare-ups are triggered by allergies or intolerances, avoiding those triggers is a key aspect of managing your condition.

	Eczema
Yes	30%
No	62%
Not Sure	8%
N/A	1%

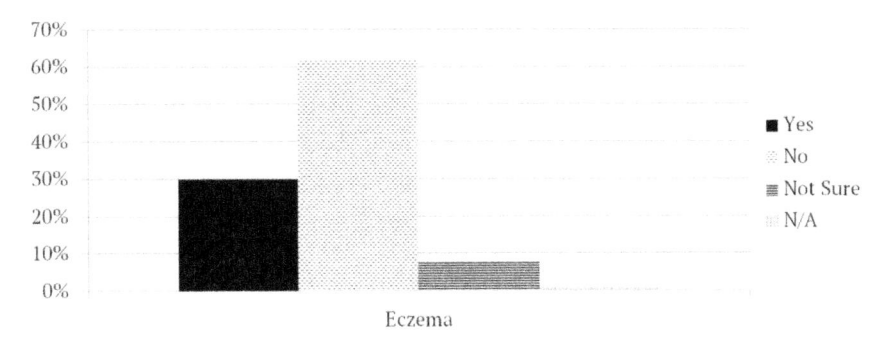

30% of survey respondents have eczema. Bearing in mind that 99.37% of respondents were adults, that's 10 times the prevalence we see in the general population.

Of these, 12% also often or always have asthma attacks in response to certain smells, and 38% often or always have food allergies or intolerances. 8% of respondents have all three.

If we look at this the other way round, 40% of respondents who often or always have asthma attacks in response to certain smells also have eczema, and so do 39% of those who often or always have food allergies or intolerances.

The survey also included a question about **anemia**:

- Do you have anemia? *Yes / No / Not sure / Not applicable*

Anemia is a deficiency in the number or quality of red blood cells. As a result, the blood of anemic people has a decreased capacity to carry oxygen around the body. This can cause fatigue, weakness, dizziness or lightheadedness, irregular heartbeats, shortness of breath, chest pain, cold hands and feet, and headaches.

Anemia can have a number of different causes, including inflammatory diseases (e.g. Crohn's disease), autoimmune diseases, bone marrow diseases, some blood diseases, genetic mutations, infectious diseases, blood loss, exposure to toxic chemicals, and some parasitic infections. The most common cause of anemia, however, is nutritional deficiencies. To produce hemoglobin and red blood cells, the body needs iron, vitamin B-12, folate, and other nutrients. A shortage of these nutrients will result in a shortage of hemoglobin and red blood cells.

Nutritional deficiencies can be caused by malnutrition – i.e., a diet lacking in certain nutrients – or malabsorption, when the body fails to absorb certain nutrients even though they are present in the diet. Malabsorption can result from any disorder that affects the function of the small intestine, including Crohn's disease and celiac disease. People with eczema, asthma, hay fever, and food allergies also have a higher risk of anemia. The odds of anemia increased with the number of disorders present. People with intestinal disturbances that cause diarrhea are also at increased risk of nutritional deficiencies.

Anemia is estimated to affects 24.8% of the world's population, with about half the cases due to nutritional deficiencies. Due to differences in food availability, the prevalence of anemia varies hugely between countries. For instance, in the US it is estimated to affect less than 6% of the total population, while in Afghanistan, Chad, Mali, and Yemen the prevalence rates are in excess of 50%.

	Anemia
Yes	22%
No	58%
Not Sure	18%
N/A	1%

Anemia

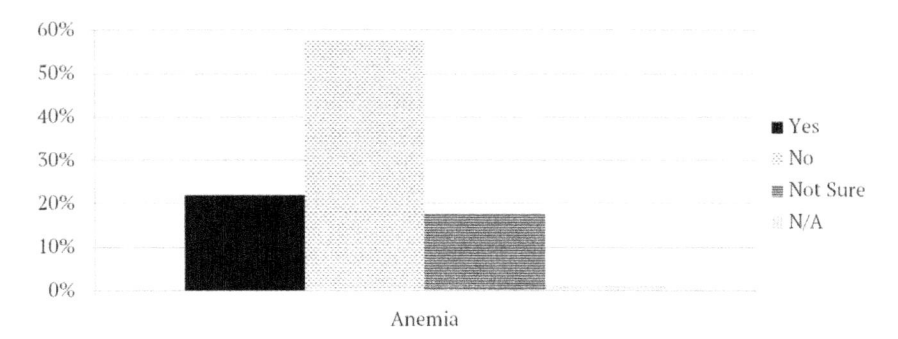

22% of respondents have anemia, while 18% are not sure. Bearing in mind that the vast majority of respondents are from the USA, UK, Canada, Australia, Aotearoa - New Zealand, and various European countries, this prevalence is higher than expected. However, these results are not surprising if we take into account the high prevalence of risk factors in the neurodivergent community. Of the respondents with anemia, 12% also have asthma, 36% also have food intolerances or allergies, 43% also have eczema, and 4% have all four conditions.

Environmental sensitivities.

This section looked at whether respondents have intolerances, allergies, or sensitivities to various stimuli. The questions were:

- Do you have food allergies or intolerances?
- Do you have food sensory issues? (e.g., you cannot eat certain foods because of their texture.)
- Do you have allergies to smells or chemicals?
- Do you have asthma attacks in response to certain smells?
- Do you get headaches in response to certain smells?
- Do you get headaches if you consume certain foods or drinks?
- Do you get headaches in response to bright lights?
- Can you hear sounds other people do not hear?

Food-related questions have been covered in the Food section. The remaining questions will be dissected here.

Environmental sensitivities fascinate me, because I have never seen them included in any study of anxieties or phobias. I have lost count of the number of times I have been asked whether certain situations cause me anxiety, and nobody ever bothered to ask me if there was a reason for that.

The logic seems to be that if something causes me undue anxiety – for instance, flying – then I must have anxiety around flying. If I avoid flying, it must be because of said anxiety. The fact that I am woefully allergic to a lot of the stuff many people routinely douse themselves in – hair sprays, deodorants, perfumes, creams, soaps, laundry products, you name it – has never made it into one of those questionnaires. Hence, my reluctance to be locked in a space where I can realistically expect to be unable to breathe magically turns into an anxiety issue. If I avoid those spaces (and I do), I must be phobic.

The same omissions on the part of researchers (and of accessibility campaigners, for that matter) affect people who have specific needs that aren't accommodated in certain environments. For instance, people who, for whatever reason, need to be able to get to a toilet very quickly may be reluctant to visit areas where toilets are scarce – say, a music festival. That isn't because they are scared of crowds, of open spaces, of loud noises, or anything like that; it's simply because they don't want to poo or pee themselves in public. People who can't stand up for long periods without passing out may be reluctant to put themselves in situations where they will have to stand up for long periods; unless they enjoy passing out, anyway. I could go on forever, but I think I made my point.

This issue is compounded when experience teaches us to anticipate certain problems, but the people responsible for our care discount the problems and focus on our state of mind. For instance, let's say that a person has been on a plane a number of times and experienced respiratory issues as a result. That person may be genuinely anxious about putting themself in that position again, because not being able to breathe is both scary and dangerous. If their breathing issues are serious or frequent, they might develop a phobia of planes, or of enclosed human-filled spaces in general. If their experiences were traumatic, they might develop PTSD responses. However, none of these issues will be alleviated by telling them that it's all in their head. That's not helpful, and it's definitely not therapy; if it's anything, it's gaslighting.

As with most things involving people, it can get worse. Many ailments have a stress component, or can be exacerbated by stress. Therefore, if a person is anxious about getting into a plane because they worry about being unable to breathe and then they have an asthma attack, a proportion of people will believe that they did that to themself. Their anxiety caused the asthma attack – or perhaps they didn't even have an asthma attack, they just thought they did because they were so worked up. Heck, maybe they pretended to have an asthma attack just to prove their point or to be the center of attention. It can't possibly be that other humans may have different reactions to the same stimuli, and that their experience, although unusual, might be just as real and as valid.

Environmental sensitivities sometimes co-occur with atypically acute sensitivities to a certain type of stimuli. For instance, sensitivities to airborne allergens can co-occur with hyperosmia – a heightened sense of smell that can cause discomfort or illness in response to certain odors.[33] However, that isn't always the case; people may be sensitive to airborne allergens they cannot smell. That means that they don't know that they are being exposed until their allergic responses kick in, which is super fun.

---

[33] If you are interested in hyperosmia and like sci-fi, I heartily recommend Spider Robinson's "Telempath." And the recommendation still stands if you don't give a hoot about hyperosmia and just like good sci-fi.

Also, prolonged exposure to allergens can irritate or obstruct the mucus membranes in the nose, leading to reduced sense of smell (hyposmia) or loss of smell (anosmia). These sensory losses can be permanent or temporary. A person can oscillate between hyperosmia and anosmia depending on how inflamed their nose is at any given point.

Environmental sensitivities are real, and they can have a real impact on people's health. Even those that aren't immediately dangerous can lead to long-term negative health outcomes. For instance, allergic rhinitis may "only" cause sneezing, a runny nose, temporary anosmia, and watery eyes. When left untreated, however, it can lead to chronic nasal inflammation and obstruction, sinusitis, ear infections, sleep apnea, upper respiratory tract infections, and Eustachian tube dysfunction. Allergic rhinitis can also increase sensitivity to substances a person isn't allergic to; quite simply, already inflamed tissues can be generally more sensitive, so it takes less to aggravate them. As a result, otherwise harmless substances can become harmful, or at the very least painful.

This kind of issue is not limited to airborne allergens. People may be sensitive to stimuli affecting any of their senses, including sight, sound, taste, and touch. As with sensitivities linked with the sense of smell, sensitivities linked to other senses may or may not coexist with a heightened ability to perceive certain stimuli. For instance, we may be able to hear noises the majority of people cannot hear, and find them distracting, disturbing, or downright painful. However, this isn't always the case. For instance, we might be negatively affected by bright lights even though our visual sensory system isn't any more perceptive than the norm.

It's a relatively well-known fact that many neurodivergent people, in particularly Autistics, are atypically sensitive to certain environmental stimuli. These issues may be pronounced enough to classify as Sensory Processing Disorders: "impairments in the detection, modulation, or interpretation of stimuli." SPDs can manifest both as over-responsivity or sensory hypersensitivity, and as under-responsivity or hyposensitivity.

I want to draw attention to one aspect of this definition: it does not make a distinction between sensitivity and responsivity – i.e., whether the issue is with how we *perceive* a stimulus or how strongly we *react* to it. This is a huge issue. It's particularly serious when it affects people who are not able to communicate the causes of their distress in ways other people will understand, believe, and respect.

	Allergies to smells or chemicals	Asthma attacks from smells	Headaches from smells	Headaches from bright lights	Atypical hearing
Never	54%	77%	24%	24%	21%
Sometimes	18%	11%	35%	37%	29%
Often	9%	4%	22%	23%	24%
Always	11%	4%	17%	15%	22%
Not sure	8%	3%	2%	2%	4%

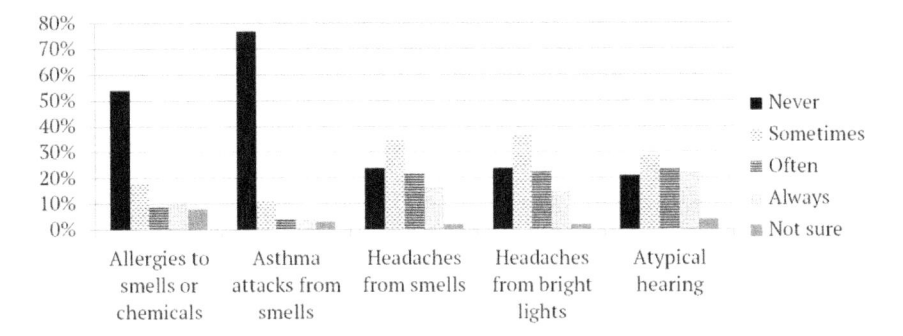

The results of this survey suggest that environmental sensitivities are not restricted to the Autistic community, although some issues seem more prevalent among Autistics.

	Allergies to smells or chemicals	Asthma attacks from smells	Headaches from smells	Headaches from bright lights	Atypical hearing
Overall	20%	9%	39%	38%	46%
Autistics	23%	5%	48%	49%	62%
Not Aut	19%	10%	36%	33%	39%

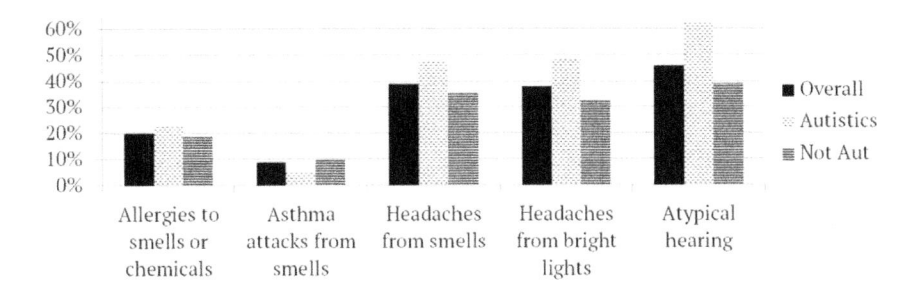

These results suggest that environmental sensitivities should be taken into account when examining neurodivergent people's aversions to certain spaces or experiences. This is particularly significant when evaluating aversions to spaces and experiences where negative sensory experiences are compounded – for instance, in places like supermarkets, which are full of smells, bright lights, and noises – or from where a person may not be able to escape – for instance, planes or schools.

These considerations become critical when trying to formulate therapeutic plans to help individuals navigate certain spaces: when the issues are sensory, rather than psychological or emotional, all proposed solutions should take that fact into account. The goal should be to find ways for people to protect themselves from the affecting stimuli – for instance, by wearing protective equipment. Learning to tolerate painful stimuli is not a valid therapeutic goal.

These considerations should also be taken into account when evaluating neurodivergent people's performance. This is particularly true of children, who may be unable to pinpoint or express the causes of their discomfort.

If a neurodivergent child is not performing well in a certain environment – for instance, at school – the fault might not lie with their neurodivergence per se, but with the fact that that particular environment literally hurts them. Schools are often full of smells, lights, and noises, all of which can trigger sensitivities in affected individuals.

It is neither fair nor reasonable to expect good performance from children in pain. It is even more unfair to chalk any resulting "failures" to their neurodivergence. The only real failure is that of the adults around them, who forced them into an environment that does not meet their needs.

Blood pressure and sugar levels.

This section looked at issues related to blood and blood circulation. The questions were:

- Do you have low blood pressure?
- Do you have postural tachycardia syndrome (POTS)?
- Do you feel dizzy, lightheaded, or faint you stand up for too long?
- Do you feel dizzy, lightheaded, or faint if you stand up too quickly?
- Do you have Reynaud's disease?
- Do you struggle to regulate your temperature in hot weather? (e.g., you become tired, faint, or dizzy, while the people around you are not affected.)
- Do you struggle to regulate your temperature in cold weather? (e.g., you shiver, lose feelings in your extremities, become tired, dizzy, or confused, while the people around you are not affected.)
- Do you have reactive hypoglycemia?
- Do you feel anxious, confused, dizzy, irritable, light-headed, faint, exhausted, weak, or shaky within four hours of eating a meal?
- Do you feel anxious, confused, dizzy, irritable, light-headed, faint, exhausted, weak, or shaky within four hours of eating certain foods?

Low blood pressure (aka **hypotension**) is defined as pressure readings below 90/60mmHg. Symptoms include lightheadedness or dizziness, feeling sick, blurred vision, weakness, confusion, and fainting.

Hypotension is an interesting condition inasmuch it is generally not considered a condition at all. Unlike hypertension (high blood pressure), it doesn't usually kill you – not directly, anyway. Getting dizzy and passing out can result in injuries or even accidental death, but that fact is often discounted. Equally discounted is the fact that having low blood pressure can make life generally unpleasant. Even readings above the official cut-off line can make you feel off. Alas, many doctors don't consider that a significant factor. If hypertension is bad, hypotension must be good, right? Therefore, it can be very hard for people with low blood pressure to receive treatment.

There are many possible causes for low blood pressure, including medical conditions, drug interactions, lifestyle issues, and genetic causes. If low blood pressure runs in your family ("familial hypotension") the chances of getting treatment are even lower than usual. If any "treatments" are recommended, these are usually lifestyle measures, such as eating and drinking more frequently, taking a nap after meals, or not sitting or standing for long periods.[34]

Anecdotal evidence suggests that low blood pressure may be unusually prevalent within the neurodivergent community.

	Low blood pressure	POTS	Dizziness from standing too long	Dizziness from standing up too quickly
Never	49%	52%	52%	14%
Sometimes	20%	4%	31%	49%
Often	8%	2%	10%	24%
Always	9%	2%	5%	12%
Not sure	13%	40%	2%	0.1%

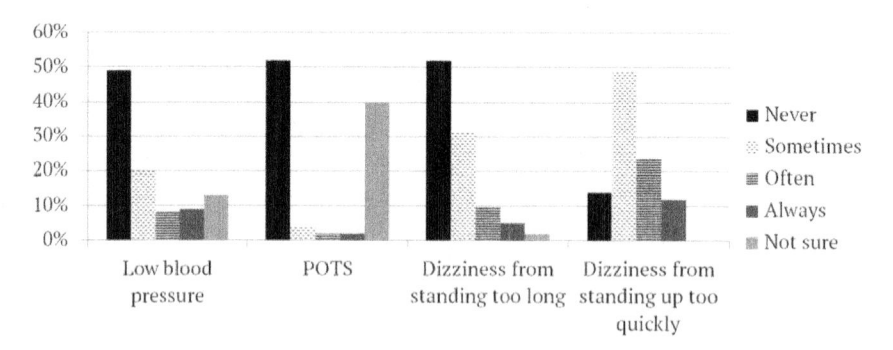

18% of respondents reported that they often or always have low blood pressure. I tried to compare this with the prevalence of the condition in the general population, but I could not find any data on it. If nothing else, this should give you an idea of how comprehensively this condition is disregarded by the medical establishment.

These results are particularly significant because of the impact of low blood pressure on our ability to function. The symptoms of chronically low

---

[34] Do I need to point out how none of these are viable solutions for schoolchildren, and for many people who work for a living? Do I really?

blood pressure include reduced drive, increased pain sensitivity, and cognitive impairments, in particular deficits in attention and memory. Given the overlap between these symptoms and ADHD traits, it would be nice to see some research as to the potential impact of treating low blood pressure in ADHDers who are struggling in these domains.

Important tangent: as I write this (March 2022), social media is practically exploding with posts about how caffeine calms ADHDers down; hence, if caffeine doesn't calm you down, you can't be really ADHD. The logic – and I use the term loosely – is that caffeine is a stimulant; stimulants calm ADHDers down; hence, if caffeine doesn't calm you down or even send you right to sleep, you're not truly ADHD. QED.

The only problem with the above theory is that it's guff, and gatekeeping guff at that. Stimulant meds do not have the same effects on most ADHDers as they do on most neurotypicals, that's true, but that doesn't mean that they have the same effects on all ADHDers. In fact, some ADHDers cannot tolerate them, while others cannot take them at all because of other health concerns. One of these health concerns is high blood pressure. As stimulants can increase blood pressure, taking them when one's blood pressure is already high can cause serious problems.

Like stimulants, caffeine can cause an increase in blood pressure. The degree of this increase differs from person to person, but consuming 200-300mg of caffeine (3-5 shots of espresso) produces a mean increase of 8.1mmHg in systolic blood pressure (the top number) and 5.7mmHg in diastolic blood pressure. If your blood pressure is high, that might be bad news for you. If your blood pressure is low, however, the resulting increase might bring it up to normal. That means that while the caffeine is active in your system (usually 3-4 hours), you may experience relief from your low blood pressure symptoms.

Sugar can also have an impact on blood pressure, both in the short and long term. Therefore, if the caffeinated product of your choice is also high in sugar, the overall impact on your blood pressure may be even greater.

If caffeinated products give you a boost, that doesn't mean that you're not ADHD. It might simply mean that your blood pressure is low, and caffeine helps bring it up to normal. And as for gatekeeping ADHDers who get a boost from caffeinated products, that's about as useful as a coffee enema.

And now, back to our regularly scheduled programming.

POTS, or **Postural Orthostatic Tachycardia Syndrome**, is taken marginally more seriously than hypotension. We've even got statistics about it! This condition is characterized by too little blood returning to the heart when moving from a lying down to a standing up position (aka, "orthostatic intolerance"). This can cause palpitations, lightheadedness, fainting, blurred vision, fatigue, sweating, nausea, and headaches. These symptoms are associated with a rapid increase in heart rate from the lying to upright position, and eased by lying back down. POTS can also cause "brain fog," a cognitive dysfunction characterized by difficulty focusing and thinking.

Estimates of the prevalence of POTS vary, ranging from 0.1 to 1%. Although POTS can affect people of all genders and ages, it is most common in AFABs between the ages of 15 and 50, who represent 80-85% of diagnoses. In people who menstruate, symptoms may increase in frequency and severity in the days before menstruation. Although most cases of POTS occur in people with no history of the condition in their family, it does run in some families. Its occurrence seems to be associated with joint hypermobility. The cause of POTS is still unknown, but episodes often begin after major surgery, trauma, a viral illness, or pregnancy.

In a shocking turn of events, POTS is still poorly understood by many medical specialists, and often poorly treated as a result. It is commonly mistaken for malingering, depression, or anxiety disorders. That this should be the case for a condition that disproportionately affects AFABs will surprise nobody who has an awareness of gender biases in medicine.

The lack of awareness on the part of doctors translates into lack of information for patients, and the results of this survey bear this out. 4% of respondents said that they often or always have POTS, while 40% were not sure. When asked about symptoms, however, 36% often or always feel dizzy, lightheaded, or faint if they stand up too quickly. Of these, 14% have a connective tissue disorder, 32% easily injure their joints, and 30% have joint hypermobility.

As usual, answering a question on a survey is absolutely not sufficient for a diagnosis. However, the presence of symptoms of POTS should warrant further investigations, particularly in people with a family history of POTS, connective tissue disorders, or joint hypermobility. Ultimately, whatever the underlying conditions ends up being, the symptoms still deserve to be taken seriously, and so do the patients reporting them.

Reynaud's phenomenon and Reynaud's disease have the same symptoms, but different causes. They are both characterized by "reversible vasospasm in peripheral arteries" – i.e., decreased blood flow to the extremities – in response to cold, stress, or emotional upset. The most common symptom is fingers that turn first pale and then blue when exposed to cold, then red when the hands are warmed. The pale color indicates that blood circulation has been cut off, and the blue color indicates low oxygen levels. This reaction is disproportionate to the actual temperature (i.e., the majority of other people will not be affected in the same way at the same temperature). Symptoms can last from a few minutes to several hours and can make it difficult to use your fingers. In severe cases, sores may develop in the affected areas. In rare cases, gangrene may develop.

If the symptoms manifest because of an underlying condition (e.g. a blood disorder, repetitive action damage, or side effect from medication) the diagnosis will be Reynaud's phenomenon. If there is no known underlying condition, it will be Reynaud's disease.

The exact cause of Raynaud's disease is unknown, but it is often linked to connective tissue or autoimmune diseases such as lupus and rheumatoid arthritis

	Reynaud's disease	Poor thermoregulation in cold weather	Poor thermoregulation in hot weather
Never	56%	42%	35%
Sometimes	4%	25%	25%
Often	3%	16%	18%
Always	5%	15%	19%
Not sure	32%	2%	3%

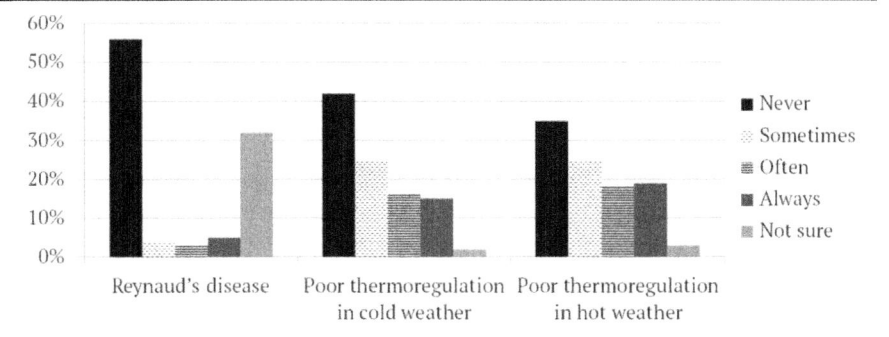

The prevalence of Raynaud's in the general population is estimated to

be between 3 and 5%. 8% of survey respondents reported that they have Raynaud's. However, 32% of respondents were not sure. It would be interesting to see whether the prevalence of Raynaud's would be higher if more people were aware of its existence.

There is no treatment for Reynaud's. Symptoms can be managed by avoiding exposure to cold, wearing warm clothing, and avoiding trauma or vibrations to the hand (e.g. from vibrating tools).

A number of other conditions can cause difficulties in thermoregulation in both cold and hot weather. These include infections, endocrine disorders, central nervous system disorders, and circulatory disorders.

31% of respondents often or always struggle to regulate their temperature in cold weather. Of these, 46% also often or always have low blood pressure. 37% of respondents often or always struggle to regulate their temperature in hot weather. Of these, 50% also often or always have low blood pressure.

The last set of questions looked at **reactive hypoglycemia**, aka postprandial (literally "after a meal") hypoglycemia. In this condition, blood sugar levels drop within 2–5 hours of eating. Symptoms include anxiety, confusion, shakiness, dizziness, irritability, lightheadedness, weakness, exhaustion, and fainting. Some people feel hungry, while others do not. Symptoms subside quickly after eating or drinking carbohydrates. However, for some people consuming sugar-rich foods can set off a short sugar rush followed by another hypoglycemic event. In that case, eating complex carbohydrates, proteins, or fats may work better.

Reactive hypoglycemia can occur because of some underlying medical conditions, such as gastrointestinal dysfunctions and hormone deficiencies. PCOS is a risk factor. It can also be a side effect of medication. However, it is often present independently of any known causes (aka, idiopathic). The causes of idiopathic reactive hypoglycemia are as yet unknown, although we know something about its mechanisms.

Anecdotally, different people seem to experience symptoms in different circumstances. Some have hypoglycemic events regardless of what they eat or what they do after eating. Some only have them after eating certain types of food; for instance, after eating sugar-rich and protein-poor meals. Some only have symptoms after eating specific foods; bananas, and in particular ripe bananas, are a common culprit. Some only have symptoms if they cannot rest after a meal.

While reactive hypoglycemia is not as dangerous as hypoglycemia caused by diabetes, it is not without consequences. Hypoglycemic events interfere with daily activities and increase the risk of accidents. Furthermore, going through frequent hypoglycemic episodes can lead to hypoglycemia unawareness: people become unable to register the symptoms that warn of low blood sugar and are more likely to experience serious hypoglycemic events, with their attendant risks.

Undiagnosed reactive hypoglycemia can lead to disordered eating as people realize, consciously or unconsciously, that eating makes them feel sick, but they don't know why. For instance, people may notice that every time they eat breakfast or lunch they end up having a terrible day, and start skipping their daytime meals in favor of a large dinner. While this may relieve their symptoms of hypoglycemia, it can cause a number of other issues.

There is no cure for reactive hypoglycemia, although people with prediabetes may benefit from taking antidiabetic drugs. For the rest of us, it's a case of managing the condition by taking whatever steps are necessary to avoid hypoglycemic events. For instance:

- Eating several small meals throughout the day, ideally 3 hours apart;
- Eating high-protein, high-fiber meals;
- Avoiding sugary foods and processed simple carbohydrates;
- Resting after meals;
- Limiting or avoiding alcohol;
- Limiting or avoiding caffeine and other stimulants;
- Eating as soon as we feel the start of a hypoglycemic event.

Basically, if we know what causes us to have a hypoglycemic event and can avoid doing that, we will still have reactive hypoglycemia but we won't be experiencing its symptoms. Unfortunately, many of us are unable to do that. How many of us can have a meal and a nap every three hours, really? This is particularly true for children, who often do not have the ability to decide what they eat, when they eat, and what they can do after eating. They may also lack the ability to explain how they feel when they are having a hypoglycemic event – and, even if they do, they might not be taken seriously by the adults around them.

	Reactive hypoglycemia	Symptoms within four hours of eating	Symptoms within four hours of eating certain foods
Never	49%	60%	62%
Sometimes	5%	20%	14%
Often	3%	9%	6%
Always	2%	3%	3%
Not sure	41%	8%	15%

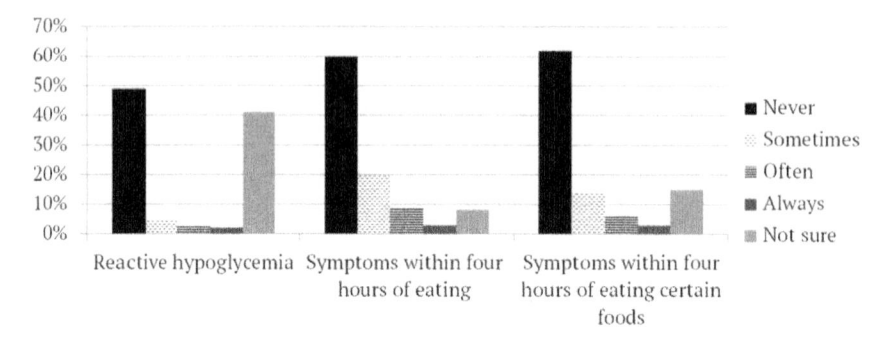

5% of respondents said that they often or always have reactive hypoglycemia, and an additional 5% have it sometimes. However, 41% of respondents answered that they were not sure. When asked about the symptoms of reactive hypoglycemia, 12% of respondents have them often or always, and 20% have them sometimes. When asked whether they have symptoms after eating certain foods, 9% have them often or always, and 14% have them sometimes.

I looked for statistics about the prevalence of reactive hypoglycemia in the general population, and I couldn't find any. What I did find was a number of studies in which a small number of patients were divided in groups according to their BMI to see whether being "overweight" increases one's chances of hypoglycemic events. That the medical establishment should ignore a condition other than to use it to attack fatness is unsurprising, yet I still managed to feel disappointed.

The lack of information about this condition can cause people to go undiagnosed. In turn, that can stop them from making the adaptations required to avoid hypoglycemic events. Personally, I have had reactive hypoglycemia all my life, and I have been aware of what triggers it since my 20s, but I only found out that it is an actual condition with an actual name when I was looking up what to include in this survey. The whole process took at least 40 years longer than it should have.

If you think this is bad, wait to see what comes next.

While I was searching for information about hypotension, I stumbled upon the following sentence:

> "(...) reactive hypoglycemia after carbohydrates may masquerade as postprandial hypotension."[35]

This was news to me. Big news, in fact, as I had never heard of **postprandial hypotension**. This condition is defined as a drop in blood pressure within two hours of consuming a meal. Symptoms are often worse after consuming sugar-rich meals, and include the usual symptoms of low blood pressure: lightheadedness, dizziness, feeling sick, blurred vision, weakness, confusion, and fainting.

Unlike reactive hypoglycemia, postprandial hypotension can be treated with medication. However, first-line treatment consists of making lifestyle and dietary changes, such as eating smaller meals throughout the day. High-sugar meals have been found to cause more severe symptoms, while high-protein meals cause the least blood pressure changes.

40-80% of people with autonomic dysfunction (aka dysautonomia) will have postprandial hypotension. Autonomic dysfunction, a condition in which the autonomic nervous system does not work properly, is more prevalent in the Autistic community and those with Ehlers-Danlos syndrome. So, it is likely that postprandial hypotension will also be more prevalent in the Autistic community, and possibly in the neurodivergent community in general. And yet, I am sitting here wondering how many of us have even heard about it.

These conditions are not mutually exclusive. It is possible to have chronic low blood pressure, reactive hypoglycemia, *and* postprandial hypotension. Given the lack of awareness about these conditions, I have to wonder how many of us are struggling with symptoms that we are so used to that we don't even realize that life could be different, and much easier. In particular, I wonder how many children are currently struggling in school not because they are not capable or willing, but because their blood pressure and blood sugar levels are making it impossible for them to function.

---

[35] https://patient.info/doctor/hypotension

Dissociative states.

This section looked at various ways in which we escape from our reality without actually moving. The questions were:

- Do you spend a lot of time daydreaming?
- Do you spend so much time daydreaming that you fail to maintain personal connections or manage your obligations?
- Do you dissociate?
- Do you have times when you feel disconnected from your thoughts, feelings, memories, and surroundings?
- Do you have times when you feel emotionally numb or detached?
- Do you have times when you feel little or no physical pain, or lose the ability to perceive other physical cues (e.g. hunger and thirst signals)?
- Do you have gaps in your long-term memory that affect certain time periods, events, or personal information?
- Do you have out-of-body experiences?
- Do you have times when you lose your sense of identity or have multiple distinct identities?

Most people escape their reality at least some of the time. We might do so by choice, for our own amusement; we pick up a book or go to a movie and allow ourselves to be transported to another reality. We might become distracted or enchanted by something we are experiencing or remembering, and momentarily disconnect with everything else. We might be so bored by whatever is going on that we zone out for a spell, or make our own entertainment by daydreaming. These are natural responses that, while they might annoy those around us, are not pathological.

However, some of us have little or no control on whether we can be present in our reality. If our disconnections with reality are involuntary or make it hard for us to function, we might need professional help. Part of getting that help might be an evaluation for a **dissociative disorder** (DD).

There are a number of DDs, varying in the type and severity of symptoms. Their classification is complex and contentious, and well outside the scope of a work like this. What I am going to do here is going through some of the symptoms of various dissociative states. As always, the information provided here is *not* diagnostic material.

Daydreaming is a mild dissociative state in which we detach from current, external tasks as our attention is pulled into a stream of consciousness. Daydreaming is perfectly natural, even for neurotypicals; studies suggest that people spend 30% - 50% of their waking time in daydreams. While daydreaming may decrease our performance on the task at hand, there is evidence that it has a positive impact on mental health and overall cognitive performance.

However, daydreaming can become problematic if it's involuntary, we can't snap out of it, or it has a detrimental impact on our life. Some neurotypicals are prone to experiencing **maladaptive daydreaming** – a newer diagnosis that has been found to be comorbid with ADHD. In maladaptive daydreaming, people become absorbed in extensive, often compulsive fantasies for several hours a day. These fantasies replace human interaction and impair everyday functioning in various domains.

	Daydreaming	**Maladaptive daydreaming**
Never	4%	29%
Sometimes	27%	39%
Often	42%	22%
Always	27%	8%
Not sure	0%	2%

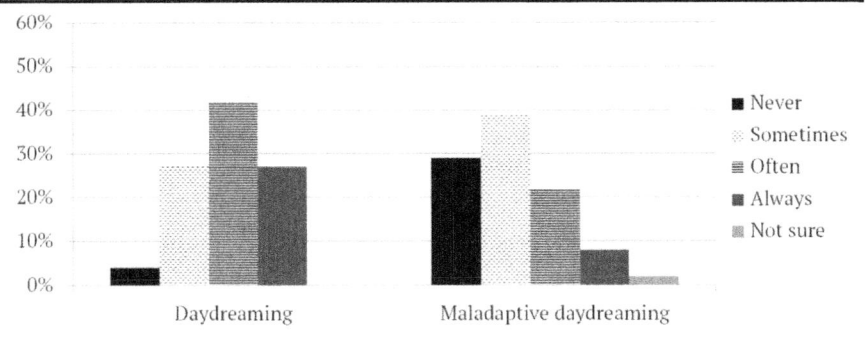

69% of respondents often or always spend a lot of time daydreaming. 31% spend so much time daydreaming that they fail to maintain personal connections or manage their obligations, which might be a symptom of maladaptive daydreaming.

A number of factors seem to correlate with increased prevalence of daydreaming and maladaptive daydreaming. The biggest increases are seen in two groups: those who, as children were often or always forced by parents or teachers to endure painful physical sensation in order to learn to get over them, and those who often or always pretend to be someone else so people will like them. As the first experience is traumatic and the second one exhausting, it isn't surprising that people learned to escape from them by daydreaming. The other factors that correlate with an increase in daydreaming are either traumatic, increase the demands placed on us, or decrease our ability to self-soothe while meeting those demands.

	Daydreaming	Maladaptive daydreaming
Whole survey	69%	31%
Routinely forced to endure unpleasant or overwhelming physical sensations in order to navigate their environment	74%	45%
Force themselves to stop their self-soothing behaviors in order to avoid getting told off	75%	41%
Redirect repetitive behaviors to less noticeable ones to look more "normal"	73%	37%
Do things you'd rather not so people will like you	74%	41%
Pretend to be someone else so people will like you	78%	47%
Punished for "tantrums"	74%	41%
"Desensitized"	79%	47%
PTSD	72%	35%
cPTSD	72%	37%

Dissociation is not daydreaming. However, it might look like it from the outside or even feel like it from the inside. For that reason, people who are prone to daydreaming may not realize when they are dissociating.

Dissociation is an umbrella term that covers a wide range of experiences, from mild emotional detachment to severe disconnection from physical and emotional experiences. During a dissociative period, we experience a degree of detachment from our reality, thoughts, feelings, memories, or sense of identity. Dissociative periods can last for mere hours to months or years. During a dissociative period, we may:

- Feel disconnected from our thoughts, feelings, memories, and surroundings.
- Feel little or no physical pain, or lose the ability to perceive other physical cues (e.g. hunger and thirst signals).
- Feel emotionally numb or detached.
- Have gaps in our memory that affect certain time periods, events, or personal information.
- Have out-of-body experiences.
- Lose our sense of identity or have multiple distinct identities.

We may experience different types of dissociation at different times in our lives, depending on our circumstances.

Dissociation is a coping mechanism that often occurs in response to excessive levels of stress or a traumatic event. If you think about the fight-or-flight response, dissociation is the mental equivalent of a flight response. We disconnect ourselves from reality in order to protect ourselves from it. While dissociation is natural, and might even be a healthy response during traumatic events, it can be pathological if it interferes with our ability to function or it becomes our default mode, regardless of our present situation.

	Dissociation	Disconnection from thoughts, feelings, memories, and surroundings
Never	14%	14%
Sometimes	36%	45%
Often	28%	30%
Always	9%	8%
Not sure	12%	3%

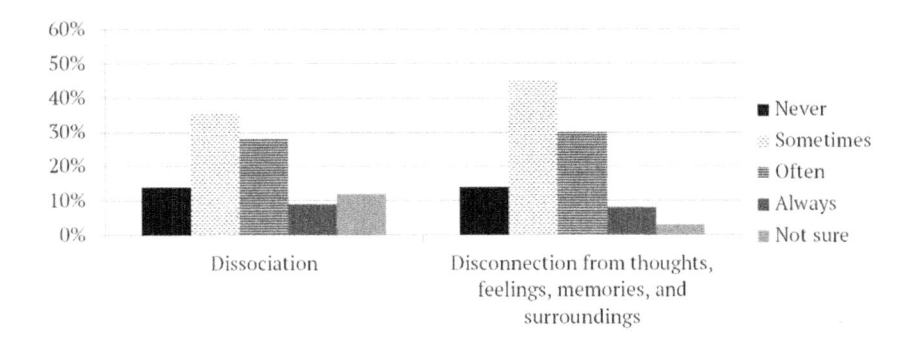

37% of respondents often or always dissociate. 38% often or always have times when they feel disconnected from their thoughts, feelings, memories, and surroundings.

Like daydreaming and maladaptive daydreaming, dissociation and disconnection from thoughts, feelings, memories, and surroundings are more prevalent in respondents who have suffered trauma, have to navigate situations that increase the demands placed on them, or have a reduced ability to self-soothe while meeting those demands.

The largest increases are seen in the respondents who are often or always routinely forced to endure unpleasant or overwhelming physical sensations in order to navigate their environment, and those who, as children were often or always forced by parents or teachers to endure painful physical sensation in order to learn to get over them. The first group likely uses dissociation as a coping mechanism. In the second group, however, it may be an entrenched habit that may be maladaptive.

	Dissociation	Disconnection from thoughts, feelings, memories, and surroundings
Whole survey	37%	38%
Routinely forced to endure unpleasant or overwhelming physical sensations in order to navigate their environment	63%	64%
Force themselves to stop their self-soothing behaviors in order to avoid getting told off	50%	53%
Redirect repetitive behaviors to less noticeable ones to look more "normal"	46%	48%
Do things you'd rather not so people will like you	47%	49%
Pretend to be someone else so people will like you	51%	53%
Punished for "tantrums"	57%	58%
"Desensitized"	64%	63%
PTSD	50%	49%
cPTSD	53%	53%

49% of respondents often or always have times when they feel emotionally numb or detached. 35% often or always have times when they feel little or no physical pain, or lose the ability to perceive other physical cues (e.g. hunger and thirst signals). Please note that the latter phenomenon isn't necessarily indicative of a dissociative state; aside from the fact that interoception is a problem for 18% of respondents, a good bout of hyperfocus can do this to us.

	Emotionally numb or detached	**Temporary loss of pain signals and interoception**
Never	7%	27%
Sometimes	43%	35%
Often	37%	25%
Always	11%	10%
Not sure	1%	2%

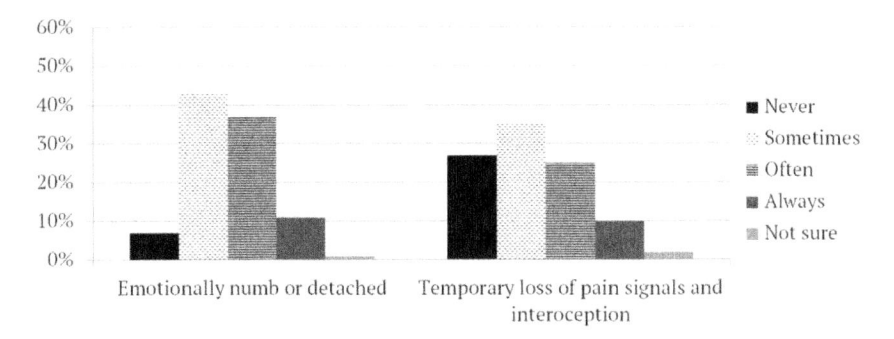

Like the other dissociative states already discussed in this chapter, emotional numbness and temporary loss of interoception are more prevalent in respondents who have suffered trauma, have to navigate situations that increase the demands placed on them, or have a reduced ability to self-soothe while meeting those demands. The largest increases are seen in the respondents who are often or always routinely forced to endure unpleasant or overwhelming physical sensations in order to navigate their environment, and those who, as children were often or always forced by parents or teachers to endure painful physical sensation in order to learn to get over them.

	Emotionally numb or detached	Temporary loss of pain signals and interoception
Whole survey	49%	35%
Routinely forced to endure unpleasant or overwhelming physical sensations in order to navigate their environment	77%	64%
Force themselves to stop their self-soothing behaviors in order to avoid getting told off	65%	49%
Redirect repetitive behaviors to less noticeable ones to look more "normal"	59%	47%
Do things you'd rather not so people will like you	61%	43%
Pretend to be someone else so people will like you	63%	46%
Punished for "tantrums"	66%	56%
"Desensitized"	71%	61%
PTSD	56%	45%
cPTSD	58%	47%

Some dissociative states are more serious, and may indicate the need for specialist support. As always, the information provided here is *not* sufficient for a diagnosis, but if you recognize yourself in the following descriptions, you might want to talk to a specialist about it.

Dissociative amnesia is a form of memory loss that affects certain time periods, events, or personal information, usually as a result of trauma or severe stress. Basically, our brains protect us by hiding certain information from us. The resulting memory gaps can span a few minutes to decades, depending on the associated events.

The information isn't actually deleted from our memories, and sometimes it can be retrieved using specialist techniques such as hypnosis and drug-facilitated interviews. However, it is critical that such retrieval happens in a therapeutic context, as people will most likely need follow-up support to deal with the trauma they uncover.

Memories that are not retrieved may still affect our behavior and mental state. For instance, we might not be able to recall the details of a traumatic event, but suffer from anxiety or panic if we find ourselves in a similar situation.

Please note that memory gaps can also have other causes. Severe sleep deprivation, for instance, can prevent or reduce memory formation. So if our stress or trauma results in sleep deprivation, or we are generally sleep-deprived due to unrelated issues, we might have genuine gaps in our memory where our brain failed to file certain information. Given that an estimated 70% of ADHDers and 80% of Autistics are chronically sleep deprived, it pays to bear this in mind.

Out-of-body experience (OBEs) are a phenomenon in which a person feels their consciousness leave their body, and continues to perceive the world from a location outside of their body. OBE can have a number of causes, including traumatic brain injuries, sensory deprivation, near-death experiences, drug use, dehydration, and sleep deprivation. In the absence of other known causes, OBEs are considered dissociative experiences.

	Gaps in long-term memory	**Out-of-body experiences**
Never	21%	55%
Sometimes	30%	27%
Often	25%	7%
Always	19%	2%
Not sure	5%	9%

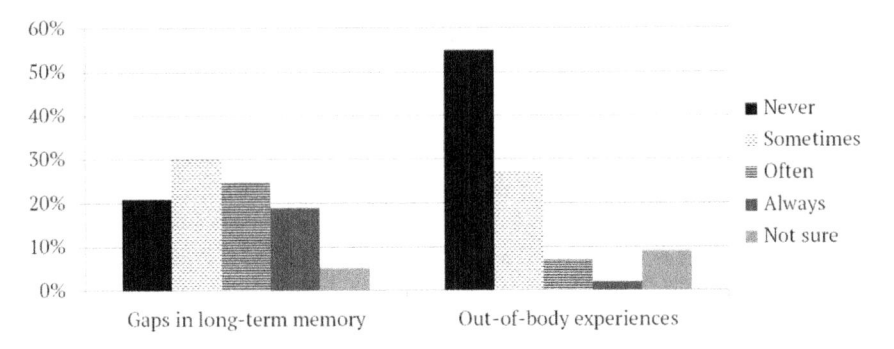

44% of respondents often or always have gaps in their long-term memory that affect certain time periods, events, or personal information. This issue is more prevalent in respondents who never sleep over 7 hours per day (50%), and lower in those who often or always sleep over 7 hours per day (36%). The limitations of this survey prevent us from establishing whether the sleep deprivation is a result of the same trauma and stress that might have caused the memory gaps, or is the cause of those gaps.

36% of respondents have out-of-body experiences at least sometimes. Given that the prevalence of OBEs in the general public is estimated at 10%, this figure seems rather high.

The factors that increase the prevalence of other dissociative states also increase the prevalence of memory gaps and OBEs. The prevalence is highest in those who are often or always routinely forced to endure unpleasant or overwhelming physical sensations in order to navigate their environment, and those who, as children were often or always forced by parents or teachers to endure painful physical sensation in order to learn to get over them.

	Gaps in long-term memory	Out-of-body experiences
Whole survey	44%	9%
Routinely forced to endure unpleasant or overwhelming physical sensations in order to navigate their environment	**63%**	**19%**
Force themselves to stop their self-soothing behaviors in order to avoid getting told off	50%	13%
Redirect repetitive behaviors to less noticeable ones to look more "normal"	50%	13%
Do things you'd rather not so people will like you	51%	12%
Pretend to be someone else so people will like you	53%	13%
Punished for "tantrums"	59%	19%
"Desensitized"	**60%**	**25%**
PTSD	53%	15%
cPTSD	58%	16%

The next section is a bit of a mess, because I lumped together two identity issues that can have very different causes and implications. The question was:

- Do you have times when you lose your sense of identity or have multiple distinct identities?

A loss of the sense of one's identity can be a symptom of **identity disturbance**: the inability to maintain one or more major components of identity. However, it can also result from situational issues, such as:

- Changes in social role (e.g. puberty, parenthood, "empty nest," career changes, retirement, etc.).
- Relationships starting or ending.
- Prolonged period of neurodivergent masking.
- Lack of opportunity to pursue personal goals and passions.
- Bullying, abusive relationships, and other forms of social trauma.
- Social isolation.

As most people go through at least some of these events, a temporary loss of one's sense of identity is very common and not necessarily indicative of an underlying problem.

Having multiple identities, on the other hand, is a symptom of **dissociative identity disorder** (DID). DID is a rare disorder that usually affects survivors of childhood abuse or neglect, although it can also result from exposure to major traumatic events. A person with DID has two or more distinct identities. As with other forms of dissociation, the disorder allows people to distance themselves from their trauma.

10% of respondents often or always lose their sense of identity or have multiple distinct identities. However, as the two phenomena have completely different implications, this result doesn't tell us much.

	Lose your sense of identity or have multiple distinct identities
Never	68%
Sometimes	18%
Often	7%
Always	3%
Not sure	4%

[Chart: Lose your sense of identity or have multiple distinct identities — Legend: Never, Sometimes, Often, Always, Not sure]

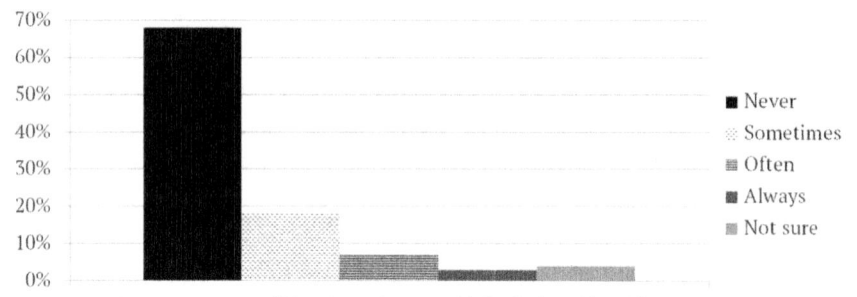

The factors that increase the prevalence of dissociative states also increase the prevalence of these identity issues. The prevalence is highest in those who are routinely forced to endure unpleasant or overwhelming physical sensations in order to navigate their environment, and those who, as children were forced by parents or teachers to endure painful physical sensation in order to learn to get over them.

	Lose your sense of identity or have multiple distinct identities
Whole survey	10%
Routinely forced to endure unpleasant or overwhelming physical sensations in order to navigate their environment	**21%**
Force themselves to stop their self-soothing behaviors in order to avoid getting told off	16%
Redirect repetitive behaviors to less noticeable ones to look more "normal"	14%
Do things you'd rather not so people will like you	14%
Pretend to be someone else so people will like you	17%
Punished for "tantrums"	17%
"Desensitized"	**20%**
PTSD	14%
cPTSD	17%

I am tired and everything hurts.

The questions in this chapter were originally split up into different section, but I decided to gather them together because their symptoms can overlap. Also, they all suck. They suck so much.

The questions were:

- Do you have any autoimmune diseases?
- Do you have a connective tissue disorder?
- Do you easily injure your joints? (e.g. sprains or strains.)
- Are your joints hypermobile?
- Do you have early onset arthritis?
- Do you have cluster headaches?
- Do you have attacks of severe pain in one side of the head?
- Do you have trigeminal neuralgia?
- Do you have sudden attacks of severe, sharp, shooting facial pain that last from a few seconds to about 2 minutes?
- Do you have tinnitus (ringing or other noises in one or both of your ears) without identifiable causes? (e.g., without hearing loss or an ear injury.)
- Do you have fibromyalgia?
- Do you have times when you experience widespread pain with no known cause?
- Are you extremely sensitive to pain? (e.g., if you suffer a minor injury, it hurts too much, or for too long.)
- Do you feel pain from something that should not be painful at all, such as a very light touch?
- Do you have times when all of your past injuries hurt, even though you have not re-injured yourself?
- Do you experience fatigue even when you haven't done anything to tire yourself out?
- Do you experience an unreasonable amount of fatigue when you exert yourself?

It is a truth universally acknowledged that a single neurodivergent person may report so many unexplainable aches and pains that writing them all down could give them a repetitive strain injury. In fact, one of the issues they might complain about is how prone they are to repetitive strain injuries. If you resemble these remarks, you might find some solace in knowing that you are not alone: we are a community with many ouches. Some of them come and go as they please, with no discernible causes, which is suboptimal. Some of them come and stay, which is even worse.

We are also tired. We are so, so tired. Some of us are tired because we don't sleep enough, or we don't sleep well, which is a subject we addressed in the "Sleep" section. Some of us are tired because of constant mismatches between our expectations and our abilities, or between our environment and our needs, as we discussed throughout this book. Managing these issues requires a ton of extra work on our part, which is draining, and can cause us significant stress, which is also draining. Some of us, however, are tired regardless. We are tired, and everything hurts. Sometimes it's impossible to disentangle whether we hurt because we are so tired, or we are tired because we hurt so much.

Both intermittent and chronic pain can have several possible causes. Different conditions may present with similar symptoms, which is super fun when it comes to diagnosing them. Even more fun is the fact that these conditions are not mutually exclusive, and their symptoms can be cumulative. So, we may have one condition with many different ouches, or we may have several conditions with overlapping ouches.

One would think that the fact that so many of us reports similar issues would have resulted in some kind of streamlining of the diagnostic process for us. If a whole bunch of us has A or B condition with X Y Z symptoms, and one of us reports X Y Z symptoms, it would make logical sense to test them for A and B conditions. Unfortunately, too many doctors seem to take the opposite approach: neurodivergents are prone to reporting chronic, unexplained pains, so their chronic pain must be all in their heads. We're just oversensitive, over-reactive, or over-complaining. To quote my very-much-ex pain management consultant, "People like you just need to learn what really hurts and what doesn't." And if it wouldn't hurt a normie, it shouldn't hurt us.

Aside from the fact that bodies just don't work that way, there is plenty of evidence to suggest that neurodivergent people are more likely to experience a number of real, diagnosable conditions that cause pain and fatigue. These include autoimmune diseases, connective tissue disorders, fibromyalgia, and neuropathies. Those of us with a uterus and ovaries may also be more likely to experience fatigue and pain caused by conditions related to hormonal imbalances, which will be discussed separately.

Autoimmune diseases are caused by a dysfunction of the immune system. Following exposure to a trigger such as a virus or a chemical, the body's natural defense system is activated, but instead of attacking the threat, it attacks normal cells. The results vary depending on which cells are being attacked:

- In rheumatoid arthritis, the immune system attacks the joints;
- In psoriasis, the immune system attacks the skin;
- In lupus, the immune system attacks joints, skin, and organs;
- In autoimmune hepatitis, the immune system attacks the liver;
- In multiple sclerosis (MS), the immune system attacks myelin, the substance that protects nerve fibers in the brain and spinal cord;
- In narcolepsy, the immune system destroys brain cells that produce a peptide called hypocretin, resulting in attacks of daytime drowsiness.
- In Myalgic Encephalomyelitis/Chronic Fatigue Syndrome (ME/CFS), a trigger causes changes in the way the immune system responds to infection or stress, resulting in widespread inflammation but no tissue damage. The exact causes and mechanisms have yet to be identified.

These are just some examples; there are more than 80 types of autoimmune disease, and all parts of the body may be affected. Some autoimmune diseases affect a single part of the body, while others have more widespread effects. Unfortunately, diagnosing them is far from simple, as many of them present with similar symptoms. These often include:

- Fatigue;
- Joint pain and swelling;
- Skin problems;
- Abdominal pain or digestive issues;
- Recurring fever;

- Swollen glands.

As these symptoms can have a variety of causes, diagnosis can be difficult. Symptom severity can also vary between patients, and can be affected by environmental and health factors.

We don't as yet know what causes autoimmune diseases, but we know that they run in families. We also know that they are more prevalent in AFAB individuals: out of the estimated 3% of the population that suffers from an autoimmune disease, 78-80% of them are AFAB.

	Autoimmune diseases
Yes	18%
No	61%
Not Sure	18%
N/A	2%

Yet again, our community exceeds expectations: despite the difficulties in getting a diagnosis of autoimmune diseases, 18% of us have one. This indicates that we are at least six times more likely to suffer from these conditions than the general population. As only 27% of respondents with autoimmune diseases are also Autistic, this is an issue affecting the neurodivergent community, not just our Autistic members.

At present, there are no cures for autoimmune diseases. However, symptoms can often be managed, and flare-ups avoided or curtailed. Treatment has to be tailored to each patient, as everyone's immune system, genetics, and environment are different. This often requires a referral to one or more specialist departments, as general practitioners may not have the required expertise. In order to get that, however, we first have to find a doctor willing to take our symptoms seriously, and be able to access the specialists who can diagnose us.

Connective tissue disorders (CTDs) share many of the most annoying features of autoimmune diseases; in particular, they can present with a variety of symptoms, they can affect most parts of the body, they can be hard to live with or manage effectively, and they are not easy to diagnose.

CTDs affect collagen and elastin – two proteins responsible for literally keeping us together. Collagen is found in the tendons, ligaments, skin, cornea, cartilage, bones, and blood vessels. Elastin is the major component of ligaments and skin.

There are more than 200 types of CTDs. Some are inherited, some are triggered by infections or exposure to chemicals, and some are of unknown cause.

In autoimmune CTDs, the collagen and elastin become inflamed, causing damage to the relevant parts of the body. We have already discussed two autoimmune CTDs; rheumatoid arthritis and lupus are autoimmune disorders affecting the connective tissue.

In heritable CTDs, defects in the synthesis of collagen or elastin may result in the production of proteins that are not strong enough, or in the production of insufficient amounts of normal proteins.

As collagen and elastin are present throughout the body, CTDs can cause a widespread range of issues. They may affect our bones, joints, skin, heart, blood vessels, lungs, eyes, ears, guts, kidneys, etc. Some of these issues manifest as obvious physical problems, such as brittle bones, over-flexible or unstable joints, skin hyperelasticity, and progressive deformities including flat feet, bow-leggedness, scoliosis, lordosis, and so on. However, less visible issues affecting other parts the body are no less important, and can have a severe impact on people's quality of life, and even on their life expectancy. Some complications, such as spontaneous arterial rupture or uterine rupture in pregnancy, can be fatal.

For most patients, however, the prognosis is nowhere near as bleak. The degree to which CTDs affect each person will depend on the severity of symptoms, which in turns will depend on a combination of genetic and environmental factors. Unfortunately, this variability has been an obstacle to diagnosis; for instance, Ehlers–Danlos syndromes were originally believed to affect 0.0002-0.0004% of the general population, but are now estimated to affect at least 0.02%. This huge jump in estimated prevalence has resulted from changes in diagnostic criteria.

Despite these changes, obtaining a diagnosis of connective tissue disorder can still be difficult. Some symptoms of CTDs can also be symptoms of other conditions or issues; for instance, frequent bruising, scarring, and dislocations in children may lead doctors to suspect and investigate abuse, rather than any physiological cause. Other symptoms, such as chronic musculoskeletal pain and frequent injuries, may be dismissed as being self-explanatories: if you injure yourself a lot, of course you'll be hurting! The fact that we don't injure ourselves on purpose, or doing overly dangerous things, is not always noted.

These diagnostic issues are most serious for those of us whose connective tissue problems are subclinical. For instance, our joints may be unstable, rather than hypermobile; we may not be able to bend them more than "normal," but we sprain, strain, or dislocate them with remarkable frequency and ease. While these issues may not seem very serious – they definitely pale into insignificance compared to the risk of a spontaneous arterial rupture – they can have a severe impact on our quality of life. This can be especially true if we are not aware of them or are not able to make the adaptations necessary to protect us from injuries. Unfortunately, without a diagnosis, we are often unable to request the school and workplace accommodations we need to prevent injuries and deformities. We may also be unable to get prompt and effective treatment when injuries do occur.

Over time, the accumulation of injuries can end up masking some of our symptoms; for instance, arthritis can make our joints less mobile, while doing nothing to promote their stability. Our back pain may be explained away because of our poor posture, even though our poor posture may be the result of back pain. We may also compensate for our structural instability by overusing our muscles; this may reduce the number of injuries we suffer, but it can manifest as fatigue and all-over aches and pains.

	A CTD	Joint hypermobility	Easily injure joints	Early onset arthritis
Never	54%	52%	49%	57%
Sometimes	2%	12%	27%	8%
Often	2%	8%	13%	5%
Always	7%	14%	7%	8%
Not sure	35%	13%	4%	22%

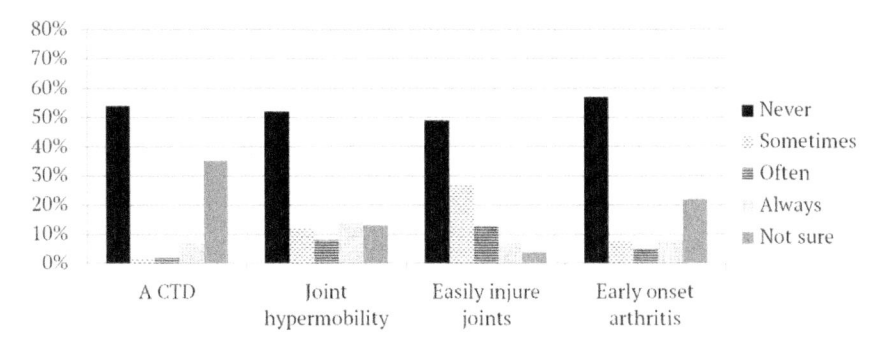

[Bar chart showing percentages for "A CTD", "Joint hypermobility", "Easily injure joints", and "Early onset arthritis" across categories Never, Sometimes, Often, Always, Not sure]

11% of respondents have a connective tissue disorder. However, 22% of them often or always have joint hypermobility, 21% of them often or always easily injure their joints, and 21% of them have early onset arthritis. These discrepancies do not mean that up to 11% of us have an undiagnosed CTD; however, it does suggest that we might be affected by joint issues that may require further investigation and treatment.

Ideally, it should also be investigated before it results in long-term or permanent damage. 71% of respondents with hypermobile joints easily injure them, and 41% have early onset arthritis. Caveat: I did not ask whether respondents have rheumatoid arthritis, so I cannot separate those whose arthritis is caused by joint diseases rather than joint injuries. However, given that the average age of survey respondents was 35 and the median 34, these results are depressing either way.

(If you have unstable or easily damaged joints and you menstruate or are taking hormonal treatment that includes estrogen, you might want to check out recent research about the impact of estrogen levels on sporting injuries. Estrogen affects ligament laxity, motor control, and timing of muscle activation. As a result, people may be at increased risk of ligament injury when their estrogen levels are higher. If you map your joint troubles against your menstrual cycle or hormonal treatment schedule and see a pattern, you might want to talk to your doctor about your options.)

Joint instability can have other impacts on our health and our abilities. Most notably, if it results in poor posture or gait, it can lead to problems with movement and coordination, trapped nerves, and loss of function. These issues are well-known to physical therapists, who have plenty of experience in dealing with the resulting problems. Unfortunately, medical practitioners aren't always as experienced or knowledgeable, and may be unable to spot the connection between, for instance, a person's flat feet and their cervical impingement or propensity for accidents. This can result in misdiagnoses, ineffective treatments, or in symptoms being wrongly attributed to psychological issues or malingering.

61% of survey respondents with a connective tissue disorder have poor gross motor skills, as do 59% of those with hypermobile joints and 71% of those who easily injure their joints. The result for the survey as a whole was 52%. While these results do not prove causation, they do suggest that there may be a connection between joint problems and poor gross motor skills.

Crunching numbers revealed another possible connection I personally did not expect – one with **trigeminal nerve conditions**. The trigeminal nerve is responsible for sensations such as heat or pain in your face. There are two trigeminal nerves, one on each side of the face, branching up to the forehead, across the cheek, down the jaw, and above the ear. If this nerve is irritated, compressed, or triggered, it can cause severe pain. There are many trigeminal nerve conditions, but this survey only looked at two.

Cluster headaches are a series of short but painful headaches affecting one side of the head, often around the eye. The pain comes on quickly, is restricted to one side of the head, is focused behind or around one eye but may spread throughout the face, and "only" lasts 30 to 90 minutes.

The cause of cluster headaches is not yet known, but we know that they can run in families. The pain is caused by a triggering of the trigeminal nerve. The signal triggering the pain starts from the hypothalamus, home of the "internal biological clock" that controls the sleep/wake cycle.

This triggering does not occur at random. Cluster headaches tend to reoccur every day for weeks or months, often at the same time(s) of day. They may go in remission for long periods only to reoccur at the same time of year.

By contrast, **trigeminal neuralgia** is a condition affecting the trigeminal nerve, but without a clear pattern. Jolts of excruciating pain can be triggered by stimulation of the face (e.g., from teeth brushing), or might just happen. These jolts can occur individually, or come in volleys lasting as long as two hours.

Trigeminal neuralgia is usually caused by compression of the trigeminal nerve, which causes damage to the myelin sheath that protects it. It can also be the result of direct injury to the nerve, from a blow, surgery, or a stroke. The condition can be progressive, with the attacks increasing in frequency, intensity, and duration.

Cluster headaches and trigeminal neuralgia can have a serious impact on people's quality of life, as the pain is so intense as to be incapacitating. Thankfully, they are rare: cluster headaches only affect an estimated 0.124% of the general population, while trigeminal neuralgia only affects 0.01-0.92%.

Remember when I was talking about autoimmune diseases, and I said that our community exceeds expectations because we have them six times as often? That was nothing. Nothing at all.

38% of respondents reported that they have cluster headaches. That means that the prevalence of cluster headaches in our community is 306 times greater than in the general population.

3% of respondents reported that they have trigeminal neuralgia. That means that the prevalence of trigeminal neuralgia in our community is somewhere between 3 and 300 times greater than in the general population.

Furthermore, these conditions are not well-known. 16% of respondents were not sure whether they have cluster headaches, and 47% were not sure whether they have trigeminal neuralgia. When we look at the people reporting the symptoms of these conditions, 51% reported the symptoms of cluster headaches, and 21% the symptoms of trigeminal neuralgia. While this does not mean that the people affected would meet the criteria for a diagnosis,[36] it does mean that more than half of our community suffers from severe attacks of facial pain. In case you were wondering, this isn't normal.

	Cluster headaches	Cluster headache symptoms	Trigeminal neuralgia	Trigeminal neuralgia symptoms
Never	46%	46%	50%	75%
Sometimes	21%	28%	2%	15%
Often	12%	16%	1%	4%
Always	5%	7%	1%	2%
Not sure	16%	3%	47%	4%

---

[36] Wanna know something funny? I currently fail to meet the diagnostic criteria for cluster headaches *or* trigeminal neuralgia because my attacks now last too long (up to 4 days) and occur too regularly (during the stages of my cycle when my estrogen levels peak). Hence, as far as my official records are concerned, I am now cured of both conditions! Party on!

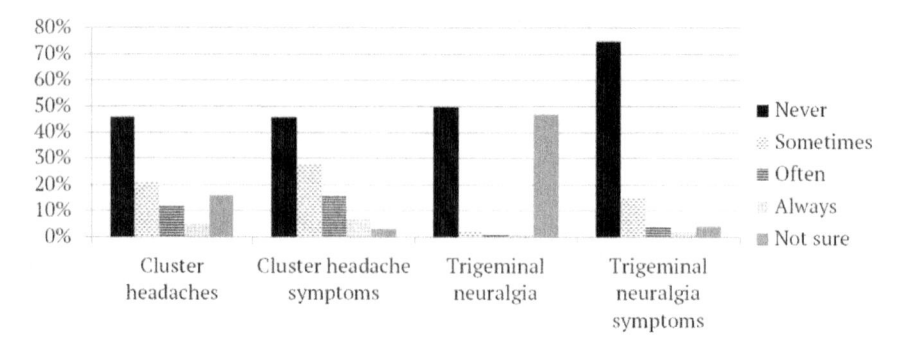

[Bar chart showing percentages for Cluster headaches, Cluster headache symptoms, Trigeminal neuralgia, and Trigeminal neuralgia symptoms, with categories: Never, Sometimes, Often, Always, Not sure]

It gets better. In respondents who easily injure their joints the prevalence of cluster headaches goes up to 51%, and that of trigeminal neuralgia to 8% Again, this does not imply causation, but you'd think that results these skewed would raise some professional curiosity.

	Cluster headaches	**Trigeminal neuralgia**
Whole survey	38%	3%
Easily injure joints	51%	8%

In the process of carrying out research for this book, I learned that in the Ehlers-Danlos community there is a well-known phenomenon referred to as facial or sinus migraines – like migraines, but in your face. Ehlers-Danlos syndrome is a group of inherited connective tissues disorders. Patients often present with various types of headaches as a result of problems with the jaw joint (temporomandibular disorders), or of cervical spine and neck instability. These issues are at present poorly studied, and often just as poorly addressed by medical professionals. The results of this survey suggest the possibility that subclinical connective tissue disorders may have a similar impact on the incidence of at least two types of headaches.

Oh, while we are at it: cervical joint instability doesn't just cause headaches and face aches. It can also manifest as trapped nerves in the arms or hands, which can be misdiagnosed as carpal tunnel syndrome.

Another symptom associated with Ehlers-Danlos is **tinnitus** (ringing or other noises in one or both of your ears) due to instability of the bones in the middle ear. Their tinnitus appears without any of the "usual" causes, such as hearing loss or an ear injury.

	Tinnitus without identifiable causes
Never	32%
Sometimes	29%
Often	16%
Always	20%
Not sure	3%

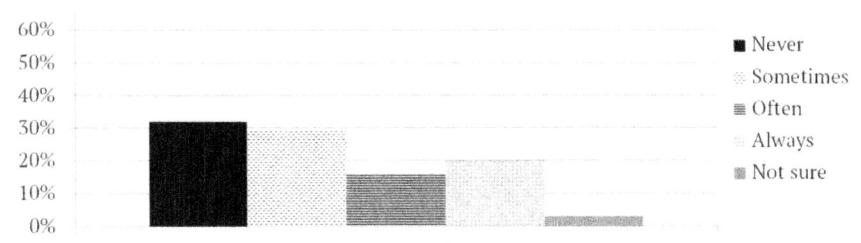

Tinnitus without identifiable causes

36% of respondents often or always have tinnitus without identifiable causes. If we include those who "only" have it sometimes, the prevalence goes up to 65%. Estimates of the prevalence of tinnitus in the general population vary between 10 and 32%, but these include people whose tinnitus has known causes, so these figures are not comparable.

The prevalence of tinnitus goes up to 49% in respondents who easily injure their joints – 75% if we include those who only have it sometimes. As for trigeminal nerve conditions, this suggests that subclinical connective tissue problems may still have a significant impact on the prevalence of otherwise unexplained tinnitus.

	Tinnitus without identifiable causes
Whole survey	36%
Easily injure joints	49%

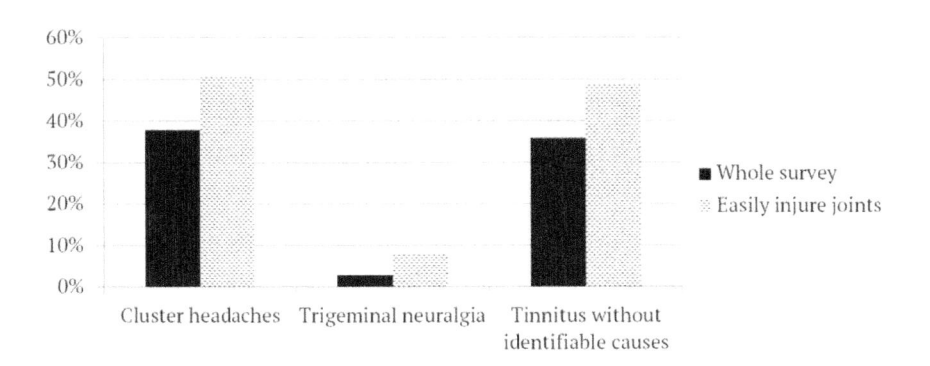

If you think this chapter has been depressing up to now, you're going to love what comes next. **Fibromyalgia** derives its name from the Latin "fibro" (for fibrous tissue) and the Greek "myo" (muscle) and "algia" (pain). It's literally "pain in the muscles and fibers." It's also a pain in the neck, both literally and figuratively.

As usual, the diagnostic criteria for fibro vary between medical systems. Unusually, however, these criteria are very new – the first set of established diagnostic guidelines dates back to 1990 – even though the condition has been known for a couple of centuries. Prior to the 1800s, the condition was considered a mental health issue. Unfortunately, many doctors these days still treat it as a mental health issue. The fact that it predominantly affects AFABs might be a factor here.

This situation isn't helped by the fact that we still have no idea of what causes fibro. We know that it runs in families, and that many patients start to experience symptoms after an infection or a physically or emotionally traumatic event. We also know that people with osteoarthritis, rheumatoid arthritis, or lupus are more likely to develop fibro. However, that's as far as we've got; we don't even know what fibro actually *does*. At present, the prevalent theory is that the brain and spinal cord of fibro patients change as a result of repeated stimulation, causing a chemical imbalance in the brain and oversensitivity of the brain's pain receptors. However, this is only a theory.

As a result of this lack of information, we don't yet have a test for fibro. The condition is diagnosed when other possibilities have been ruled out. Unfortunately, this process isn't simple because fibro presents with a variety of symptoms, many of which could be caused by a number of other conditions. Current diagnostic criteria include:

- Widespread muscle and joint pain that has persisted for at least three months and has no other identifiable causes.

- Tender points -- specific spots around the joints that hurt when pressed. The same amount of pressure in the same locations would not hurt a person without fibro. Not everyone with fibromyalgia has tender points, but some doctors still consider them an essential requirement for diagnosis.

- Fatigue. Patients often wake up tired, even if they have had plenty of sleep, and do not feel refreshed after resting.

- Sleep problems. Patients might fall asleep, but sleep lightly and wake up easily. Alternatively, patients might wake up exhausted, even though they have slept long enough. Sleep may be simply disrupted by pain, but many patients also have other sleep disorders, such as restless legs syndrome or sleep apnea. Sleep studies indicate that the brains of people with fibro switch on while they're asleep, reducing the amount of restorative deep sleep they can get.

- Cognitive difficulties or "fibro fog," causing difficulties with concentration and short-term memory. As these faculties are an essential part of executive functioning, carrying on a normal life with fibro can be difficult.

Because these symptoms are hard to quantify and may be associated with a number of other conditions, fibro is often misdiagnosed and misunderstood. Fibro is also commonly co-morbid with a number of other conditions, including:

- Mood disorders, in particular depression or anxiety. It is unclear whether these are a part of the condition, or the result of the impact of fibro on people's lives.
- Morning stiffness, similar to that experienced by people with rheumatoid arthritis. This stiffness can last from a few minutes to hours.
- Numbness, tingling, or burning sensations in hands and feet (paresthesia) with no identifiable causes. These are often worst in the morning, and can last a few minutes or persist throughout the day.
- Headaches, including migraines and tension headaches. These may be associated with neck and back problems, in particular with overtight neck muscles.
- Postural tachycardia syndrome (POTS).
- Gastrointestinal problems, including constipation, diarrhea, Irritable Bowel Syndrome (IBS), acid reflux, and gastroesophageal reflux disease (GERD).
- Urination problems, such as needing to go a lot, painful urination, or a leaky bladder.
- Unusually painful menstrual cramps.
- Temporomandibular joint disorders (TMJs)

    Whether these symptoms are actual comorbidities or part of fibro is still under debate.

So we have a condition with widespread, pervasive, vague symptoms that could be attributed to a variety of other conditions, which may also be present at the same time. And that's only part of the current diagnostic issues around fibro.

In some countries, a diagnosis of fibro may be sufficient for a person to be classified as disabled and entitled to the relevant benefits. There is nothing wrong with that, as many people with fibro are disabled. However, as a result, some doctors are reluctant to diagnose fibro if they suspect a patient to be malingering. Conversely, some doctors use fibro diagnoses as a way to get complicated patients out of their way. Instead of carrying out in-depth investigations, they "diagnose" them with fibro and leave it at that. Some doctors may also use fibro to cover up the impact of past misdiagnoses or failures in treatment. Patients aren't in pain as the result of medical malpractice: they just developed fibro as a result of their past injuries or diseases, which is unfortunate but not actionable.

For people wondering whether to seek a diagnosis of fibromyalgia, there are two additional considerations. Firstly, there is at present no cure for fibro, and specific treatment options are very limited and not available in all countries or from all doctors. While some patients are able to access targeted treatments that can make a huge impact on their symptoms and quality of life, many are only offered painkillers, usually opioids. The treatments offered may be no different to those that would be offered to patients with similar symptoms but no fibro diagnosis.

On the other hand, having a diagnosis of fibro can make it difficult to get a diagnosis of anything else. If new symptoms arise, it can be hard to convince doctors to carry out the appropriate investigations instead of just attributing them to fibro. As a result, whether a diagnosis of fibro results in better or worse medical treatment depends on a patient's circumstances and the quality of their doctors.

	Fibromyalgia	**Widespread pain with no known cause**
Never	66%	56%
Sometimes	2%	23%
Often	2%	12%
Always	6%	8%
Not sure	25%	2%

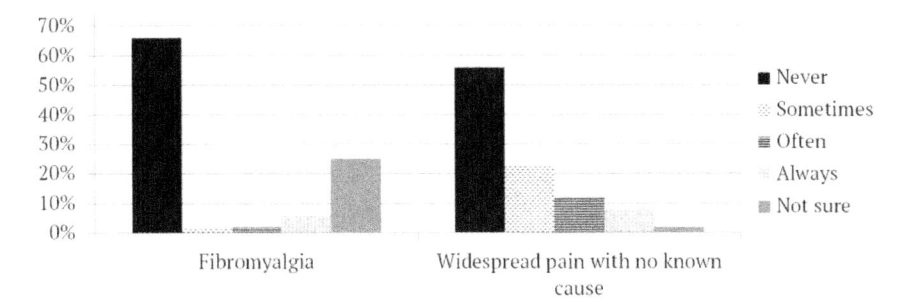

As fibro and fibro-related symptoms are significant even when they aren't present 24/7, I will include those who "only" experience them sometimes in the following calculations.

9% of respondents have fibro. As current estimates for prevalence in the general population are 3-6%, we are, yet again, exceeding expectations.

42 % of respondents have times when they experience widespread pain with no known cause. This is one of the diagnostic criteria for fibro, but it could be caused by other conditions – after all, the reason the pain has no known causes could simply be the lack of suitable medical investigations. Either way, this is a significant symptom that should be taken seriously by doctors.

	Extremely sensitive to pain	Feel pain from something that should not be painful	"Pain flashbacks"
Never	66%	62%	60%
Sometimes	19%	23%	23%
Often	7%	9%	10%
Always	5%	5%	4%
Not sure	3%	2%	3%

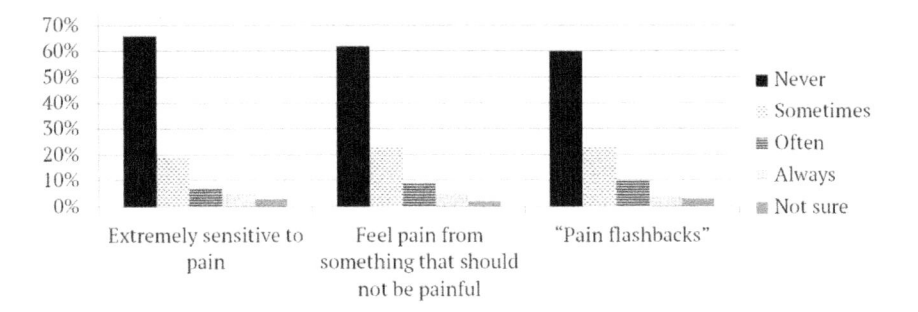

31% of respondents are extremely sensitive to pain. 36% feel pain from something that should not be painful at all, such as a very light touch. 37% have times when all of their past injuries hurt, even though they have not re-injured themselves. While these symptoms are not currently part of the diagnostic criteria for fibro, they often affect fibro patients. And regardless of whether they indicate fibro or not, they still suck, and they should still be investigated by doctors.

Fatigue is a symptom of fibro, but it can be a symptom of many of the conditions prevalent within our community. If you recall the chapter on sleep, only 6% of respondents are always able to sleep the recommended minimum of seven hours per day, while 16% of respondents have sleep apnea. When we also consider the prevalence of chronic pain conditions and sundry other issues that might negatively affect the quantity and quality of our sleep, it's unsurprising that 78% of respondents often or always wake up tired, even when they get enough sleep.

	Unexplained fatigue	**Excessive fatigue after exertion**
Never	8%	20%
Sometimes	30%	31%
Often	34%	24%
Always	27%	23%
Not sure	1%	2%

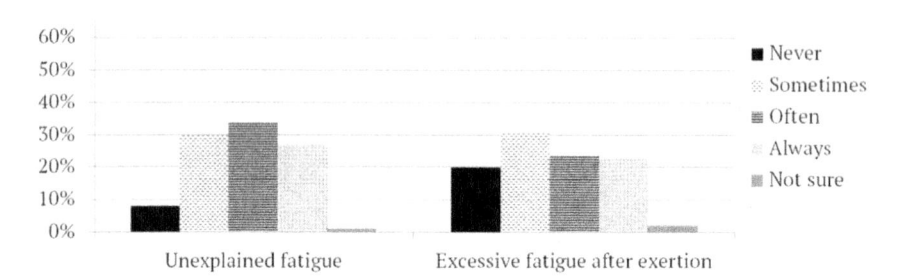

62% of respondents often or always experience fatigue even when they haven't done anything to tire themselves out, and 47% often or always experience an unreasonable amount of fatigue when they exert themselves.

These two groups overlap. 94% of those who experience an

unreasonable amount of fatigue when they exert themselves also experience fatigue even when they haven't done anything to tire themselves out.

The prevalence of these issues is different in groups that get different amounts of sleep. Those who never sleep more than seven hours show the highest prevalence of both issues (73% and 56% respectively). On the other hand, those who often or always sleep more than seven hours show the lowest prevalence (53% and 41% respectively).

	Whole Survey	Never sleep 7hrs	Often or always sleep 7hrs
Experience fatigue even when you haven't done anything to tire yourself out?	62%	73%	53%
Experience an unreasonable amount of fatigue when you exert yourself?	47%	56%	41%

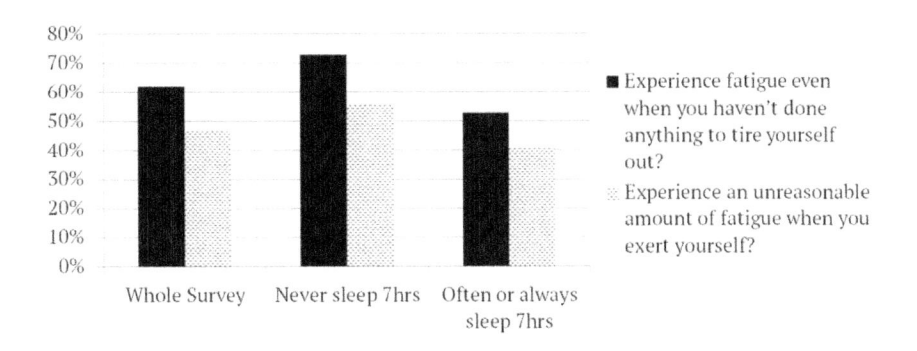

Hormonal imbalances

This section looks at some conditions that affect people who have a uterus, ovaries, or breast tissue. The questions were:

- Do you have endometriosis?
- Do you have uterine fibroids?
- Do you have uterine polyps?
- Do you have fibrocystic breast disease?
- Do you have polycystic ovary syndrome (PCOS)?

All these conditions have one thing in common: they are linked to hormonal imbalances. Unfortunately, they have something else in common: they are all grossly underdiagnosed in the general public. There is no reason to believe that diagnostic rates are more accurate within the neurodivergent community; in fact, there are plenty of reasons why they might be worse, particularly for those of us with chronic pain conditions or at the receiving end of medical biases. Therefore, while anecdotal evidence suggests that these conditions may be unusually common in our community, comparing prevalence between us and the general population is a fairly futile exercise.

That doesn't mean that this chapter is a waste of space, though. There are issues associated with the way in which these conditions are often (mis)handled that may affect us worse than they do neurotypicals, and being aware of these issues may be helpful.

"Estrogen dominance" is currently a very popular subject in the pseudoscientific community, and there is a lot of inaccurate and dangerous information about it out there. I do not want to add to it by giving my readers the impression that rebalancing your hormonal levels is a cure-all; it isn't, particularly if your ailments don't have anything to do with hormones. Having said that, there are a number of conditions that are linked to high levels of estrogen. These include endometriosis, uterine cancer, uterine fibroids, uterine polyps , fibrocystic breast disease, and breast cancer. Polycystic ovary syndrome (PCOS) may also be linked to estrogen dominance, but it is primarily linked to other hormonal imbalances and will be discussed separately.

Endometriosis is a condition where the lining of the uterus (endometrium) grows in areas where it doesn't belong, most commonly the ovaries, fallopian tubes, and the tissue lining the pelvis.

This can result in heavy or irregular bleeding and a lot of pain: painful periods, pain around ovulation, pain during or after sex, pain with bowel movements or urination, and pain in the pelvic area, lower back, or legs. Endometriosis hurts, and it hurts a lot of people: it is currently believed to affect 10% of AFABs worldwide.

Unfortunately, there is no cure for endometriosis. Fortunately, however, there are ways of controlling symptoms and reducing the progress of the disease. They all hinge on reducing the level of estrogen in order to reduce inflammation and pain. Endometrial tissue can be removed by surgery, but not every patient can access this. Also, endometriosis recurs at a rate of 20% to 40% within five years following surgery unless it is combined with hormonal treatments.

Uterine fibroids (leiomyomas) are noncancerous growths of the uterus. They are very common (the estimated prevalence is 70%-80% of AFABs, depending on ethnicity) and are not necessarily dangerous or problematic. Many people have fibroids without even knowing it, because they don't have any symptoms. The impact of fibroids depends on their size, number, and position. While small fibroids may not cause any symptoms, large fibroids can push against the sides of the uterus, changing its shape and pressing against other internal organs.

When fibroids cause symptoms, these often include heavy menstrual bleeding, excessively long menstrual periods (over a week), pelvic pressure or pain, frequent urination, difficulties emptying the bladder, constipation, backache, or leg pains. In rare cases, fibroids can outgrow their blood supply and begin to die off, causing acute pain. Large or numerous fibroids can also interfere with fertility. Submucosal fibroids (growing in the uterine cavity, under the surface of the endometrium) can cause infertility and pregnancy loss.

The cause of fibroids has not yet been established, but they are currently believed to result when an abnormality in the uterus multiplies rapidly under the influence of estrogen.

There is no cure for fibroids, but they can be treated. Treatment options are very varied and include:

- Procedures to destroy the fibroids without removing them.
- Procedures to surgically remove the fibroids from the uterus.

- Endometrial ablation, which destroys the lining of the uterus.
- Hysterectomy, which removes the uterus altogether.

Hysterectomy is the only proven permanent solution for uterine fibroids. Unless the uterus is removed, there is a chance that it will develop new fibroids. Alas, people considered to be "of reproductive age" are often precluded from having a hysterectomy or endometrial ablation, because those cause infertility. Whether the people in question are able or willing to have children isn't always treated as a significant factor.

There are also non-surgical treatment options. These include hormonal and non-hormonal treatments that provide symptom relief, as well as hormonal treatments that control fibroid growth by reducing or blocking the production of estrogen. These treatments do not remove existing fibroids, but may cause them to shrink and reduce the chances of new ones developing.

Uterine polyps are soft growths on the inside of the uterus. They can range significantly in size and number. Small polyps may cause no symptoms, but large polyps can cause infertility and pregnancy loss.

The cause of endometrial polyps is not yet known, but their growth appears to be a response to swings in hormone levels and high estrogen levels. Polyps are believed to affect 24% of the general population, but their prevalence is higher in postmenopausal people. The prevalence of malignant or pre-malignant polyps is also higher in postmenopausal people. However, as a general rule, uterine polyps are rarely cancerous.

Polyps can be asymptomatic. When they cause symptoms, these can include irregular periods, prolonged or excessive bleeding, bleeding between periods, bleeding after menopause, and infertility.

If polyps are not causing symptoms, they are usually just monitored. However, if they cause symptoms, treatment is indicated. This usually consists of surgical removal of the polyps (polypectomy). If the polyps are found to be cancerous, a hysterectomy may be indicated. Hormonal treatments are available to shrink polyps and ease symptoms, but symptoms return if the treatments are stopped.

Fibrocystic breast disease is caused when an imbalance between estrogen and progesterone results in proliferation of connective tissue (fibrosis) in the breasts. This results in the development of fibrocystic plaques, nodularity, cysts, and fibrocystic lumps in the breast tissue. These abnormalities are classified as benign (i.e., not cancerous), but they can be extremely painful. Also, the risk of breast cancer is 2-4 times higher in patients with fibrocystic breast disease.

Although estimates of the prevalence of fibrocystic breast disease vary hugely, this disease is believed to be quite common, affecting up to 50% of AFABs over the age of 30. However, "only" 20% of them develop painful macrocysts (large cysts) that can have a severe impact on their quality of life.

There is no cure for fibrocystic breast disease. Cysts can be aspirated – the fluid inside is removed with a fine needle, which may collapse the cyst and relieve discomfort. Unfortunately, cysts can fill up again. Persistent or recurring cysts can be removed via surgery, but this is not available to all patients. Fortunately, however, the symptoms and progression of fibrocystic breast disease can be controlled by reducing estrogen levels through hormonal treatments.

As you can see, these conditions are very different, but they all have one thing in common: unless the affected organ is removed, managing hormonal levels is a key aspect of managing the symptoms and progression of these conditions.

Unfortunately these conditions have something else in common: most of their symptoms are hard to quantify. Many of them could be assumed to be the symptoms of severe period discomfort or premenstrual syndrome (PMS) – or, if the doctor in question does not trust their patient, the symptoms of a regular menstrual cycle as related by a whiner or a malingerer.

Technically, this misdiagnosis should not be possible. PMS is not a throwaway term; it's a formal diagnosis that should only be given once conditions that can cause similar symptoms have been ruled out. However, all too often doctors assume PMS and treat patients accordingly, and only carry out further investigations if the symptoms get worse, or if the patient tries and fails to conceive for a set period of time.

There are several major problems with this. Aside from the fact that these conditions can have a far greater impact on a person's quality of life than regular periods or PMS, they are progressive. Failing to diagnose and treat them early can mean having to deal with far greater problems. Furthermore, many of the treatments recommended for managing periods and PMS are either obvious (e.g., if you're in pain, take painkillers), irrelevant (e.g., don't drink or smoke), or ineffective (e.g., many "natural" remedies). Those which do have a relevant impact are often geared towards *increasing* estrogen levels. As the conditions we are discussing here are caused by high estrogen levels, persevering with treatments that increase estrogen can exacerbate them. For people with fibrocystic breast disease, high estrogen levels also increase the risk of breast cancer.

This isn't a neurodivergent problem; it's a potential problem for anyone with a uterus or breasts. However, there is a possibility that it might disproportionately affect neurodivergent people for two reasons. Firstly, many of us are at the receiving end of medical stigma because of our neurodivergence or of the co-occurring conditions we live with. This can make some doctors less likely to take our symptoms seriously.

Secondly, as a community, we are habitually sleep-deprived. Lack of sleep and irregular sleeping patterns have been proven to have deleterious effects on people's hormonal balance, with dangerous results; for instance, night shift work may be linked to an increased risk of breast cancer. This may be due to the suppression of melatonin production, confusion in the body circadian system, and the weakening of the immune system resulting from disordered sleep.

In the section about sleep, I mentioned that many doctors are reluctant to prescribe melatonin supplements for long-term use because melatonin affects the timing and release of female reproductive hormones. Specifically, melatonin affects estrogen synthesis and inhibits the activity of estrogen receptors – in a nutshell, more melatonin, less estrogen. This is a problem if a person's hormonal balance is as it should be, because melatonin supplements can make it go out of whack. However, if a person's melatonin production is not what it should be, it is reasonable to expect that their hormonal balance will also be off, because the effects of melatonin on estrogen will be missing. And as for patients who have conditions linked to estrogen dominance *and* sleep disturbances, not considering that the two may be linked is just incompetent.

	Endometriosis	Uterine fibroids	Uterine polyps	Fibrocystic breast disease
Yes	11%	10%	5%	8%
No	68%	68%	73%	77%
Not Sure	20%	20%	20%	14%
N/A	1%	1%	2%	2%

[Bar chart showing percentages of Yes, No, Not Sure, N/A responses for Endometriosis, Uterine fibroids, Uterine polyps, and Fibrocystic breast disease]

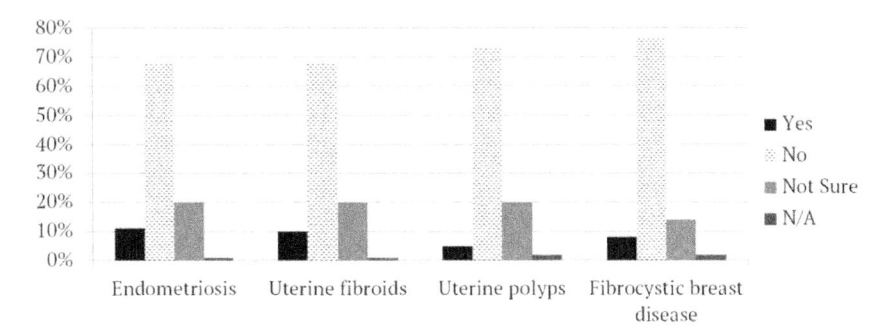

Polycystic ovarian syndrome (PCOS) differs from the rest of the conditions described in this section as it is caused by the ovaries producing unusually high levels of androgens (aka "male hormones"). The underlying cause is as yet unknown, but PCOS has a genetic component and is co-morbid with insulin resistance and chronic low-grade inflammation.

Despite the name of the condition, not all patients with PCOS have ovarian cysts. Common symptoms include erratic menstrual cycles, abnormal hair growth (hirsutism), hair loss, and skin problems including acne, skin tags, and dark skin patches. As the condition runs in families, some patients may not realize that they are experiencing symptoms of a condition; to them, it's all normal. There is also considerable variability in how patients present, and some patients have no symptoms.

This makes diagnosis difficult. Current estimates suggest that up to 75% of patients with PCOS may remain undiagnosed even after consulting their doctor. It isn't uncommon for patients to only be diagnosed when they try and fail to conceive for some time, spurring doctors to conduct further investigations. For those who never try, the condition may go undiagnosed, regardless of the presence of symptoms.

This can have a significant negative impact on people's health because PCOS puts patients at a higher risk of several health conditions, including diabetes, high blood pressure, cardiovascular disease, endometrial hyperplasia, endometrial cancer, sleep disorders, depression, and anxiety. Therefore, early diagnosis and appropriate interventions can make a significant difference to patients' long-term health outcomes.

Unlike the other conditions discussed in this chapter, PCOS isn't easily misdiagnosed for regular period discomfort or PMS. However, it has an even more fun feature. The hormonal imbalances linked with PCOS cause weight gain and make weight loss incredibly difficult. However, patients with PCOS are routinely told that they need to lose weight to manage their condition – or, worse, that they caused the condition by putting on weight. Similar issues apply to other conditions that cause weight gain (e.g., sleep apnea, depression, etc.) or make weight loss hard (e.g., any chronic pain condition, joint disorders, etc.). Evidently, fatphobia can cause doctors to get turned around when following a causal link.

	PCOS
Yes	16%
No	64%
Not Sure	19%
N/A	1%

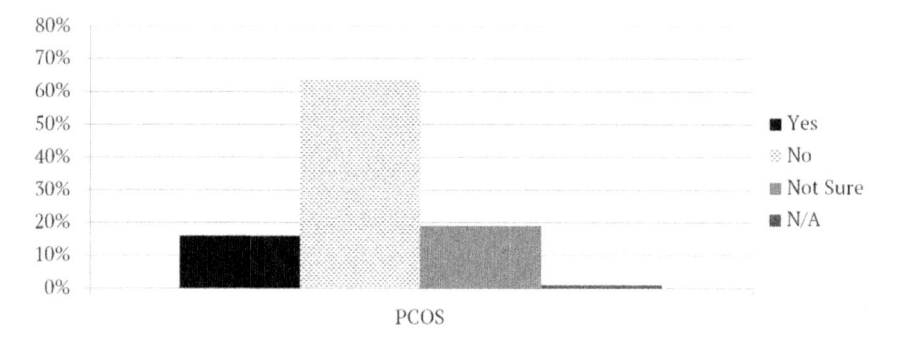

As I already discussed, due to the fact that these conditions are routinely under- or misdiagnosed, comparing the prevalence in the neurodivergent community and in the general population is a losing proposition. However, there is something else we can look at: the prevalence of these conditions in survey respondents who are getting different amounts of sleep.

	Whole Survey	Never sleep 7hrs	Often or always sleep 7hrs
Endometriosis	11%	19%	11%
Uterine fibroids	10%	11%	10%
Uterine polyps	5%	6%	4%
Fibrocystic breast disease	8%	9%	6%
PCOS	15%	21%	11%

[Bar chart showing prevalence percentages for Endometriosis, Uterine fibroids, Uterine polyps, Fibrocystic breast disease, and PCOS across three groups: Whole Survey, Never sleep 7hrs, and Often or always sleep 7hrs]

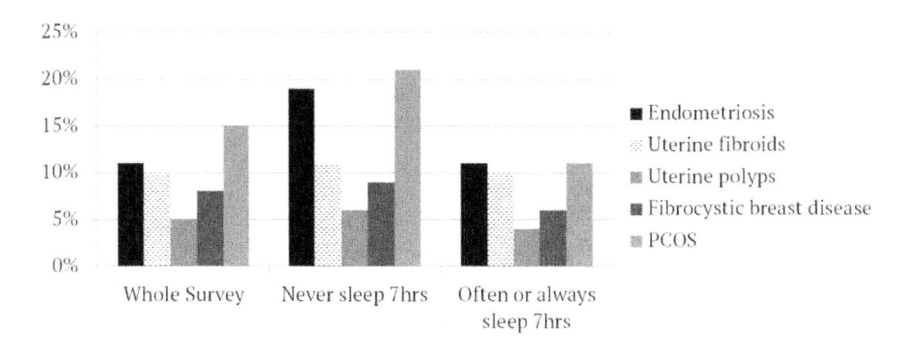

The prevalence of all of these conditions is highest in respondents who are never able to sleep at least 7 hours per night and lowest in those who often or always sleep at least 7 hours per night. These differences are most pronounced in endometriosis and PCOS. These results are not surprising given what we know about the impact of sleep deprivation on melatonin production and hormonal balance, and the link between hormonal balance and these conditions.

Relationships and trauma.

I lumped these two subjects together because, horrible as that might sound, they are all too often related. The questions were:

- Do you struggle to make new friends?
- Do you struggle to keep your friends?
- Do you struggle in your relationships with partners and relatives?
- Do you have a history of abusive or neglectful relationships?
- Were you bullied as a child?
- Are you bullied now?
- Do you have PTSD?
- Do you have symptoms caused by exposure to a traumatic event?
- Do you have cPTSD?
- Do you have symptoms caused by exposure to long-term trauma, abuse, or neglect?
- Do you experience intrusive thoughts?
- Do you experience repetitive thoughts that pop into your head without warning, at any time, and you cannot control?

Friendship is a bit of a contentious issue in the context of therapeutic interventions for neurodivergence. Not all neurodivergents are as gregarious as the average neurotypical, for a variety of reasons. We may have fewer friends than our peers, interact with them less often, prefer to interact with them one-on-one or in small groups rather than at larger gatherings, or prefer to interact online rather than in person. Depending on our diagnoses, these differences may be considered pathological by the "experts" responsible for our care. This is particularly true for children, who may be measured against arbitrary standards of socialization regardless of whether they enjoy certain forms of socializing. The goal of therapeutic interventions should be to help us achieve the quantity and quality of social contact that meets our needs; instead, some of them focus on making us go through the motions of socialization, regardless of whether we derive any satisfaction from doing so.

Not all neurodivergents want to be as gregarious as is expected of them.

By framing the question in terms of whether we struggle with friendship or not, I hope to have gathered results that reflect our dissatisfaction in this domain, rather than how well we meet some arbitrary standards.

	Struggle to make friends	Struggle to keep friends
Yes	72%	68%
No	23%	25%
Not Sure	5%	7%
N/A	0%	0%

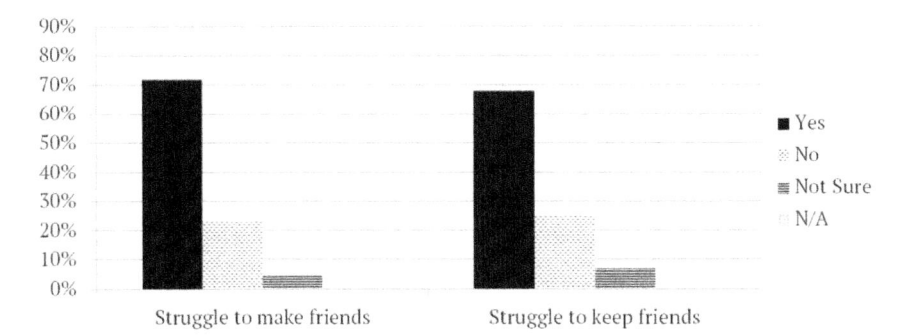

72% of respondents said that they struggle to make new friends, and 68% that they struggle to keep their friends. Now, there are no national statistics I can compare these values to, so I cannot categorically state that they are not "normal," but they do seem rather high.

Making and keeping friends requires a whole bunch of different personal qualities and skills. I could have reasonably tried to run correlations between these two questions and about half the questions in the survey. That would have been the end of me, though, so I consulted my personal ND hive mind, asked why they struggle to make and keep friends, and ran those correlations.

The results confirmed their thoughts on the subject. Aside from the correlation with Rejection Sensitive Dysphoria, which is discussed in the relevant chapter, the highest correlation is with a question about memory: "Do you forget that you own things if you put them out of sight?" Of the respondents who answered often or always, 74% struggle to make friends, and, 79% struggle to keep friends.

Other correlations came in much lower:
- 61% of those who struggle to make or keep friends have an interest or

passion that captures the majority of their interest and is not common for people of their age/gender/socioeconomic status

- 49% of those who struggle to make or keep friends struggle to identify or respond to phatic communication.
- 48% of those who struggle to make or keep friends have symptoms caused by exposure to long-term trauma, abuse, or neglect.
- 32% of those who struggle to make friends pretend to be someone else so people will like them, as do 31% of those who struggle to keep their friends.
- 23% of those who struggle to make friends struggle to recognize other people's feelings, as do 24% of those who struggle to keep their friends.

When looking at these results, it's important to remember that 94% of respondents were ADHDers, so our results are very much skewed. Other neurotypes may be affected by different issues, or by the same issues to a greater or lesser extent. For ADHDers, though, it looks like our inability to remember that things exist when we can't see them may extend to people. Forging and maintaining friendships requires a degree of contact. If we are constantly dropping the ball because we plumb forgot that X person exists, or that they sent us a message that we totally meant to answer but never actually got around to, that can't be helping us.

Other factors may also be in play. Sociologist Han Koehle coined the terms "social pitcher plant" in reference to those who are capable of keeping friends if said friends come along, but cannot go forth and catch them, so to speak.[37] This is likely to be of particular significance to those of us who, for whatever reason, find it hard to meet or interact with new people. Koehle also coined the term "friendship bottom" for those who enjoy being at the receiving end of friendship and are happy to reciprocate it, but are not comfortable taking a dominant role in the relationship.

The next question didn't quite go as planned, for hilarious reasons. I was planning to see whether there is a correlation between the relationships we have with our family of origin and the relationships we form as adults. Unfortunately, my lysdexia had other plans. Instead of asking people whether they struggle in their relationships with PARENTS

---

[37] Please note that digesting said friends is generally considered a no-no.

and relatives, I asked about PARTNERS and relatives. Oops.

	Struggle in relationships with partners and relatives	A history of abusive or neglectful relationships
Yes	70%	59%
No	25%	35%
Not Sure	5%	6%
N/A	0%	0%

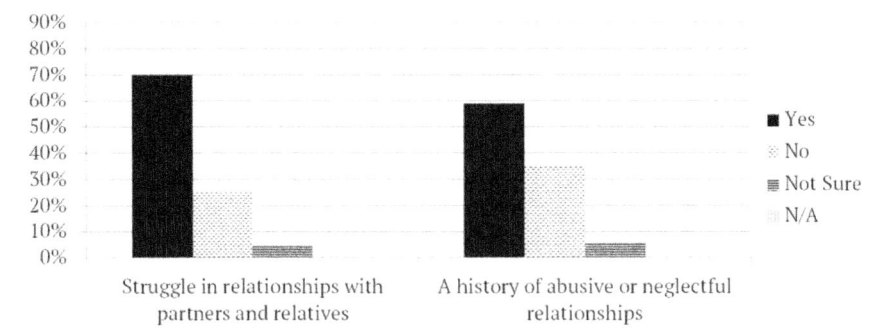

70% of respondents struggle in relationships with partners and relatives, and 59% have a history of abusive or neglectful relationships. These variables are subjective, and available statistics about the prevalence of these issues in the general population vary wildly depending on the metrics used. As a result, running comparisons with "official" statistics would be almost pointless. None of this should detract from the results themselves, though, because these numbers suck. They really do.

Correlation-wise, 68% of those who struggle in relationships with partners and relatives also have a history of abusive or neglectful relationships, and 80% of those with a history of abusive or neglectful relationships also struggle in relationships with partners and relatives. Unfortunately, this doesn't tell us as much at it might have done if I had formulated the question correctly.

If you are personally affected by these issues, please remember: your neurodivergence isn't doing this. It takes two people to have a good relationship, but it only takes one person to make a relationship go to hell. And being neurodivergent doesn't make you the designated person-at-fault here.

We can be ND and have neglectful, abusive, or just plain shitty parents.

We can be ND and have incompatible, unsupportive, or abusive partners. We can be ND and have exploitative bosses. We can be ND and have unsupportive or backstabbing colleagues. We can be ND and be at the receiving end of literally every kind of mistreatment: physical abuse, intimate partner violence, sexual abuse, psychological or emotional abuse, financial or material abuse, discriminatory abuse, organizational or institutional abuse, and literally everything else. We can be ND and find ourselves in dire straits because of socio-demographic variables utterly outside of our control. We can also be ND and have literally any ailment, injury, or condition. The only thing being ND makes us immune to is neurotypicality.

Neurodivergence doesn't stop bad things from happening to and around us, and it doesn't cause all of them, either. Our neurodivergence might be a contributing factor, to be sure, but it doesn't mean that we are magically responsible for everyone else's thoughts, feelings, words, or actions. We might be klutzy, ditzy, flaky, socially inept, and so on and so forth, but that doesn't mean that every bad thing people do to us is our fault. Our fallibilities do not obliterate other people's personal responsibility, and to say otherwise is not just ableism; it's victim blaming. And yes, it's still victim blaming if we say it about ourselves.

The same concept applies to the next subject: being bullied. **Bullying** is unwanted physical or verbal aggression directed at a specific person, repeated over a period, involving an imbalance of power, and aimed at excluding the victim from a group.

Neurodivergent traits may make us more likely to be picked on by bullies because many bullies are attracted to anyone who behaves or looks different from the norm. That doesn't mean that we get bullied because we are neurodivergent, though. We get bullied because bullies want to bully people, and we make convenient targets. The responsibility for the bullying sits entirely with the bullies.

	Bullied as a child	**Bullied now**
Yes	78%	8%
No	18%	85%
Not Sure	3%	7%
N/A	0%	0%

[Chart: Bar chart showing "Bullied as a child" and "Bullied now" with legend: Yes, No, Not Sure, N/A]

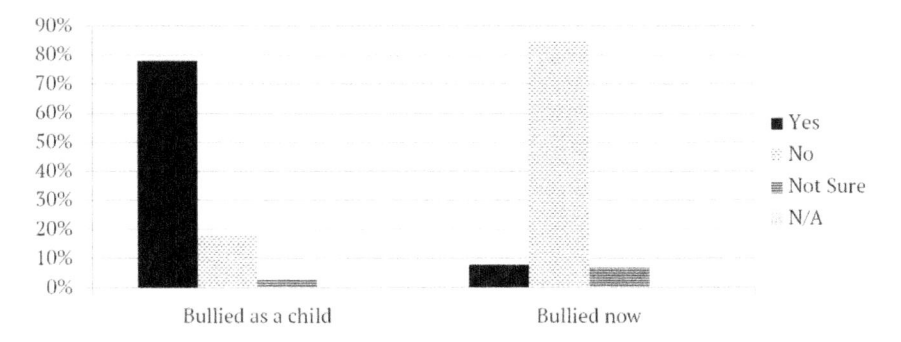

78% of respondents were bullied as children. 8% of respondents are still bullied now. Of these, 93% were also bullied as children. As correlations go, that's pretty damn high.

Statistics about bullying are subject to similar caveats as those about abusive or neglectful relationships. Worse, they rely on people reporting that they are being bullied, and that's not something everyone is willing or able to do. Unless the bullying has been so egregious that it would cause the bully to be removed from the situation, reporting can carry serious risks of retaliation. Furthermore, zero-tolerance policies in schools and workplaces can actually prevent people from reporting acts of violence. If the policy is that anyone who has taken part in a physical altercation is at fault, regardless of who started it, all parties will be punished. That punishment is likely to be more of a deterrent for people who are concerned about their reputation as good people; therefore, it is more of a punishment for the victims than for the bullies.

These caveats notwithstanding, we do have some estimates about the prevalence of bullying in the general population. This problem is believed to affect 20% to 46% of schoolchildren. While these numbers are a bit shaky, there is no arguing that 78% is a hell of a lot higher than 46%. Therefore, these results suggest that there may be a correlation between being neurodivergent and being bullied. If anyone is surprised by this, then they don't understand either issue.

The results for adults are more surprising. Estimate for the prevalence of adult bullying in the general population are as high as 40%. So, neurodivergent people may actually be bullied less than our neurotypical counterparts. However, this could have less to do with how often people try to bully us, and more with how thick-skinned we grew to be through sheer practice. Many workplaces do not allow their staff the same degree of latitude one might enjoy in school, and the consequences of being reported for bullying can be far more severe. If we get so accustomed to people mistreating us that we learn to ignore anything short of a physical assault, this can make us effectively impregnable to any bully not willing to go that far.

Developing a skin that thick takes time and practice, though, and is neither risk-free nor cost-free. Bullying isn't just unpleasant; it is a serious social issue that can lead to negative performance and health outcomes. Bullying shows a negative correlation with academic and job performance – i.e., when we are bullied, our performance suffers. Bullying also results in higher rates of absenteeism and people quitting their school or job. Bullied people who stick it out are at elevated risk of stress, anxiety, depression, loss of confidence, sleep loss, headaches, muscle tension, chronic pain, mental breakdowns, and burnout. Depending on what it involves and how long it goes on for, bullying can also result in PTSD or cPTSD.

Post-traumatic stress disorder (PTSD) is an anxiety disorder caused by exposure to a traumatic event. By contrast, **complex post-traumatic stress disorder** (cPTSD) results from exposure to long-term trauma, abuse, or neglect. PTSD is a recognized diagnosis. cPTSD is not currently included in the DSM-5 (The Diagnostic and Statistical Manual of Mental Disorders), but it is included in the ICD-11 (International Classification of Diseases), and is becoming more widely recognized by doctors.

The symptoms of these conditions are similar, and can include:

- Re-experiencing events as flashbacks or nightmares.
- Intrusive thoughts about the events.
- Hyperarousal – constantly being on alert.
- Sleeping problems, such as insomnia.
- Difficulties concentrating.
- Somatic symptoms – physical symptoms related to trauma triggers that don't have any underlying medical cause.
- New, negative beliefs and feelings about the self and others.
- Avoidance of certain situations.
- Artificial, compulsive distractions, ranging from the excessive performance of constructive activities (e.g. overworking or overtraining) to the use of substances or self-harm.

After being exposed to a traumatic event, it's natural to experience some emotional repercussions. These are not indicative of a traumatic stress disorder. For a diagnosis of PTSD/cPTSD to be applicable, symptoms must be severe and persistent enough to have a significant impact on the person's day-to-day life.

Anyone can develop a traumatic stress disorder. However, there are risk factors that increase the chances of this, including pre-existing mental health conditions (e.g. anxiety or depression) and the lack of a support system. Resilience factors, on the other hand, reduce the likelihood of developing a traumatic stress disorder. These include being prepared and able to respond to a traumatic event and having coping strategies for getting through and learning from the experience. In essence, we are more likely to develop a traumatic stress disorder when we lack the resources to respond to or recover from traumatic events.

Neurodivergence per se is not a cause of trauma. However, being neurodivergent in a neurotypical world can result in greater chances of being at the receiving end of abuse and neglect, particularly during childhood. This is due to systemic failures in accommodating the basic needs of neurodivergent children (neglect) and increased chances of being targeted by bullies and predators (abuse). For those of us whose families' love and care is conditional upon our constant mimicking of neurotypical behaviors, these issues are compounded: not only we have to endure the stress of maintaining a neurotypical persona in order to receive the care and love we need, but we cannot rely on our families to support and comfort us when we struggle. In fact, our failures to meet neurotypical demands may result in punishment.

In this section, I did my usual trick and asked about each issue twice, first by label, and then by description. This was not a waste of effort, as respondents answered the two questions differently.

	PTSD	Symptoms caused by a traumatic event	cPTSD	Symptoms caused by long-term trauma
Yes	35%	49%	25%	45%
No	35%	31%	35%	36%
Not Sure	30%	20%	40%	20%
N/A	0%	0%	0%	0%

[Chart showing percentages for PTSD, Symptoms caused by a traumatic event, cPTSD, and Symptoms caused by long-term trauma, with categories Yes, No, Not Sure, N/A]

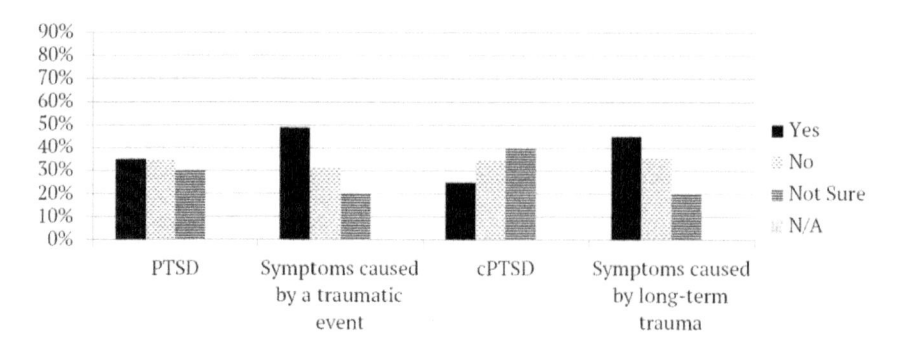

35% of respondents said that they have PTSD, while 49% said that they have symptoms caused by exposure to a traumatic event. Similarly, 25% of respondents said that they have cPTSD, while 45% said that they have symptoms caused by exposure to long-term trauma, abuse, or neglect. 54% of those with PTSD also have cPTSD, while 69% of those with symptoms of PTSD also have cPTSD.

These differences aren't necessarily the result of a lack of information; a person may have *some* symptoms of PTSD or cPTSD, but not enough to qualify for a diagnosis, or to consider themselves as suffering from these conditions. I think these differences should be considered when drafting future surveys, and the questions worded in order to reveal the information we are looking for. What are we interested in, whether people have these conditions, or whether they have suffered trauma that has left them with long-term symptoms?

Either way, these values are horrendously high. Official statistics about PTSD are somewhat shaky as different medical systems use different criteria, and there is no knowing how many people live with the condition without ever reporting it, but its prevalence is currently estimated at 3.5-9.2%. Statistics about cPTSD are even shakier as the condition isn't recognized by all doctors, but its prevalence is currently estimated at 0.5-7.7%. According to these figures, we are roughly five times more likely to experience symptoms of PTSD or cPTSD than the general population. So, yeah, this isn't great.

It isn't a great mystery, though. Like bullying, PTSD and cPTSD are most likely to affect those who don't have the resources to fight against them. The connection between these issues runs deeper, though: when we look at the correlation between bullying in childhood and PTSD and cPTSD, we find that 86% of respondents with PTSD were bullied, as were 85% of those with symptoms caused by exposure to a traumatic event., and 88% of those with cPTSD and those with symptoms caused by exposure to long-term trauma, abuse, or neglect. It could be that these results are directly connected, and the bullying itself caused the PTSD or cPTSD. It could also be that the same risk factors contributed to people being bullied and developing post-traumatic symptoms. These statements are not mutually exclusive, and both could be true.

The next section looked at something that can be a symptom of PTSD or cPTSD, of mental health conditions such as anxiety, depression, or obsessive-compulsive disorder (OCD), or exist on its own: **intrusive thoughts**. These are unwanted thoughts that pop into our heads without warning, at any time, and that we cannot switch off at will.

Intrusive thoughts are often repetitive and can be disturbing or even distressing. They can be about any subject – worries about doing something inappropriate or embarrassing, disturbing or violent ideas, distressing memories, or just random stuff. Everyone has them from time to time, and they are usually harmless. However, if they occur so often that they interfere with our day-to-day activities or severely affect our mood, this could be a sign of an underlying mental health condition.

Unfortunately, I fudged this section as I only allowed this question to have yes/no answers. Therefore, the results do not tell us how often respondents experience intrusive thoughts.

	Intrusive thoughts	**Repetitive, uncontrollable thoughts**
Yes	78%	73%
No	15%	20%
Not Sure	6%	8%
N/A	0%	0%

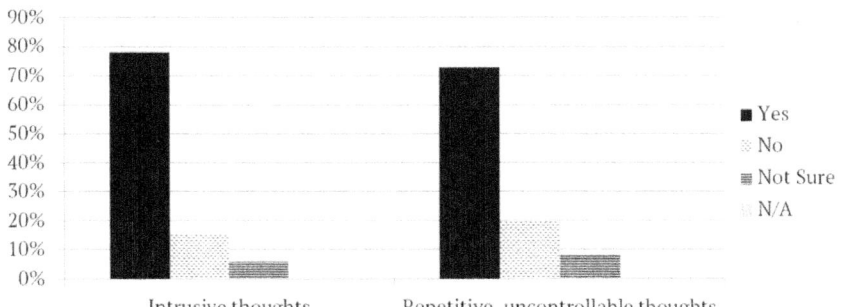

78% of respondents stated that they experience intrusive thoughts, and 73% that they experience repetitive thoughts that pop into their head without warning, at any time, and they cannot control. As these results are too vague to be useful, I won't dissect them further.

Mental health.

With the exception of dissociation, PTSD, and cPTSD, the survey did not include any questions about mental health. This omission raised a lot of queries and quite a few complaints. There were several reasons why I didn't cover this topic, and it's not because it isn't relevant – quite the opposite, in fact. Mental health issues are rife within the neurodivergent community. However, disentangling whether these issues are caused by mental distress or mental health conditions is not always straightforward.

Let's take anxiety and depression as examples. Many of us are anxious and depressed, which can lead doctors to assume that we have anxiety and depression. However, that's not always the case. Being neurodivergent in a neurotypical world provides us with plenty of reasons to feel anxious and depressed. Constantly underperforming is stressful and depressing. Being punished for things outside of our control is stressful and depressing. Going into situations when experience teaches us that we will probably mess up, no matter how hard we try, is stressful and depressing. Constantly repressing our basic physical needs is stressful and depressing. Hiding our real self in the vain hope of gaining social acceptance is exhausting, isolating, stressful, and depressing.

That doesn't mean that we *have* anxiety and depression – as in, our "symptoms" could be the natural response to our situation, rather than the result of a neurochemical imbalance or inaccurate and unhelpful thinking patterns. If that is the case, trying to medicate us or talk us out of our feelings is unlikely to work, and could make matters worse.

This problem is particularly obvious in the case of Cognitive Behavioral Therapy (CBT), a talking therapy that aims to teach patients to change the way they think and behave. The basic principle of CBT is that our thoughts, feelings, physical sensations, and actions are interconnected. When that connection works to our disadvantage, we can take steps to address that. For instance, we might find that faulty ways of thinking have a negative impact on our feelings, or that learned patterns of behavior steer us towards inappropriate actions. In essence, we are all creatures of mental, emotional, and behavioral habits; by changing these habits, we may improve our life.

CBT works for a lot of people and makes good scientific sense. However, it has one major pitfall: its practitioners do not always take the time to check the accuracy of their patients' "negative" thoughts, or the appropriateness of "unhelpful" behaviors in their personal context. This problem is not unique to CBT; therapists using other techniques are just as likely to fail to investigate the accuracy of their patients' concerns, particularly when such concerns are totally alien to them. This becomes particularly critical when patients are disabled, marginalized, or oppressed, and their therapists are not.

A therapist unfamiliar with the impact of neurodivergence on daily life may believe that their neurodivergent patients are showing signs of paranoia when they discuss instances of discrimination or ostracism, or signs of unfounded anxiety when they raise concerns about the health of their relationships, their financial security, or their ability to navigate adulthood and its responsibilities. When those patients are also marginalized and oppressed in other ways, uninformed therapists may understand them even less; if they are unaware of the impact of single discriminations and disadvantages, negotiating intersectionality is going to be completely beyond them. The issue is further compounded when therapists hold unexamined biases; until they accept their own part in the problem, they will be unable to admit that it has a real, negative impact on the lives of their patients. The bottom line is that until therapists become aware of the impact of disability, marginalization, and oppression, they will not be able to fully support their disabled, marginalized, and oppressed patients.

This disconnect is particularly significant in CBT, because CBT works by teaching people to change their way of thinking. Unhelpful, incorrect, negative thoughts should be replaced with helpful, accurate, positive thoughts. The problem is that not all negative thoughts are incorrect. A patient may think that their colleagues find them weird, and be right. They might think that their family members love them but do not like them, and be right. They might think that their boss only tolerates them because they work twice as hard as everyone else, and that if they ever stopped driving themself into the ground they'd be fired, and be right. They might not be able to provide proof for any of this, though, because most people don't say stuff like that out loud; but that doesn't mean that they are wrong. Insisting that they are, and that their life would magically fix itself if only they could think about it differently, is gaslighting – a form of persistent brainwashing that causes the victim to doubt themself, their perceptions, their sanity, and their self-worth. Needless to say, that's not what most people look for in a therapeutic intervention.

Similar concerns apply to the behavioral aspect of CBT. Some habits that are deemed inappropriate or unhelpful are actually adaptations to a particular situation or environment. A person might have learned to be "excessively" restrained around their colleagues because letting their neurodivergence show has caused them problems in the past. They might have learned to "overplan" and "overthink" because when they don't, they mess up, and their mistakes are too expensive. They might behave differently from their therapists simply because they belong to a different culture or subculture, with different criteria for what is "normal." Therapists who are unfamiliar with the social milieu of their patients and don't take the time to investigate it might push for behavioral changes that would be maladaptive.

As I said, this is not a problem unique to CBT. It is also not a problem inherent to CBT; the issue is not with the practice itself, but with individual therapists and their unwillingness to listen to and learn from their patients' experiences. Unfortunately, though, this issue seems very pervasive in not only in CBT and other therapies, but also in medicine and research.

Personally, I have yet to see a mental health assessment that takes into account the fact that different people live different lives that present them with different challenges and different risks. I touched on this issue in the section on environmental sensitivities, but many other factors can have similar implications. Anything that increases our risks is likely to increase our anxiety in certain situations, and while that might have an impact on our mental health, it isn't primarily a mental health issue. Anything that increases our discomfort is likely to increase our unhappiness and decrease our enthusiasm, and that's also not primarily a mental health issue. For instance, chronic pain and fatigue can make us feel depressed, and over time can lead to actual depression, but attempting to treat our mood without addressing its cause is a losing proposition. The same goes for attempting to overcome our reluctance to engage in certain activities without addressing the fact that we might find them excruciatingly painful or simply impossible to access. And this is just an easy example of a pervasive issue.

Then there's another issue: many of us cultivate atypical behavioral and mental habits as coping mechanisms. For instance, we might engage in repetitive behaviors that might resemble OCD, because we need to check several times that we haven't lost or forgotten something. We might awfulize the consequences of the slightest failures to keep ourselves on track, use last-minute panic as a boost to overcome our executive dysfunction, over-plan to make up for what we might forget or mess up, and generally live in a constant state of tension. We may also be so paralyzed by the potential consequences of speaking or acting inappropriately that we stop ourselves from speaking or acting at all.

We learn these behaviors growing up, and we might never consider them problematic because, from a practical point of view, they work. The anxious schoolchild who stays up all night to study may get good grades. The child so paralyzed by social anxiety that they hardly speak beyond the most structured formalities may be considered a paragon of politeness and a credit to their family. The employee who is so terrified of not being good enough that they constantly overwork may be praised for their achievements. The person who overthinks, overplans, oversaves may reach retirement in a better financial position than many of their cohort. The problem is that all these achievements come at a cost: we end up living our lives as a constant, enervating struggle for performance. And if that wasn't depressing in and off itself, there's the fact that no matter how hard we try, we still mess up sometimes.

Over time, we might develop better, healthier coping mechanisms and be able to jettison the old, unhealthy ones. For many of us, that happens when we finally get diagnosed or get constructive support. Sometimes, however, unhealthy coping mechanisms can become entrenched habits which may persist way past the point when they stop being useful. At that point, treating them as mental health issues makes perfect sense. Until then, however, I'd argue that treating the underlying problems would be a better bet.

There is another reason why I omitted mental health from this survey: it was already very long. While this was unavoidable in order to include all the subjects I wanted to cover, it made the survey inaccessible to some would-be participants who either refused to engage with it because of its size, or gave up during it because they ran out of oomph. Adding mental health would have hugely increased the size of the survey, particularly if I wanted to try and disentangle symptoms of distress, coping mechanisms, and actual mental health conditions. And, to be honest, I am not confident that a standardized survey could do that.

Lastly, there are nearly 300 mental disorders listed in the DSM-5 (Diagnostic and Statistical Manual of Mental Disorders), and we can have any of them. The only thing our neurodivergence makes us immune to is neurotypicality. I could have included the most common co-occurring conditions – anxiety and depression – but I didn't really see the point.

These conditions are so prevalent that they deserve a study of their own. I would argue that the study should focus on the societal changes that might prevent us from developing these conditions, because that might actually *help us*, but I have lost the ability to be that optimistic.

Stress.

I did not ask about stress in this survey because it is too vague a concept. Different people have different ideas of what it means, so a comparison between results would be very difficult. However, I asked about a lot of stressors and about a lot of diseases that are known to be affected by stress. Their incidence should be enough to inform us as to the level of stress our community is affected by.

Stress is a state of threatened homeostasis provoked by a psychological, environmental, or physiological stressor – i.e., our bodies go temporarily out of whack in response to a threat. This isn't a bug in the system: our bodies are designed to activate a bunch of physiological changes designed to help us deal with the threat. These changes include the release of a bunch of neurotransmitters and hormones.

One of the better-known chemicals released during this kind of event is adrenaline; in fact, many popular sources talk about the "adrenaline dump" as a shorthand for the sudden chemical change we experience when under threat. I will do so here.

Adrenaline dumps affect both our bodies and our minds. You might have heard stories about people who have managed amazing feats in emergencies: lifting cars off children, rescuing people from burning buildings, and so on. However, for most of us, most of the time, adrenaline is not a source of superpowers. In fact, an adrenaline dump can negatively affect our perceptions and reactions, making us unable to respond effectively to dangerous or stressful situations. These changes include:

- Increased heart rate and blood pressure.
- Increased speed and strength.
- Decreased sensitivity to pain.
- Decreased co-ordination, in particular fine motor skills.
- Decreases blood flow to the surface of the skin.
- Tunnel vision.
- Impaired or reduced hearing.
- Clouded thinking.
- Misperception of time (everything slows down).
- Repetitive behavior loops (e.g. repeating the same sentence or

movement, regardless of whether it's working).

As you can probably guess, this doesn't always work out great for us. It really depends on the situation. If we are trying to fend off a hungry wolverine that has attached itself to our leg, being able to repeatedly hit it harder and faster than we normally could, without being distracted by our pain or our environment, while bleeding less than usual, can give us enough of an edge to survive the encounter.[38] If we are trying to deal with a different type of threat, however, being temporarily incapable of hearing, seeing, thinking, and moving properly might not work to our advantage. What saved our ancestors gathering food in the savanna might not help us do our shopping in the supermarket.

Unfortunately, our bodies don't know that. They have been honed over millennia to deal with threats a certain way, because it kept our ancestors alive. Even though our environments and demands have changed, our bodies will continue to work as they are designed to do, whether we like it or not.

Having said that, it is possible for us to train for a greater degree of control during adrenaline dumps. Targeted training can help us recognize the effects of adrenaline, to accept them as normal, and to manage them as well as possible. This can help us function more efficiently in stressful situations, and it is why we can have professional paramedics, surgeons, firefighters, and so on: they work hard to learn to be calm and competent in the middle of situations that would send most of us into a spin. The process requires effective training and exposure, combined with good results. Over a period of time, it can increase competence and confidence under stress. Increased competence and confidence decrease the stress response, creating a positive feedback loop.

However, the results of this training aren't always transferrable. Even those of us who successfully learn to deal with one set of stressors might be unable to deal with another – for instance, a surgeon might find themself at the mercy of an out-of-control adrenaline dump when faced with a burning building. And none of this can help us if we do not have the opportunity to learn how to manage our adrenaline dumps in an environment where we can succeed. Success is essential to the process, because it's essential to building our confidence. Repeatedly being dumped in situations where we fail to achieve a goal while adrenalized is

---

[38] Please, do not test this theory.

not going to help us.

Also, this cannot help us when our stress is chronic – or, rather, it might help us manage our response to adrenaline, but it might not affect our response to the rest of the neurochemicals, neurotransmitters, and hormones that our body is chucking at us. Over time, the chemical out-of-whackness that is the normal and natural response to stressors can make us very sick, or even kill us.

Stress is currently believed to be a risk factor for 75% to 90% of diseases, including cardiovascular diseases, metabolic diseases, neurodegenerative disorders, cancer, mental health conditions, and a whole bunch of fun stuff. It can also interfere with our immune system, increasing our susceptibility to contagious diseases. The mechanisms for these effects have not been established yet, but they are currently believed to involve cortisol, the primary stress hormone.

Cortisol has a whole bunch of far-ranging effects on the body. For instance, it increases blood sugar levels, alters immune system responses, and suppresses the digestive and reproductive systems. It also affects the brain regions that control mood, motivation, and fear. Cortisol isn't bad for us, the same way that adrenaline isn't bad for us; what hurts us is being exposed to elevated cortisol levels for prolonged periods of time.

The body's stress response is supposed to be a short-term affair. Once a threat has passed, our hormone levels return to normal, and so do our body's functions. When stressors are always present, however, our body doesn't have a chance to return to normality. The long-term activation of the stress response system and the resulting overexposure to cortisol and other stress hormones can disrupt almost all our body's processes. And this can make us very sick indeed.

Now, it is true that different people may handle stressors differently; what turns me into a gibbering mess might hardly affect you, and vice versa. Our ability to handle our stressors will depend on a number of factors, including genetic predisposition, past life experiences, and current circumstances. However, it's unarguable that most people find it easier to avoid becoming stressed when they are exposed to fewer stressors. Anything that increases exposure to stressors increases our risks of becoming stressed. Prolonged exposure to stressors increases our risk of prolonged stress. And prolonged stress increases our chances of developing a number of diseases.

This is relevant here because some neurodivergences have an effect on the stressors we face. Sometimes, this is a direct effect; for instance, if we have a number of environmental sensitivities or allergies, every trigger is a potential stressor. Sometimes the causal chain is a bit longer; for instance, if we can reliably anticipate that something bad will happen to us if we do X, because every time we do X something bad happens to us, then doing X will be a stressor. Being naturally predisposed to messing stuff up, being misunderstood, or failing to meet our regular demands are all sources of stressors.

Ultimately, anything that makes us different from the norm is a potential stressor – or, more accurately, increases our chance of being exposed to stressors. This isn't because being different is inherently bad, but because it is so often punished, overtly or covertly.

If we look, speak, move, or act differently from the majority of other people, we are more likely to find ourselves at the receiving end of negative social repercussions. Most of the times, for most of us, these won't put us in physical danger, but that doesn't have as big an impact on our stress levels as some might guess. Humans are social animals, designed to survive in groups. As far as our brains are concerned, anything that threatens our chances of belonging to a group is a threat to our survival. Social exclusion and isolation might not kill us, but they would have killed the vast majority of our ancestors, so they register as significant threats. And being constantly exposed to these threats can make us unwell.

While learning not to care about everyone's opinion is a valuable skill, learning to tolerate being disliked by the majority is a whole other story. Humans are just not designed for that. As a result, any trait that puts us at risk of widespread social rejection forces us to make a choice: do we hide that aspect of ourselves to gain a modicum of acceptance, or do we face the risk of ostracism? Both of these choices carry significant costs, and both can cause us chronic stress.

This issue has been shown to affect sexual and gender minorities, who are at higher risk of lower immune responses and chronic inflammation, which can lead to a variety of ailments. I don't believe any studies have been carried out about the impact of neurodivergences per se on our stress levels, but I would be very surprised if the conclusions were different.

Crisis points.

This section looked at ways in which people react if they are forced to endure sensorily, socially, or emotionally overwhelming situations. The questions were:

- Do you experience meltdowns?
- Do you have intense physical or emotional responses to overwhelming situations? (i.e., you become unable to control your own body or speech.)
- Do you experience shutdowns?
- Do you become unresponsive or stop processing information in response to overwhelming situations?
- Do you have selective mutism?
- Do you become temporarily unable to speak in response to stressful social situations or when your senses are overwhelmed by your environment? (e.g., in crowded places.)
- Do you experience burnouts?
- If you become overtaxed by your obligations, do you experience periods of fatigue, heightened stress, and diminished capacity to cope with daily life?

Meltdowns, shutdowns, and selective mutism are three reactions to overwhelming situations. They are typically associated with Autism, but they also affect other neurotypes.

In a **meltdown**, people experience a temporary loss of control that can be expressed as verbal and/or physical reactions: shouting, screaming, crying, kicking, hitting, biting, self-harm, and so on. A meltdown is not a temper tantrum; it's a fight response.

In a **shutdown**, people still experience a temporary loss of control, but this is manifested as withdrawal and inaction. They may lose the ability to process information, communicate, respond to stimuli, move, stand, and so on. A shutdown is not a refusal to participate; it's a freeze response.

Selective mutism is a rather unfortunate term, as it suggests an element of choice that is wholly absent from the phenomenon. People experiencing selective mutism become temporarily unable to speak. They might be able to think of what they want to say, but just cannot say it at that point. Selective mutism isn't stonewalling; it's a freeze response that takes away a person's ability to speak.

These three responses occur when a person is exposed to triggers they cannot avoid or escape. Different people have different triggers; for instance, they may be triggered by certain sensory experiences, by certain social situations, by changes in routine, and so on. However, virtually anything can be a trigger. Triggers can be highly personal; if something routinely triggers meltdowns in a person, then it is a meltdown trigger for that person, regardless of how other people respond to it.

People have no control whatsoever over what triggers them, or over how much exposure to the trigger they can tolerate before they go into crisis mode. Once the meltdown/shutdown/episode of selective mutism has started, they do not have the power to stop it or control it. However, many people go through a warning stage before an episode starts; in this stage, they may manifest their distress, engage in self-soothing behaviors (aka stims), or try to leave the area. If they aren't able to self-soothe or leave and the trigger is not removed, an episode will ensue.

	Meltdowns	Intense physical or emotional responses when overwhelmed
Never	16%	26%
Sometimes	61%	46%
Often	17%	20%
Always	2%	6%
Not sure	4%	2%

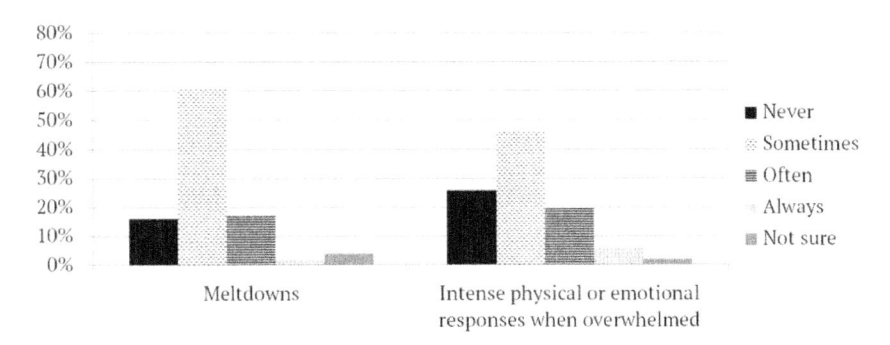

19% of respondents reported that they often or always have meltdowns, while 26% reported that they often or always have intense physical or emotional responses to overwhelming situations. Without making further inquiries, I cannot tell what caused this discrepancy. It could be because people are unfamiliar with the term, because they believe meltdowns to only affect Autistic people, because their reactions are not energetic enough for them to label them as meltdowns, or many other reasons.

As for the connection between Autism and meltdowns, 40% of respondents who experience meltdowns are Autistic, as are 43% of those who have intense physical or emotional responses to overwhelming situations. These numbers may seem high, but they still leave well over half of respondents who have meltdowns unaccounted for.

Aside from Autism, a number of other factors correlated with an increase in the prevalence of meltdowns. These included:

- Being routinely forced to endure unpleasant or overwhelming physical sensations in order to navigate your environment;
- Forcing oneself to stop self-soothing behaviors in order to avoid getting told off;
- Redirecting repetitive behaviors to less noticeable ones to look more "normal";
- Increased need to make repetitive or unusual movements when under stress;
- Doing things you'd rather not so people will like you;
- Pretending to be someone else so people will like you;
- In childhood, getting into trouble for having "tantrums"• when one was trying to avoid painful physical sensations;
- In childhood, being forced by parents or teachers to endure painful physical sensations in order to learn to get over them (labelled as "desensitized" – why this kind of intervention is not desensitization is explained in details in the relevant section.)

The greatest increase in the prevalence of meltdowns is shown in respondents who are routinely forced to endure unpleasant or overwhelming physical sensations in order to navigate their environment. This is unsurprising, as being exposed to more triggers is likely to result in more meltdowns.

The second largest increase is shown in respondents whom, as children, were forced by parents or teachers to endure painful physical sensation in order to learn to get over them. If you hark back a the section about emotional regulation, these "desensitization therapies" correlate with a higher prevalence of rapid, pronounced changes in mood with very little reason, struggles to control one's behavior when experiencing strong emotions, and getting in trouble for behaving impulsively when emotional. It looks like their effects also increase the likelihood of the affected people experiencing meltdowns when they hit crisis mode.

	Have meltdowns	Intense physical or emotional responses when overwhelmed
Whole survey	19%	26%
Autistic	24%	37%
Routinely forced to endure unpleasant or overwhelming physical sensations in order to navigate their environment	39%	53%
Force themselves to stop their self-soothing behaviors in order to avoid getting told off	29%	41%
Redirect repetitive behaviors to less noticeable ones to look more "normal"	25%	35%
Need to make repetitive or unusual movements increases under stress	25%	35%
Do things you'd rather not so people will like you	27%	33%
Pretend to be someone else so people will like you	31%	37%
Punished for "tantrums"	31%	44%
"Desensitized"	36%	51%

The responses to the questions about shutdowns show a different pattern, and I don't quite know why. 32% of respondents said that they often or always experience shutdowns, but only 19% that they often or always become unresponsive or stop processing information in response to overwhelming situations. I can only surmise that the problem lies in the wording of the questions, but why that is I cannot guess.

	Shutdowns	Unresponsive or stop processing information when overwhelmed
Never	16%	48%
Sometimes	44%	30%
Often	27%	13%
Always	5%	7%
Not sure	7%	3%

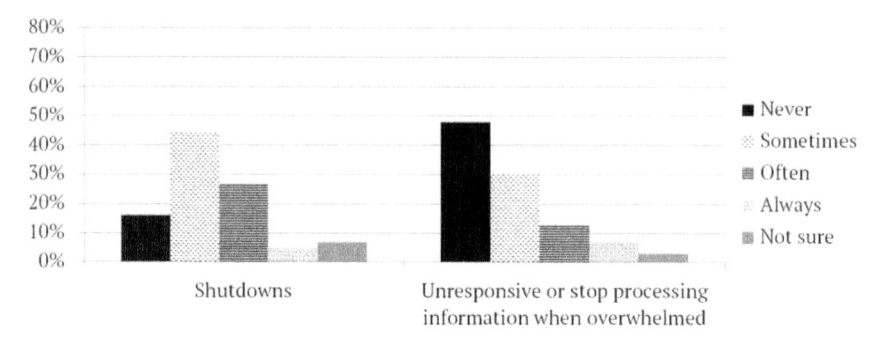

As for the connection between Autism and shutdowns, 46% of respondents who experience shutdowns are Autistic, as are 44% of those who become unresponsive or stop processing information in response to overwhelming situations.

The factors that correlate with an increase prevalence of meltdowns also correlate with an increase prevalence of shutdowns. As with meltdowns, the greatest increases in the prevalence of shutdowns is shown in respondents who are routinely forced to endure unpleasant or overwhelming physical sensations in order to navigate their environment. The second largest increase is shown in respondents who, when they were children, were forced by parents or teachers to endure painful physical sensation in order to learn to get over them.

	Shutdowns	Unresponsive or stop processing information when overwhelmed
Whole survey	32%	19%
Autistic	48%	54%
Routinely forced to endure unpleasant or overwhelming physical sensations in order to navigate their environment	55%	61%
Force themselves to stop their self-soothing behaviors in order to avoid getting told off	44%	52%
Redirect repetitive behaviors to less noticeable ones to look more "normal"	43%	48%
Need to make repetitive or unusual movements increases under stress	40%	46%
Do things you'd rather not so people will like you	42%	47%
Pretend to be someone else so people will like you	43%	51%
Punished for "tantrums"	52%	58%
"Desensitized"	53%	58%

Selective mutism is not as prevalent as meltdowns and shutdowns: only 10% of respondents often or always have selective mutism, and 19% often or always become temporarily unable to speak in response to stressful social situations or when their senses are overwhelmed by their environment. 54% of the former are Autistic, as are 49% of the latter.

	Selective mutism	Temporarily unable to speak when overwhelmed
Never	53%	48%
Sometimes	18%	30%
Often	7%	13%
Always	3%	7%
Not sure	18%	3%

[Chart showing Selective mutism and Temporarily unable to speak when overwhelmed with categories: Never, Sometimes, Often, Always, Not sure]

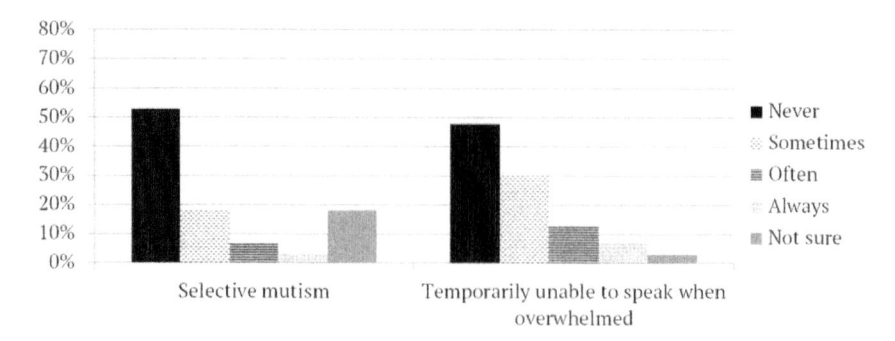

The factors that correlate with an increase prevalence of meltdowns and shutdowns also correlate with an increase prevalence of selective mutism. At the risk of repeating myself, forcing children to endure painful physical sensation in the name of desensitization is bad. It's really bad.

	Selective mutism	**Unable to speak when overwhelmed**
Whole survey	10%	19%
Autistic	18%	31%
Routinely forced to endure unpleasant or overwhelming physical sensations in order to navigate their environment	25%	**43%**
Force themselves to stop their self-soothing behaviors in order to avoid getting told off	17%	29%
Redirect repetitive behaviors to less noticeable ones to look more "normal"	16%	27%
Need to make repetitive or unusual movements increases under stress	13%	26%
Do things you'd rather not so people will like you	15%	27%
Pretend to be someone else so people will like you	18%	30%
Punished for "tantrums"	20%	34%
"Desensitized"	23%	**39%**

Burnout is a different, but related issue. It's a reaction to prolonged exposure to stressful or triggering situations without the ability to decompress, rest, and recover. A person is forced to endure sensorily, socially, or emotionally overwhelming experiences until they are pushed beyond a certain tolerance point, and as a result, their system crashes.

People in burnout experience a loss of function which can last days or weeks. Their symptoms can include:

- Increased emotional volatility;
- Increased executive dysfunction;
- Increased sensitivity to sensory stimuli, leading to an increase in the frequency of meltdowns/shutdowns/selective mutism;
- Decreased communication abilities (both verbal and written/spelled);
- Memory loss;
- Physical and mental fatigue;
- Lethargy.

	Burnouts	Fatigue, stress, and diminished coping skills after being overtaxed
Never	2%	2%
Sometimes	28%	15%
Often	47%	42%
Always	20%	40%
Not sure	3%	1%

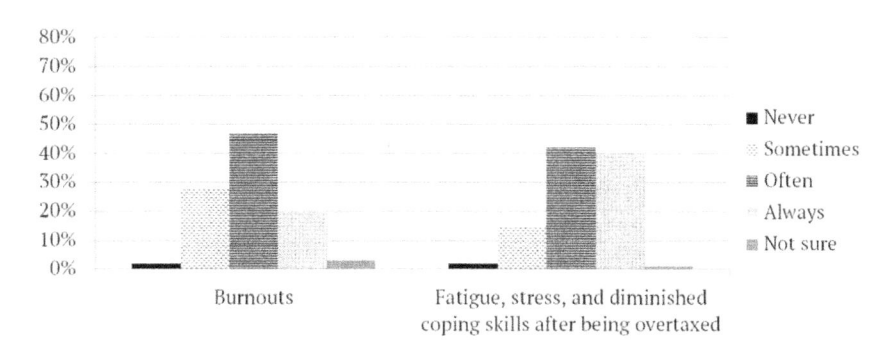

67% of respondents often or always experience burnouts. 82% experience periods of fatigue, heightened stress, and diminished capacity to cope with daily life if they become overtaxed by their obligations. Establishing whether people who experience the latter are affected severely enough to meet the criteria for burnout would require further investigations.

34% of respondents who experience burnouts are Autistic, as are 32% of those who experience periods of fatigue, heightened stress, and diminished capacity to cope with daily life if they become overtaxed by their obligations

Unsurprisingly, the factors that correlate with an increased prevalence in meltdowns, shutdowns, and selective mutism also increase the prevalence of burnouts. Most notably, 86% of those who are routinely forced to endure unpleasant or overwhelming physical sensations in order to navigate their environment experience burnouts, as do 83% of those who, as children, had to suffer through attempts at "desensitization therapies."

	Burnouts	Fatigue, stress, and diminished coping skills after being overtaxed
Whole survey	67%	82%
Autistic	75%	86%
Routinely forced to endure unpleasant or overwhelming physical sensations in order to navigate their environment	86%	94%
Force themselves to stop their self-soothing behaviors in order to avoid getting told off	78%	89%
Redirect repetitive behaviors to less noticeable ones to look more "normal"	75%	88%
Need to make repetitive or unusual movements increases under stress	73%	87%
Do things you'd rather not so people will like you	75%	88%
Pretend to be someone else so people will like you	78%	90%
Punished for "tantrums"	81%	91%
"Desensitized"	83%	92%

Meltdowns, shutdowns, selective mutism, and burnouts are easier to avoid than to manage – as in, they can be avoided by avoiding exposure to the relevant triggers, but once a person is in that state, all they can do is ride it out until it passes. However, avoiding exposure to triggers is more easily said than done. This is one of those issues where "awareness" campaigns won't help us; what we need is actual changes in our environment, the demands put upon us, and our ability to decompress. Thoughts and prayers won't fix this.

Achievements, or lack thereof.

This section looked at underachievement. The question was:

- Have you underachieved at work or in education (i.e., have you achieved less than people believed you capable of)?

The current diagnostic system for neurodivergences centers on failures. In order to be put forward for testing, children have to fail to meet age-appropriate standards in their academic work, socialization, communication, or behavior. In order to obtain a diagnosis of neurodivergence in adulthood, patients have to prove that their symptoms started in childhood, were and are age-inappropriate, and cause consistent impairment in multiple domains.

There are two obvious problems with this approach. First of all, it discounts the fact that many neurodivergents put a lot of effort into compensating for their traits or suppressing them altogether. Undiagnosed adults, in particular, spend years learning how to function in neurotypical environments. These adaptations may enable us to achieve at least some of our goals, but they are not cost-free. In fact, many of them require a lot of effort.

Some coping mechanisms are downright damaging. For instance, we might compensate for our tendency to make mistakes by obsessively checking and re-checking our work; we might learn to dissociate when we need to stay still for prolonged periods; we might have developed social anxiety so paralyzing that we no longer talk out of turn, because we struggle to talk at all; we might have channeled our physical restlessness into a constantly racing mind. This kind of coping mechanism reduces the impact of our neurodivergence... but only on the people around us. We are just as affected by our neurodivergence – in fact, we now have to deal with our traits *and* with our coping mechanisms. We have learned to suffer in silence, though, and for some people, that's all that matters.

Secondly, failures to achieve neurotypical results in certain domains are not the only symptoms of neurodivergence, or even the ones with the greatest impact on our well-being. We could charitably say that current diagnostic criteria are based on the symptoms that are most obvious to an outside observer, which is why they are used for diagnosis. We could be snarky and say that diagnostic criteria that focus primarily on how much our neurodivergence affects those around us rather than ourselves are less than ideal, and are a sad indictment of how the medical system views our existence.

These considerations notwithstanding, there are plenty of proofs, both statistical and anecdotal, that our neurodivergent traits and the way they are perceived by neurotypicals can cause problems in a variety of domains, and that these problems can have negative impacts on our lives.

	Have you underachieved at work or in education
Yes	77%
No	15%
NS	8%
N/A	0%

Have you underachieved at work or in education

77% of respondents reported that they have underachieved at work or in education. This does not come as a huge surprise and is in line with the results shown by other studies. What is surprising and more than a little depressing (for me, anyway) is what we find when we correlate age at diagnosis and underachievement. Most respondents were ADHDers, so I will focus on this group first as the results are more numerous and therefore more reliable.

	% of ADHD underachievers by age at diagnosis
<12	74%
<18	78%
>18	78%
Self-diagnosed	80%

% of ADHD underachievers by age at diagnosis

74% of ADHDers diagnosed under 12 self-identify as underachievers, compared to 77% of those diagnosed under 18, 77% of those diagnosed over 18, and 80% of those who are self-diagnosed.

As this survey was not a scientific study and the results of self-reporting on broad concepts like underachievement aren't terribly rigid, it would be pointless to calculate whether these differences are statistically significant. It makes more sense to look at these results as suggesting that age at diagnosis isn't much of a factor. If anything, being diagnosed under 12 may correlate with a slightly lower chance of underachieving and being self-diagnosed may correlate with slightly higher chances, but the differences aren't staggering.

Autistic respondents reported a different pattern of results:

	% of Autistic underachievers by age at diagnosis
<12	80%
<18	64%
>18	79%
Self-diagnosed	80%

% of Autistic underachievers by age at diagnosis

80% of Autistic diagnosed under 12 self-identify as underachievers, compared to 64% of those diagnosed under 18, 79% of those diagnosed over 18, and 80% of those who are self-diagnosed. These results are far less robust as the number of respondents is much smaller, but they suggest that being diagnosed over 12 but under 18 may correlate with a lower chance of underachieving. However, the number of respondents is so small (11) that the results are not reliable enough to make any kind of statement on the subject.[39]

There is an ongoing argument within the neurodivergent community as to whether early diagnoses are actually helpful. One the one hand, growing up undiagnosed means not only having to cope without adaptations at school and at work, but also without an explanation as to why we are different from our cohorts. It can be hard for us to get help, or even to help ourselves, because we don't know what we need, or why. On the other hand, getting an early diagnosis does not necessarily mean that we will get the support we need to achieve our potential. On the contrary, getting an early diagnosis can mean getting written off early. We may receive no actual support, because we are deemed beyond help. Worse than that, we may be forced through therapeutic interventions that are borderline abusive. Furthermore, all our problems may end up being chalked down to our neurodivergence.

In trans circles, there is a phenomenon known as "trans broken arm syndrome," where medical providers assume that the health concerns of trans people must be either a reflection of our transness or of hormonal therapies we are undertaking. It doesn't matter whether the health concern in question has obviously nothing to do with gender or gender-affirming care; if you are trans, even a broken arm is a trans issue. Medical providers may refuse to give you aid because they are not qualified to offer trans care, or they might refuse to give you aid unless you magically stop being trans first. Fat people suffer from a similar issue, referred to as "fat broken arm syndrome." Medical providers may not carry out adequate investigations because they wrongly assume that any health problem experienced by fat patients must be caused by weight, or refuse to provide care until fat patients have lost weight, even for conditions which are known to cause weight gain or prevent weight loss. Although there isn't as yet a name for this kind of issue in neurodivergence, there ought to be,

---

[39] Only one participant less than no-longer-Dr. Wakefield's seminal "study" of the link between MMR vaccine and Autism, though. I guess I lack his gumption. Or his profit motive.

because it's totally a thing.

As soon as we are diagnosed as neurodivergent, every possible life issue we have ever experienced magically becomes an issue of neurodivergence. This is particularly obvious on parents' forums, where the answers to "how do I get my child to do/stop doing X" are markedly different for neurotypical and neurodivergent children, but other settings are not immune from this bias. Whether at home, at school, at work, or anywhere else, if we have problems and we are neurodivergent, our issues will be reframed as issues of neurodivergence, regardless of what they are and who is actually causing them. No matter what happens to us, no matter who is responsible, no matter the degree of control we actually have on a situation, our neurodivergence must be the cause of our problems, or at the very least a contributing factor. And if we cannot handle the resulting issues, that must also be down to our neurodivergence. In this context, receiving an early diagnosis just gives us the chance to be blamed for everything for a few more years.

One could look at the results of this survey and come to the conclusion that early diagnoses don't actually help us that much. However, this would be a very superficial conclusion. There is likely to be a lot more going on.

First of all, we need to consider the factors that facilitate people getting an early diagnosis. In order to get tested for neurodivergence, children have not only to show clear traits, but also to be "failing" in one or more domains. Children who struggle but achieve "normal" results may not be put forward for testing. Neither are children who are not expected to succeed, which is one of the reasons why societal biases have such an impact on diagnostic rates.

The pressure and demands of school change as we get older. As a result, neurodivergent children who coped reasonably well with kindergarten and elementary school may hit a wall in secondary school.[40] Some of us cope reasonably well with structured academic systems, but go to pieces when we reach university and we are suddenly expected to self-organize. The age at which we were diagnosed could therefore indicate the stage in our life when our coping mechanisms became insufficient and we started to struggle. However, it could also indicate the stage in our life when our struggles became too obvious for the authorities to ignore, rather than when we actually started struggling.

---

[40] That's what I did.

Getting diagnosed later might mean that our coping skills and support were sufficient to meet earlier demands. In this context, getting diagnosed as soon as we start struggling may help maximize our potential if it gets us the support we needed to develop appropriate coping skills to handle current and future challenges.

These are conjectures, though. There are many factors at play, and they affect different people in very different ways because the playing field isn't level. Measuring the impact of early diagnosis on each individual would require trawling the multiverse for answers, and I can't do that. Furthermore, all these arguments can distract us from the most important take-home from these results: that three quarters of us consider ourselves to be underachievers.

I want to stress something: underachieving means that we did not attain a predicted level of achievement in a certain domain. It does not necessarily indicate that we aren't living our best lives. It's a discrepancy between what is expected of us and what we actually end up doing, and it has nothing to do with what makes us happy. We might know that we could have put our talents and energy towards achieving certain goals – having a certain career, owning a certain amount of stuff, forming a certain type of family – and we might also know that doing so would have sucked for us.

It is possible to be an underachiever and to be perfectly happy with where we are and what we are doing. It is also very possible to be an underachiever and feel terrible about it, particularly if we live in a capitalist culture and have internalized its values. We can be perfectly content underachievers, though; it might fly in the face of social conventions, but hey, so does a whole bunch of stuff that makes us happy and comfortable.

Future surveys should look at both aspects of this subject: whether we have underachieved by conventional standards, and whether we are reasonably satisfied with our achievements to date. The second issue is at least as important.

Conclusion.

The first and most obvious conclusion is that there's quite a bit going on with us, and most of it isn't included in current diagnostic criteria or addressed by the support we get post-diagnosis, assuming we get any. This raises a number of issues.

- A lot of us struggle with long-term problems with basic functioning that are not included in current diagnostic criteria. We are effectively disabled in ways we might not even realize, because nobody bothers to tell us that the vast majority of people don't share our struggles. Given how common these issues are, are the current diagnostic criteria appropriate? Do they address the issues that most affect our lives, or those that most affect the lives of those around us?

- Going a step beyond, should support be allocated to us on the basis of our diagnoses or our needs? Are needs not "validated" by a diagnosis less real or less worthy of consideration and support?

- The physical conditions covered by this survey are known to be common co-occurring conditions in Autism, as made evident by the work produced by the #ActuallyAutistic community. Why are the results of this work not reflected in medical care and medical research? Specifically, why are certain patterns obvious to lay people yet invisible to "experts"?

- If these conditions commonly co-occur with other neurodivergences, why are these commonalities not reflected in the way different neurodivergences are diagnosed, treated, and studied? Most specifically, why are Autism and ADHD treated as two completely unrelated conditions when we share so many mental and physical traits that have a huge impact on our ability to function?

- And, going back around to the first point, why are these traits not automatically included in the support we get post-diagnosis? Screening for common co-occurring conditions would save us a lot of suffering, save doctors a lot of time, and save hospitals a lot of money. So why isn't this happening?

This is most notable in the case of sleep deprivation. Research shows that up to 70% of ADHDers and 80% of Autistics are habitually sleep-deprived. Research also shows that sleep deprivation not only correlates with a number of short-term psychoemotional and cognitive issues and with long-term health conditions, but actually causes them. For instance, it has been demonstrated that sleep and chronic pain are related, but that that relationship isn't reciprocal, as previously believed – i.e., chronic pain doesn't cause sleep deprivation, which in turn worsens chronic pain. While this reciprocal connection makes perfect sense in theory, it isn't supported by current findings. It turns out that sleep impairments are a stronger, more reliable predictor of pain than pain is of sleep impairments. So, bad sleep comes first, and chronic pain is its result. A feedback loop may then be created, but addressing the pain while ignoring the sleep is unlikely to resolve the situation.

The results of this survey support these theories. Respondents who never manage to sleep the recommended minimum of 7 hours per day have a greater prevalence of... basically everything. In contrast, those who often or always manage to sleep 7 hours a day have a lower prevalence of all issues. And this includes physical issues that most people would not consider to be sleep-related, as well as psychoemotional issues that are currently believe to be inevitable aspects of our neurodivergence.

	Whole Survey	Never sleep 7hrs	Often or always sleep 7hrs
Wake up tired, even when you get enough sleep?	78%	85%	67%
Easily injure your joints? (e.g. sprains or strains.)	20%	32%	13%
Experience fatigue even when you haven't done anything to tire yourself out?	61%	73%	53%
Experience an unreasonable amount of fatigue when you exert yourself?	47%	56%	41%
Feel pain from something that should not be painful at all, such as a very light touch?	13%	19%	10%
Times when you experience widespread pain with no known cause?	19%	26%	14%
Times when all of your past injuries hurt, even though you have not re-injured yourself?	14%	20%	9%
Tinnitus without identifiable causes?	36%	43%	31%
Cluster headaches?	17%	24%	13%
Polycystic ovary syndrome (PCOS)?	17%	19%	11%
Endometriosis?	12%	16%	11%

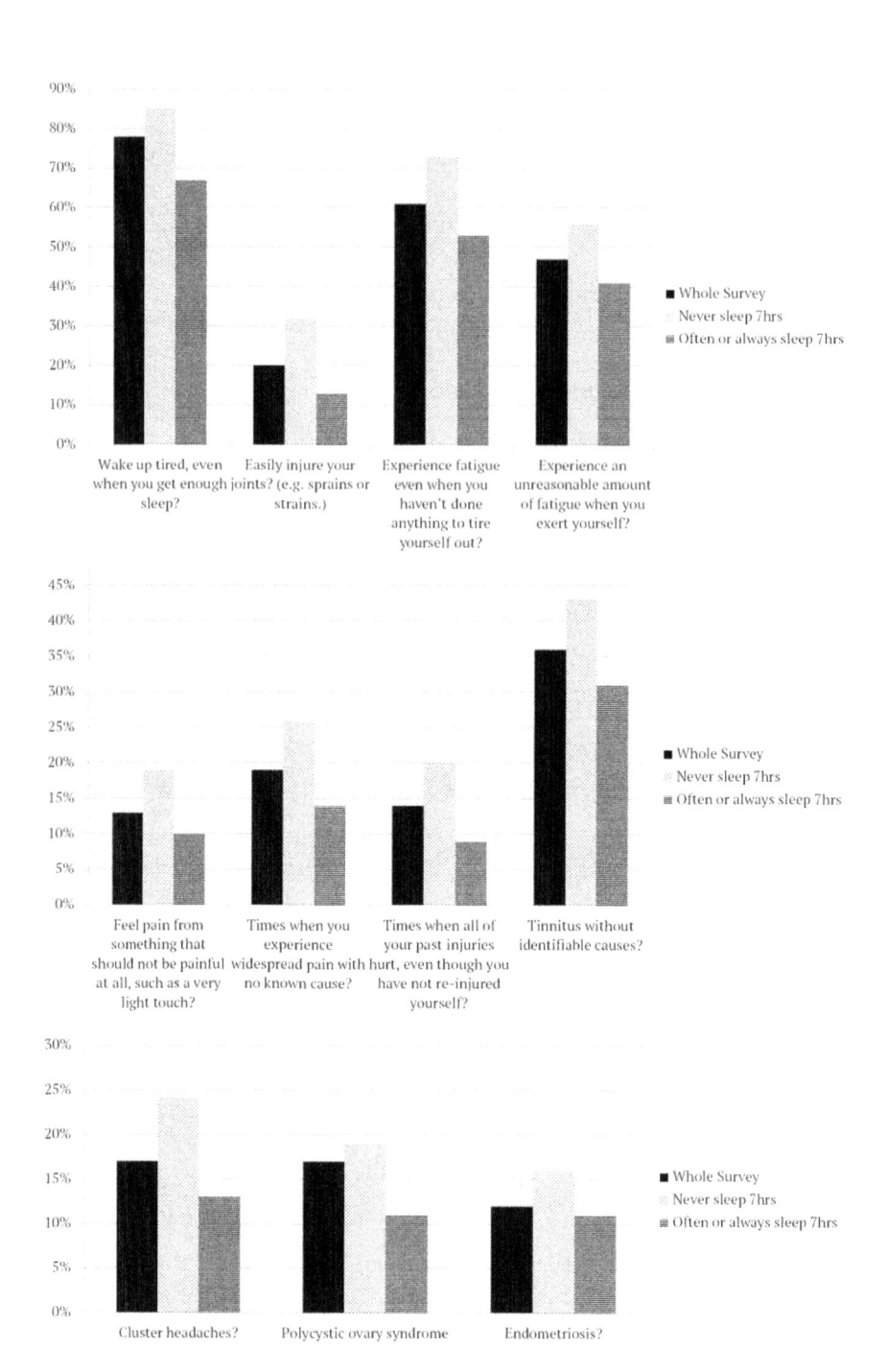

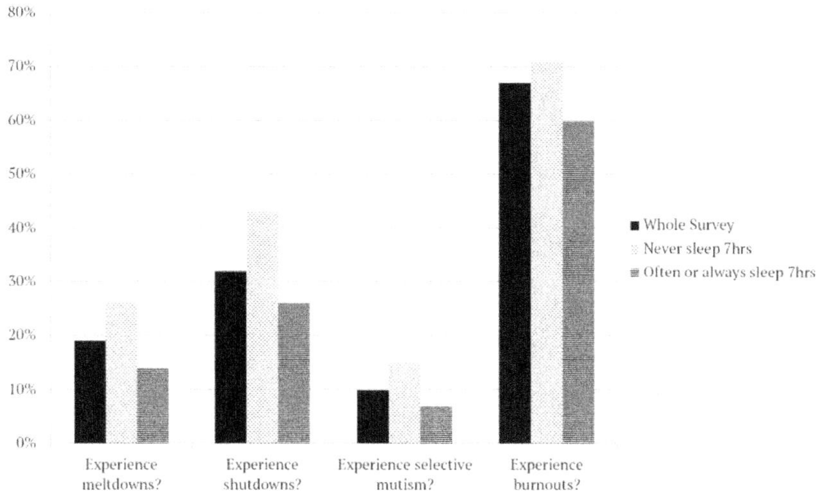
80%
70%
60%
50%
40%
30%
20%
10%
0%
Whole Survey
Never sleep 7hrs
Often or always sleep 7hrs
Experience meltdowns?
Experience shutdowns?
Experience selective mutism?
Experience burnouts?

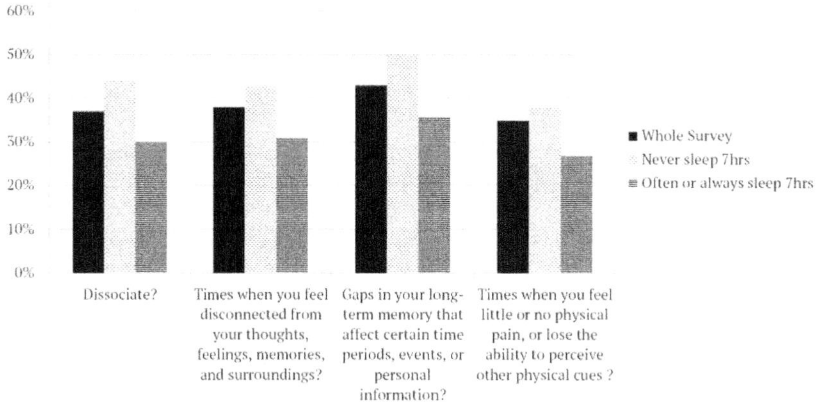
60%
50%
40%
30%
20%
10%
0%
Whole Survey
Never sleep 7hrs
Often or always sleep 7hrs
Dissociate?
Times when you feel disconnected from your thoughts, feelings, memories, and surroundings?
Gaps in your long-term memory that affect certain time periods, events, or personal information?
Times when you feel little or no physical pain, or lose the ability to perceive other physical cues ?

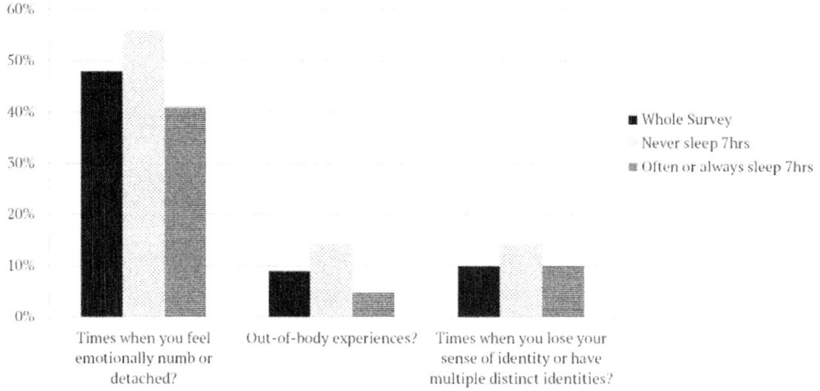
60%
50%
40%
30%
20%
10%
0%
Whole Survey
Never sleep 7hrs
Often or always sleep 7hrs
Times when you feel emotionally numb or detached?
Out-of-body experiences?
Times when you lose your sense of identity or have multiple distinct identities?

	Whole Survey	Never sleep 7hrs	Often or always sleep 7hrs
Experience meltdowns?	19%	26%	14%
Experience shutdowns?	32%	43%	26%
Experience selective mutism?	10%	15%	7%
Experience burnouts?	67%	71%	60%
Dissociate?	37%	44%	30%
Times when you feel disconnected from your thoughts, feelings, memories, and surroundings?	38%	43%	31%
Gaps in your long-term memory that affect certain time periods, events, or personal information?	43%	50%	36%
Times when you feel little or no physical pain, or lose the ability to perceive other physical cues?	35%	38%	27%
Times when you feel emotionally numb or detached?	48%	56%	41%
Out-of-body experiences?	9%	14%	5%
Times when you lose your sense of identity or have multiple distinct identities?	10%	14%	10%

So, we know that the neurodivergent community is generally sleep-deprived, and that sleep deprivation is a key contributor to many of the psychoemotional, cognitive, and physical symptoms we struggle with. Why then is addressing our sleep not automatically included in the care we receive post-diagnosis?

There is another element to this. Many sleep disturbances are known to be linked to issues with melatonin production. In turn, melatonin production is known to be negatively affected by sleep deprivation. Still, many doctors are against the long-term use of melatonin supplements because they might interfere with our melatonin production – so, they refuse to prescribe us the thing we need to sleep, which we can't produce because we can't sleep. This position is both illogical and unsupported by current research, yet it persists.

There is more. Melatonin supplements have been found to be beneficial for the treatment and management of a number of conditions, including:

- Treating circadian sleep disorders.

- Reducing abdominal pain in people with Irritable Bowel Syndrome.
- Controlling the symptoms of fibromyalgia, neuropathies, and other chronic pain conditions.
- Managing the symptoms of migraines, trigeminal neuralgia, cluster headaches, and temporomandibular disorders (painful conditions affecting the jaw joint and surrounding muscles).
- Controlling the symptoms of tinnitus without known causes.
- Lowering the risk of endometriosis.
- Managing chronic pelvic pain in patients with endometriosis.
- Controlling the symptoms of fibrocystic breast disease, including the growth and proliferation of cysts and the associated pain.

Given the prevalence of these conditions in our community, why isn't anyone connecting the dots?

The next question is just as significant. Adverse childhood experiences (ACEs) are potentially traumatic events that occur in childhood. Examples of ACEs include experiencing violence, abuse, neglect, traumatic events, or growing up in a family with mental health or substance misuse problems. ACEs are known to have a significant negative impact on long-term health and life outcomes, including underachievement in multiple domains, chronic health problems, mental illness, substance misuse, and a greater likelihood becoming the victims or perpetrators of violence. The toxic stress resulting from ACEs has been shown to affect brain development and change how the body responds to stress.

In this survey, we looked at one potential ACE, bullying in childhood, as well as two trauma conditions that can affect people at any age, PTSD and cPTSD. We also looked at another factor: whether in childhood our respondents were forced by parents or teachers **to endure painful physical sensation in order to learn to get over them.** The latter group shows a greater prevalence of psychoemotional and physical issues than the first three. Let me reiterate that: "desensitization" attempts made to "help" us get over our issues may have a worse long-term impact on our emotional, mental, and physical health than PTSD, cPTSD, or childhood bullying. Yet "desensitization" is still marketed as a suitable or even desirable therapeutic intervention for ND children. How in the hell is this still a thing?

	Whole Survey	Bullied	PTSD	cPTSD	"Desensitized"
Experience meltdowns?	19%	20%	25%	26%	36%
Experience shutdowns?	32%	35%	41%	43%	53%
Experience selective mutism?	10%	11%	15%	17%	23%
Experience burnouts?	67%	69%	75%	79%	83%
Dissociate?	37%	39%	50%	53%	64%
Times when you feel disconnected from your thoughts, feelings, memories, and surroundings?	38%	40%	49%	53%	63%
Gaps in your long-term memory that affect certain time periods, events, or personal information?	43%	45%	53%	58%	61%
Times when you feel little or no physical pain, or lose the ability to perceive other physical cues	35%	38%	45%	47%	60%
Times when you feel emotionally numb or detached?	48%	52%	56%	58%	71%
Out-of-body experiences?	9%	10%	15%	16%	25%
Times when you lose your sense of identity or have multiple distinct identities?	10%	11%	14%	17%	20%
Reactive hypoglycemia?	5%	5%	6%	8%	8%
PoTS	4%	4%	6%	6%	8%
Allergies to smells or chemicals?	20%	21%	26%	26%	31%
Asthma attacks in response to certain smells?	9%	9%	12%	11%	13%
Easily injure your joints? (e.g. sprains or strains.)	20%	22%	25%	27%	34%
Experience fatigue even when you haven't done anything to tire yourself out?	61%	63%	72%	77%	80%
Experience an unreasonable amount of fatigue when you exert yourself?	47%	50%	61%	63%	69%
Extremely sensitive to pain?	12%	13%	17%	18%	22%
Feel pain from something that should not be painful at all, such as a very light touch?	13%	14%	20%	24%	29%
Times when you experience widespread pain with no known cause?	19%	21%	26%	31%	37%

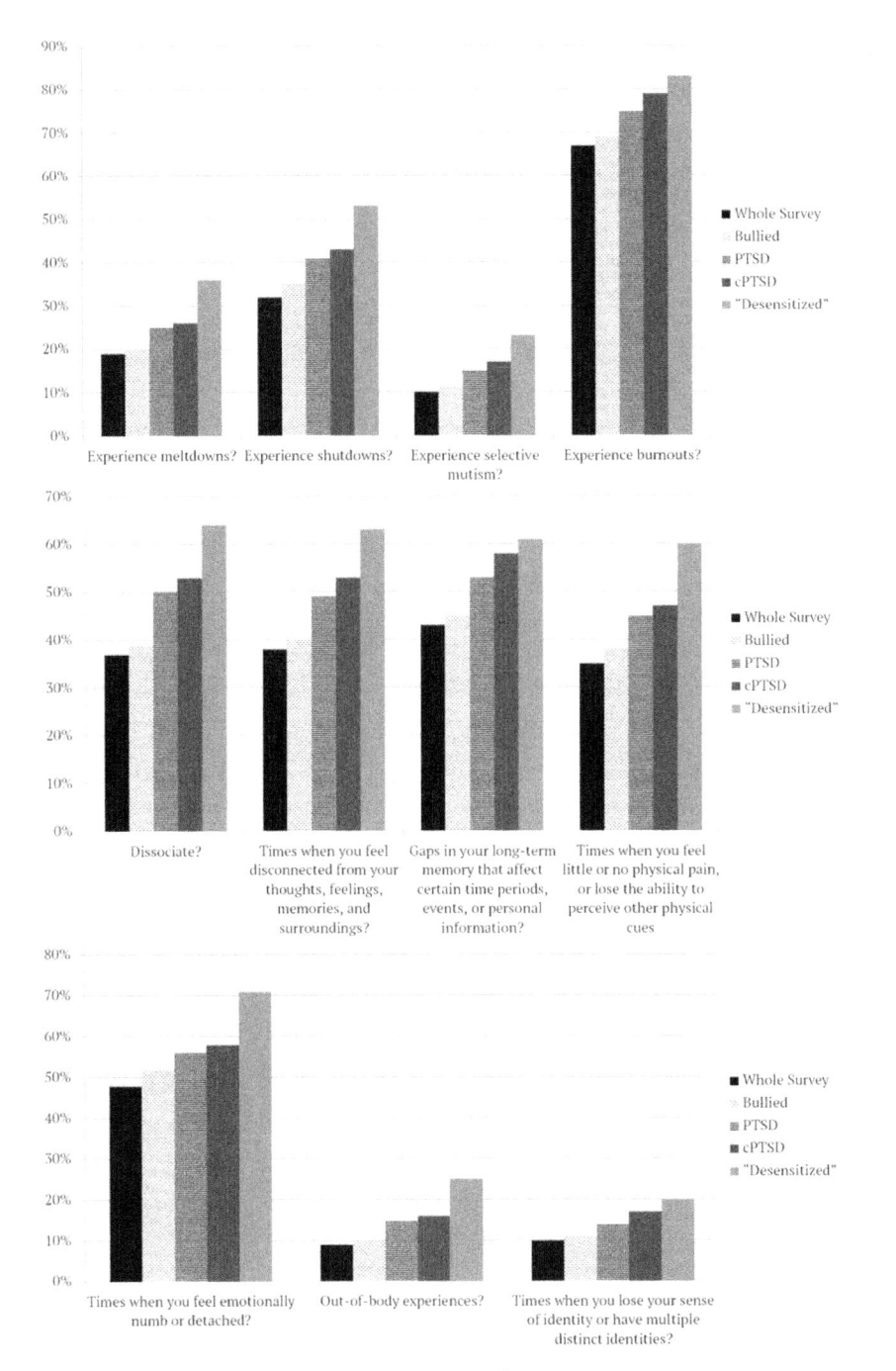

There is another issue related to the "support" given to neurodivergent children (and plenty of adults, too). A lot of "therapies" are not geared towards making our life easier by helping us narrow the gap between our demands and our abilities. They are geared towards teaching us how to act neurotypically, so we'll blend in better. This is allegedly aimed at helping us function better; in reality, it often *reduces* our ability to function by increasing our demands while depriving us of the ability to explore workarounds, use support tools, express our discomfort, or self-soothe.

There is plenty of anecdotal evidence that neurodivergents who force themselves to stop stimming in order to avoid getting told off, do things they'd rather not so people will like them (which I rephrased as "people-pleasing"), or pretend to be someone else so people will like them (which I rephrased as "masking") experience worse mental health outcomes. There is also some evidence indicating that they experience worse physical health outcomes – unsurprising, given the impact of chronic stress.

As I was already crunching numbers, I decided to have a look at how bad this was. Results suggest that stopping stims, people pleasing, and masking are all linked with increases in the prevalence of a number of physical and psychoemotional issues. Masking tends to result in the greatest increases in prevalence, but the other two factors aren't far behind, and stopping stims comes on top for a couple of outcomes.

Redirecting stims, which is usually considered a much safer option than stopping them, shows an only marginally lower prevalence of these issues. However, that doesn't necessarily indicate that the fault lies in the stim redirection per se. People who redirect stim also stop themselves from stimming (55%), do things they'd rather not so people will like them (50%), and pretend to be someone else so people will like them (43%).

It is not inconceivable that the issue with these strategies is that they come as part of a package of unnatural behaviors that are taught to us or forced on us in an attempt at making us look like someone we're not, or that we learn to perform as a way to avoid being punished by our caregivers or peers. We do not take them up because we want to change, but because we need to have better relationships with those around us. Repressing our true self becomes the only way we can live our lives without facing a variety of punishments.

Teaching ND children to mask, people-please, and stop or redirect stims is still the core of many "therapies" designed to "help" us. Given that these unnatural behaviors are all linked with increases in the prevalence of serious long-term negative psychoemotional and physical health outcomes, how is this still a thing?

	Whole Survey	Stop stims	Redirect stims	People please	Mask
Experience meltdowns?	19%	29%	25%	31%	**36%**
Experience shutdowns?	32%	44%	43%	43%	**53%**
Selective mutism?	10%	17%	16%	18%	**23%**
Burnouts	67%	78%	75%	78%	**83%**
Dissociate?	37%	50%	46%	51%	**64%**
Times when you feel disconnected from your thoughts, feelings, memories, and surroundings?	38%	53%	48%	53%	**63%**
Gaps in your long-term memory that affect certain time periods, events, or personal information?	43%	50%	50%	53%	**61%**
Times when you feel little or no physical pain, or lose the ability to perceive other physical cues	35%	49%	47%	46%	**60%**
Times when you feel emotionally numb or detached?	48%	65%	59%	63%	**71%**
Out-of-body experiences?	9%	13%	13%	13%	**25%**
Times when you lose your sense of identity or have multiple distinct identities?	10%	16%	14%	17%	**20%**
Easily injure your joints? (e.g. sprains or strains.)	20%	**26%**	24%	**26%**	**26%**
Experience fatigue even when you haven't done anything to tire yourself out?	61%	72%	69%	**73%**	**73%**
Experience an unreasonable amount of fatigue when you exert yourself?	47%	**58%**	56%	57%	57%
Fibromyalgia?	7%	7%	8%	9%	9%
Extremely sensitive to pain?	12%	14%	**15%**	**15%**	**15%**
Feel pain from something that should not be painful at all, such as a very light touch?	13%	16%	17%	**18%**	**18%**
Times when you experience widespread pain with no known cause?	19%	**25%**	**25%**	23%	23%

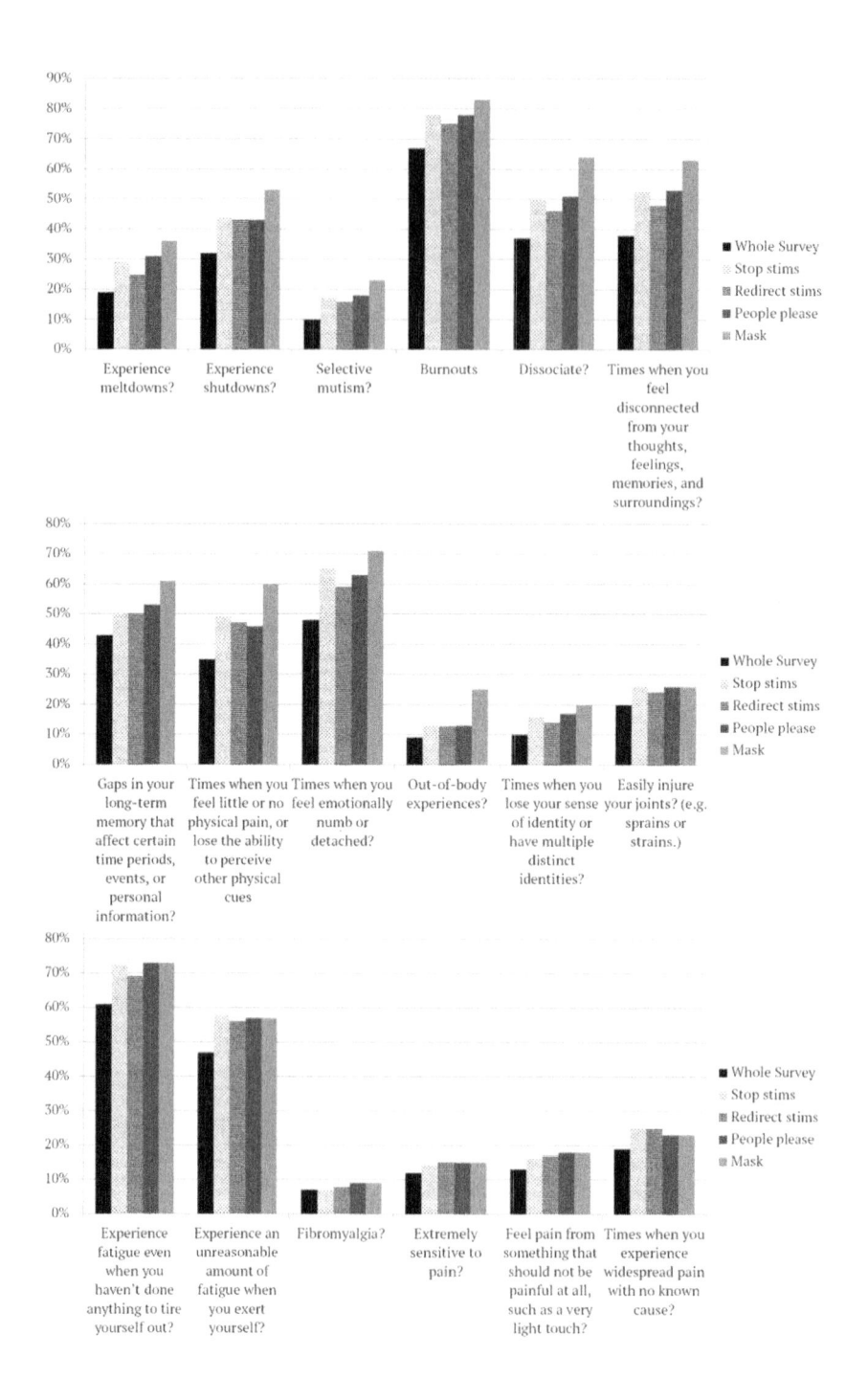

	Whole survey	Punished for "tantrums"	"Desensitised	Bullied as a child	Bullied now
Stop stims	31%	47%	**51%**	34%	44%
Redirect stims	49%	66%	**69%**	52%	66%
People please	41%	55%	54%	43%	**61%**
Mask	32%	43%	46%	33%	**47%**

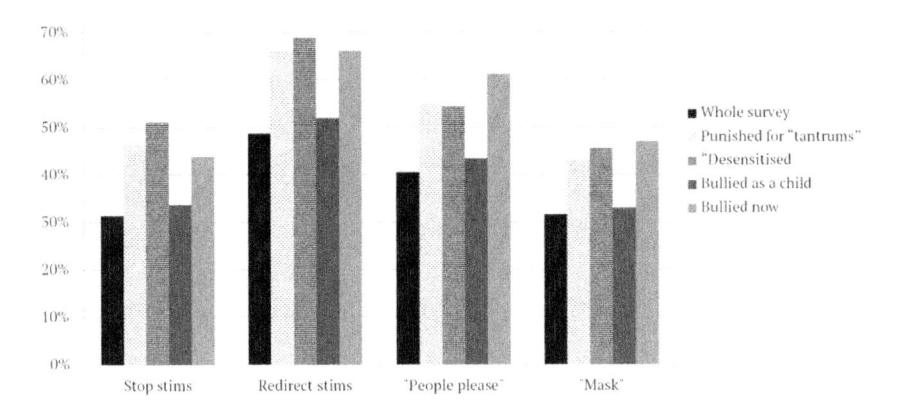

Ultimately, these are the conclusions I personally come to:

- The link between the diagnostic criteria used to classify us and our experience is tenuous at best.
- The link between our diagnoses and our support needs is no stronger.
- The link between the "therapies" we are put through and our actual needs is pretty much nonexistent.
- The vast majority of current strategies designed to help us not only don't do that, but can have serious negative impacts on our long-term health.
- This situation is unlikely to improve until medical experts start listening to neurodivergent voices.

Where do we go from here?

That depends on what we mean by "we."

As a community, I think it'd be nice if we collectively popped over to where the #ActuallyAutistic content creators hang out and said "Thank you" – not literally, though, because some of them might not like that. Maybe we could just send them snacks or something? They are owed some kind of thank you, anyway. This project is my work, granted, but it's based on information the #ActuallyAutistic community produced and circulated. If they hadn't already done a ton of work, I wouldn't have known which questions to include. So, yeah, thank you snacks seem in order.

As individuals, I guess where we go depends on what we discovered, if anything. If you think that you have found out something new about yourself, or connected some dots that you think may form a picture, please remember that this book is not a diagnostic manual, and it cannot be used as such. Seriously, don't even go there. If you are concerned because some of your symptoms resemble those described here, the only way to know for sure and to get help, if appropriate, is to take those concerns to a medical professional.

Unfortunately, that's more easily said than done. Too many of us can't get the medical care we need, either because we can't see a medical specialist, or because the medical specialists we see are somewhat lacking in the "care" department.

If you are able to see a doctor but you do not trust that they'll take your symptoms seriously, I strongly advise you to go to your appointment bearing a letter including the following:

- A detailed list of your symptoms;
- When they started and how often they manifest;
- Their severity and their impact on your life;
- Anything that triggers your symptoms or makes them worse;
- If applicable, whether they are affected by your menstrual cycle or hormone treatment schedule;
- Your family health history, if relevant;
- Any remedies you have already tried, and whether they worked;
- Whether you have already reported your symptoms to medical

professionals and what the outcome was.

Putting this information in writing can make doctors less willing to brush off our symptoms without investigating them, as they don't like to get sued. You don't have to present it like that, though, particularly if you want to avoid antagonizing them. You could say that you wrote everything down so you wouldn't forget anything or make a mistake. Heck, it's about time that we make our memory problems work for us.

Mentioning the prevalence of certain issues in the neurodivergent community may or may not help, depending on how your doctor feels about neurodivergence and "new" medical discoveries. Saying that you think that you have a condition because you answered an online survey, however, is almost guaranteed not to help.

If this survey did raise some concerns, but they aren't medical, I promise you, you are in good company. A lot of our issues aren't medical and shouldn't be medicalized. If you need help dealing with them, you might want to consider enlisting the support of a neurodivergence-competent therapist or coach. And hey, did you know that neurodivergent therapists and coaches exist? And that getting support from people whose neurotype matches ours is a lot easier, because we don't have to teach them how to help us?

If hiring help is not an available option, there are some good, free resources out there. NeuroClastic is a good place to start from.

If you decide to fix things all on your lonesome, I would advise you to prioritize the basics first: sleep, nutrition, hydration, and air. If this also sounds more easily said than done, that's because it is! But those are the basic requirements of every body, and if this survey has shown anything, it's that neurodivergence isn't confined to our brains. Until our bodies are getting sufficient oxygen, water, nutrients, and rest, every other measure we implement is going to be nothing more than re-filling a leaky bucket. And yes, that applies to ADHD meds, too.

Once the basics are in place, I'd advise you to check your stress levels, but that's based on the assumption that they are an issue, and that you can do something about them. My basic approach is to deal with the stuff likely to have the most significant impact for the least possible effort; I like things to be efficient, and I often struggle to implement big changes. However, you might have other priorities.

If you have discovered absolutely nothing new about yourself, congratulations: you are either much better informed than most of us, or have fewer problems. Either way, I am sorry if I wasted your time, but I am not sorry that you are already in a relatively good place.

As for me, what I'm planning to do is nothing – nothing constructive, anyway, because I'm one of those for whom resting is far from restful. This has been one of the most interesting, challenging, and depressing projects I've ever worked on. While I'm glad I did it, I never want to do it again. I'm going back to writing neuroqueer fiction,[41] playing with puppies, and learning stuff that doesn't make me want to headbutt the nearest wall.

...so, yeah, I will probably rejig the survey and do this again, because the structure didn't work as well as I wanted, and the holes in it annoy me. But I will have to forget how much this sucked first. Watch this space, but don't hold your breath.

If you have enjoyed this book, please consider contributing towards the creation of an audiobook version, which will be published through Audible. Ideally the reader will be Jacob McNatt, who did a sterling job recording "Going Official!" However, if within six months of starting this pot we haven't reached the minimum amount required to pay his fees, I will look for the best possible replacement we can afford.

https://ko-fi.com/modgoblin

---

[41] Which you can buy for moneys! https://www.amazon.com/Robin-Banks/e/B01MU5VWGL/

Appendix 1: The original survey.

This is the original version of the survey. It has some serious flaws, described in the main text.

Facets of Neurodivergence

This survey aims to explore three aspects of neurodivergence:

1. The most frequent traits;
2. The most frequent co-occurring conditions;
3. The availability of information about co-occurring conditions within the neurodivergent community.

As I am looking at the experiences of neurodivergent people, neurotypicals cannot participate. Self-diagnosed neurodivergents are welcome. If you have a problem with this, then you do not understand the structural barriers that prevent the vast majority of neurodivergent people from obtaining a formal diagnosis, and YOU are not welcome. (Just kidding: fill in the survey if you want, but seriously, do us all a favour and find out more about this. Gatekeeping undiagnosed neurodivergents is harmful, and it disproportionately affects already marginalized people.)

This survey is long. It needs to be, in order to gather the information needed. If you struggle to complete long tasks, you don't have to do it in one sitting! The survey is broken up in sections of about 10 questions each, each of which can be easily completed while you're waiting for the kettle to boil or sitting on the loo.

This survey may include terms you have never heard of. If that's the case, please answer "Don't know" rather than looking them up. The availability of this type of information is part of what I am trying to find out!

This survey has not been reviewed by an ethical committee because it is run by an individual - Ash Banks, author of "Going Official! On getting a diagnosis of adult ADHD, and what to do with it" and a number of works of fiction and non-fiction. I am not affiliated with any institution; I am purely trying to get some figures to shed light on a pattern I am seeing within the neurodivergent community.

The results of this survey will be made public. As I am not collecting any information regarding people's identity, they will be strictly anonymous.

If you wish to be kept abreast of the results of this survey, please email going.official.ADHDgmail.com

Section 1: Personal Information

Are you heterosexual?

Yes / No

What gender were you assigned at birth? Tick all that apply.

Male / Female / Intersex

Do you still identify with the gender you were assigned at birth?

Yes / No / Partly

How old are you?

<insert age>

In which country/countries did you spend your childhood until the age of 12?

<insert country>

Section 2: Cognitive and learning styles

What is your main mode of thinking? Choose the option(s) that best describes you.

- Verbal/logic thinker: you think verbally, with your mind narrating your experiences as you go through them. You might have an affinity for words, literature, or languages.
- Visual thinker: you think in pictures and need to see things—either in your mind or physically—in order to process information. You use language as a secondary tool to narrate the photo-realistic pictures that pop up in your imagination.
- Pattern thinker: this is a more abstract form of visual thinking. Thoughts are in patterns, rather than photorealistic pictures. You might have an affinity for finding seemingly meaningful patterns in both meaningful and meaningless data.
- 3-D or spatial-mechanical thinker: you automatically create a 3-D model of the world around you in your head, and can rotate and manipulate the resulting picture so you can view it from all angles. You might have an affinity for spatial problem solving (e.g., solving visual puzzles, rotating or arranging objects so they fit in small spaces.) You might be able to mentally picture something with such detail that you can run mental experiments on your creation, tweaking it until it works.
- Not sure

How do you learn best?

Tick all that apply

- Visual learning: understanding and retaining information presented in a visual way – e.g. as pictures, diagrams, written directions, visual demonstrations, and more.
- Reading/writing learning: understanding and retaining information presented in writing – e.g. as text only.
- Auditory learning: understanding and retaining information presented verbally rather than visually – e.g. as a spoken lecture rather than written notes.
- Kinesthetic learning: understanding and retaining information through physical activities - e.g. carrying out manual tasks, physically handling objects, acting out events, or translating concepts, even abstract ones, into physical sensations in your body.
- Combined: when the same information is presented in multiple formats at the same time.

Section 3: Types of neurodivergence

Please tick all the boxes that apply to you.

Mark only one oval per row.

Self-diagnosed / Diagnosed under 12 / Diagnosed under 18 / Diagnosed over 18 / Not sure

- ADHD
- Aphasia/dysphasia
- Autism
- Dyscalculia
- Dysgraphia
- Dyslexia
- Dyspraxia
- Hyperlexia
- Sensory Processing Disorders
- Auditory Processing Disorder
- Synesthesia
- Tourette's
- Other

Section 4: Traits you have had since childhood

Mark only one oval per row.

Never / Sometimes / Often / Always / Not sure

- Difficulties writing
- Difficulties reading
- Difficulties with math
- Poor gross motor skills (i.e., are you uncoordinated or "clumsy.")
- Poor fine motor skills (i.e., do you struggle to pick up, hold, or manipulate small things.
- Synesthesia
- Cross-overs between sensory or cognitive pathway? (e.g., you can see music or smell colours.)
- Alexithymia
- Inability to recognize your feelings
- Inability to recognize other people's feelings
- "Mental juke-box" that plays a constant soundtrack

Section 5: Sleep

Mark only one oval per row.

Never / Sometimes / Often / Always / Not sure

- Are you able to sleep at least 7 hours every night?
- Does it take you longer than 20 minutes to fall asleep after you go to bed?
- Do you have delayed sleep phase syndrome?
- Are you unable to fall asleep at a socially acceptable time even though you get to bed on time?
- Do you wake up in the middle of the night for no reason?
- Do you have long spells of insomnia in the winter?
- Do you have long spells on insomnia in the summer?
- Do you wake up tired, even when you get enough sleep?
- Do you have sleep apnea?
- Do you have narcolepsy?

Section 6: Restlessness, fidgets, and stims

Mark only one oval per row.

Never / Sometimes / Often / Always / Not sure

- Are you fidgety or restless? (mental restlessness counts!)
- Do you stim?
- Do you make repetitive or unusual movements or noises when you need to calm down?
- Do you make repetitive or unusual movements or noises when you are understimulated?
- Are any of the repetitive behaviors you engage in harmful to yourself?
- Are any of the repetitive behaviors you engage in harmful to others? (annoying them does not count!)
- Do you get told off because of your repetitive behaviors?
- Do you force yourself to stop your repetitive behaviors to avoid getting told off?
- Do you redirect your repetitive behaviors to less noticeable ones to look more "normal"?
- Do you find that your need to make repetitive or unusual movements increases under stress?

Section 7: Focus and stimulation

Mark only one oval per row.

Never / Sometimes / Often / Always / Not sure

- Do you find it hard to focus on a task when there is activity or noise around you?
- Do you find it hard to focus on a task if there isn't enough going on around you?
- Do you find it hard to focus on one thing at a time? (e.g., you can only listen to a lecture if you can doodle or fidget.)
- Do you try to avoid situations that require you to wait?
- Do you feel exhausted, drained, or agitated if you are forced to do nothing?
- Do you interrupt during conversations or lectures?
- Do you space out during conversations or lectures?
- Have you engaged in risky or illegal behaviours just "for the buzz"?
- Do you feel depressed or agitated if your life is running too smoothly?

Section 8: Memory

Mark only one oval per row.

Never / Sometimes / Often / Always / Not sure

- Do you forget important appointments or obligations?
- Do you use multiple reminders to remember important appointments or obligations?
- Do you have difficulty concentrating on people when they are speaking to you?
- Do you frequently misplace things or have difficulty finding them?
- Do you use a strict storage system to avoid losing things?
- Do you perform repeated checks to make sure that you have not lost or forgotten things?
- Do you forget that you own things if you put them out of sight?
- Do you have problems with your working memory? (e.g., if you needed to pick up five ingredients for a recipe, could you remember them without a written list?)
- Do you have problems storing information in your long-term memory? (e.g., you have to go over the same bit of information a number of times before it is stored, or you fail to store chunks of your life.)
- Do you have problems accessing your long-term memory? (e.g., you know that you know something, but you cannot access that specific bit of information at will.)

Section 9: Organisation and decision-making

Mark only one oval per row.

Never / Sometimes / Often / Always / Not sure

- Do you find it hard to organize your time effectively?
- Do you stick to a strict schedule because it's the only way you can get everything done?
- Do you stick to a strict schedule because you find it comforting?
- Do you try to stick to a schedule, but you just can't?
- Do you find living under a strict schedule suffocating?
- Are you able to correctly gauge the passing of time (e.g. what time it is, how long a routine task takes) without checking a watch?
- Do you struggle to make small decisions when you have too many options? (e.g., you spend an unreasonable amount of time reading reviews before buying a cheap item.)
- Do you make big decisions too quickly? (You don't "look before you leap.")
- Do you struggle to make decisions if you do not have enough information to work out the possible risks and effects?

Section 10: Interest and hyperfocus

Mark only one oval per row.

Never / Sometimes / Often / Always / Not sure

- Do you find daily tasks boring or repetitive?
- Do you find it hard to stay focused on tasks you find boring or repetitive, even when they are important to you?
- Do you tend to avoid or delay starting tasks that are new, complicated, or important?
- Do you abandon tasks if they turn up to be too complicated?
- Do you find it hard to complete tasks once you know you can do them?
- Do you pick up new hobbies only to abandon them if you don't get good at them fast enough?
- Do you pick up new hobbies only to abandon them once you get good at them?
- Do you have an interest or passion that captures the majority of your interest?
- Is that interest or passion common for people of your age/gender/socioeconomic status?
- Do you make money from your interest or passion?
- Do you get into trouble with the people around you for getting too sucked in into your passion or interest?
- Do you feel upset or agitated if you are pulled away from being engaged in your tasks or passion?

Section 11: Communication

Mark only one oval per row.

Never / Sometimes / Often / Always / Not sure

- Do you have a passion for learning new words or languages?
- Do you have to translate your thoughts into simpler language to communicate with those around you?
- Do you get into trouble for using words that are "too complicated"?
- Do people misinterpret what you are saying or make incorrect assumptions as to the intentions behind your words?
- Have you been told that your body language, facial expression, or tone of voice are inappropriate?
- Do you struggle to notice or interpret non-verbal communication cues (e.g., body language, facial expressions, tone of voice)?
- Do you struggle to give out socially appropriate non-verbal communication cues (e.g., body language or facial expressions)?
- Are you uncomfortable with "small talk"• ? (i.e., social pleasantries designed for politeness rather than the transfer of information.)
- Do you struggle to identify or respond to phatic communication? (i.e., things people say to establish or maintain social relationships rather than to exchange information.)

Section 12: Functioning in groups

Mark only one oval per row.

Never / Sometimes / Often / Always / Not sure

- Do you struggle to identify or negotiate social hierarchies?
- Do you struggle to function in group situations, even though you would enjoy the company of the same people one-to-one?
- Do you struggle to function in group situations that do not center around a defined activity? (e.g., working, playing a board game or a sport, etc.)
- Do you enjoy informal, unstructured group situations? (e.g., a party at someone's house.)
- Do you enjoy formal, unstructured group situations? (e.g., a formal social function.)
- Do you avoid social events because you find them unpleasant?
- Do you attend social events even though you find them unpleasant?
- Do you find yourself drained after attending social events, even when they went well?
- Are you able to follow a conversation in a room with background noise?

Section 13: Eye contact and facial recognition

Mark only one oval per row.

Never / Sometimes / Often / Always / Not sure

- Do you find direct eye contact unpleasant?
- Do you have to consciously regulate the amount of eye contact you make in order to appear "normal"• ?
- Do you pretend to make eye contact in order to appear "normal,"• but you are actually focusing on something else?
- Do you have prosopagnosia?
- Do you struggle to recognize people out of context?
- Do you struggle to recognize people if they change their hair or clothes?
- Do you worry about the possibility of not recognizing someone or not remembering their name?

Section 14: Emotional regulation

Mark only one oval per row.

Never / Sometimes / Often / Always / Not sure

- Do you have mood lability?
- Do you experience rapid, pronounced changes in mood with very little reason?
- Do you struggle to control your behavior when you are experiencing strong emotions?
- Do you get in trouble for behaving impulsively when you feel emotional?
- Do you have Rejection-Sensitive Dysphoria?
- Do you tend to anxiously expect social rejection?
- Do you believe that people are going to reject you even though they haven't done anything concrete to show that?
- Do you find rejection very painful, even when it comes from people you do not really like or care for?
- Do you do things you'd rather not so people will like you?
- Do you pretend to be someone else so people will like you?

Section 15: Crisis points

Mark only one oval per row.

Never / Sometimes / Often / Always / Not sure

- Do you experience meltdowns?
- Do you have intense physical or emotional responses to overwhelming situations? (i.e., you become unable to control your own body or speech.)
- Do you experience shutdowns?
- Do you become unresponsive or stop processing information in response to overwhelming situations?
- Do you experience burnouts?
- If you become overtaxed by your obligations, do you experience periods of fatigue, heightened stress, and diminished capacity to cope with daily life?
- Do you have selective mutism?
- Do you become temporarily unable to speak in response to stressful social situations or when your senses are overwhelmed by your environment? (e.g., in crowded places.)

Section 16: Dissociative states

Mark only one oval per row.

Never / Sometimes / Often / Always / Not sure

- Do you spend a lot of time daydreaming?
- Do you spend so much time daydreaming that you fail to maintain personal connections or manage your obligations?
- Do you dissociate?
- Do you have times when you feel disconnected from your thoughts, feelings, memories, and surroundings?
- Do you have gaps in your long-term memory that affect certain time periods, events, or personal information?
- Do you have times when you feel little or no physical pain, or lose the ability to perceive other physical cues (e.g. hunger and thirst signals)?
- Do you have times when you feel emotionally numb or detached?
- Do you have out-of-body experiences?
- Do you have times when you lose your sense of identity or have multiple distinct identities?

Section 17: Body awareness

Mark only one oval per row.

Never / Sometimes / Often / Always / Not sure

- Do you have poor interoception?
- Do you struggle to read your body's hunger signals, so you forget to eat until you feel sick from hunger?
- Do you struggle to read your body's thirst signals, so you forget to drink?
- Do you struggle to know when you need to pee or poo until you are desperate, or have an accident?
- When you were a child, did you get into trouble for having "tantrums" • when you were trying to avoid painful physical sensations?
- When you were a child, were you forced by your parents or teachers to endure painful physical sensation in order to learn to get over them?
- Are you routinely forced to endure unpleasant or overwhelming physical sensations in order to navigate your environment?

Section 18: Connective tissue and pain

Mark only one oval per row.

Never / Sometimes / Often / Always / Not sure

- Do you have a connective tissue disorder?
- Do you easily injure your joints? (e.g. sprains or strains.)
- Are your joints hypermobile?
- Do you have early onset arthritis?
- Do you experience fatigue even when you haven't done anything to tire yourself out?
- Do you experience an unreasonable amount of fatigue when you exert yourself?
- Do you have fibromyalgia?
- Are you extremely sensitive to pain? (e.g., if you suffer a minor injury, it hurts too much, or for too long.)
- Do you feel pain from something that should not be painful at all, such as a very light touch?
- Do you have times when you experience widespread pain with no known cause?
- Do you have times when all of your past injuries hurt, even though you have not re-injured yourself?

Section 19: Sensitivities and neuropathies

Mark only one oval per row.

Never / Sometimes / Often / Always / Not sure

- Do you have food allergies or intolerances?
- Do you have food sensory issues? (e.g., you cannot eat certain foods because of their texture.)
- Do you have allergies to smells or chemicals?
- Do you have asthma attacks in response to certain smells?
- Do you get headaches in response to certain smells?
- Do you get headaches if you consume certain foods or drinks?
- Do you get headaches in response to bright lights?
- Can you hear sounds other people do not hear?
- Do you have tinnitus (ringing or other noises in one or both of your ears) without identifiable causes? (e.g., without hearing loss or an ear injury.)
- Do you have cluster headaches?
- Do you have attacks of severe pain in one side of the head?
- Do you have trigeminal neuralgia?
- Do you have sudden attacks of severe, sharp, shooting facial pain that last from a few seconds to about 2 minutes?

Section 20: Blood pressure and sugar levels

Mark only one oval per row.

Never / Sometimes / Often / Always / Not sure

- Do you have low blood pressure?
- Do you have postural tachycardia syndrome (POTS)?
- Do you feel dizzy, lightheaded, or faint you stand up for too long?
- Do you feel dizzy, lightheaded, or faint if you stand up too quickly?
- Do you have Reynaud's disease?
- Do you struggle to regulate your temperature in hot weather? (e.g., you become tired, faint, or dizzy, while the people around you are not affected.)
- Do you struggle to regulate your temperature in cold weather? (e.g., you shiver, lose feelings in your extremities, become tired, dizzy, or confused, while the people around you are not affected.)
- Do you have reactive hypoglycemia?
- Do you feel anxious, confused, dizzy, irritable, light-headed, faint, exhausted, weak, or shaky within four hours of eating a meal?
- Do you feel anxious, confused, dizzy, irritable, light-headed, faint, exhausted, weak, or shaky within four hours of eating certain foods?

Section 21: Co-occuring conditions

Mark only one oval per row.

Yes / No / Not sure / Not applicable

- Do you have eczema?
- Do you have anemia?
- Do you have polycystic ovary syndrome (PCOS)?
- Do you have endometriosis?
- Do you have uterine fibroids?
- Do you have uterine polyps?
- Do you have fibrocystic breast disease?
- Do you have chronic pain associated with non-cancerous abnormalities in your breasts?
- Do you have any autoimmune diseases?
- Do you have restless legs syndrome?
- Do you have an overwhelming urge to move your legs, particularly in the evening or at night?

Section 22: Life and trauma

Mark only one oval per row.

Yes / No / Not sure

- Have you underachieved at work or in education (i.e., have you achieved less than people believed you capable of?)
- Do you struggle to make new friends?
- Do you struggle to keep your friends?
- Do you struggle in your relationships with partners and relatives?
- Do you have a history of abusive or neglectful relationships?
- Were you bullied as a child?
- Are you bullied now?
- Do you have PTSD?
- Do you have symptoms caused by exposure to a traumatic event?
- Do you have cPTSD?
- Do you have symptoms caused by exposure to long-term trauma, abuse, or neglect?
- Do you experience intrusive thoughts?
- Do you experience repetitive thoughts that pop into your head without warning, at any time, and you cannot control?

The end!

And not a moment too soon!

Thank you for participating in this questionnaire! If you would like to be kept abreast of results, please email us at

going.official.ADHDgmail.com

About the author

Hi! My name is Ash. I picked it myself. You might know me as Modgoblin from The ADHD Gift. I have written some non-fiction books[42] and maintained a blog[43] about self-defense and recovery from violence and trauma. I also write sci-fi and fantasy.[44] Most of my characters are neurodivergent, but that's not a deliberate slight against the neurotypical community; I just have no idea how their brains function. I do, however, have at least two straight characters in each book, because representation matters! This is the second book I write under my first name.

I currently live in rural Lincolnshire with an unreasonable number of dogs. I have had several careers, including agriculture, genetics, nature conservation, and animal care. Evidence suggests that I have to go through a total life reboot every 5-10 years. If that theory holds, next year is going to be interesting. I have already run away with the circus and from the circus; I am not sure what stunt I'll pull next, but I hope I will enjoy it.

My path to finding out that I am neurodivergent has been convoluted, to put it mildly. I started showing signs of hyperactivity as a fetus – no, seriously. My mom reckons that once I started moving, I just didn't stop. My behavior did not improve until I was made to develop a paralyzing degree of social anxiety. That, combined with my family's belief that 100% was the passing grade, meant that I had a whole load of fun in school.

I discovered that I have a number of sensitivities in my late teens, when moving into a university dorm caused me such a bad reaction that I ended up in the emergency room. I discovered that I'm dyslexic in my early 20s, when I started tutoring students with learning difficulties. I discovered that my mother had known all about it in my mid-30s. I would say that put a crimp in our relationship, but our relationship was mostly crimps anyway. Shortly after that, I discovered that I am dyspraxic, which is jolly good fun when you are trying to learn martial arts. The working memory issues and sleeping disorders became apparent a couple of years after that, when my insomnia caused me a level of cognitive decline so profound that I ended up being referred to the local dementia clinic. While all that was going on, I signed up with a life coach to try and get my life into a resemblance of order. I didn't realize that at the time, but a lot of the work

---

[42] https://www.amazon.com/A-R-Banks/e/B09JHP4FT5
[43] https://godsbastard.wordpress.com/
[44] https://www.amazon.com/Robin-Banks/e/B01MU5VWGL

we did was around unmasking and addressing my needs, rather than my faults. It was pretty rough at the start, but it got easier over time, and now it's good fun. I enjoy my own company now, although I still wish I was a better cook.

There I was, trying to fix my real life while writing fiction to escape it, when an idea occurred to me: what if the part of me that craves spontaneity and adventure and the part of me that needs to overplan everything were two separate people? And what if they met, and instead of detesting each other like they do in my head, they fell in love? That caused me to drop the perfectly good manuscript I was working on and embark on a two-year-long escapade with my two favorite characters to date. Yes, I wrote a love story between my ADHD and my anxiety. And at the time, I didn't know that I was neurodivergent and anxious.

Those discoveries were made at the behest of an Autistic friend, who suggested that my brain didn't quite work as most brains do, and that I might want to look into that. A hyperfocus and a whole bunch of tests later, my life suddenly made sense.

The funniest thing was telling my friends about it. With no exception, their reaction was utter surprise... at the fact that I had only just found out. I'm still not sure if the issue was that I don't mask around them or that most of them are also neurodivergent. We sure have a way of finding our own, even when we don't have a name for what we are looking for.

It took me another two years to get a diagnosis valid in this country. I didn't see the point, to be honest: I am self-employed, so workplace adaptations are all up to me, and I absolutely did not want meds. I didn't need meds. I had been without them all my life and had managed perfectly well. I liked my brain the way it was, thank you! Then something shifted inside me, and I started to listen to what other ADHDers had to say on the subject. A lot of stress and an exorbitant diagnostic bill later, I discovered what all the fuss was about. Shortly thereafter, I discovered that meds are not for me: I can adult better when I'm medicated, but I can't write. That's not a trade-off I am willing to make. I'm glad I got to try them, though.

I really hope this book didn't suck for you. It just took me so very long to get here, and I don't want that to happen to anyone else. Too much wasted life, you know? Nobody should have to wait four decades to find out that they're different – not weak, not broken, not defective, just different. Our needs matter. Our abilities matter. We matter. (Unless we are going really, really fast, in which case we energy.)

Printed in Great Britain
by Amazon